Head *and* Heart

Head *and* Heart

A Personal Exploration
of Science and the Sacred

VICTOR
MANSFIELD

Quest Books
Theosophical Publishing House

Wheaton, Illinois ♦ Chennai (Madras), India

The Theosophical Society wishes to acknowledge the generous support of The Kern Foundation in the publication of this book.

First Quest Edition 2002

For additional information write to

The Theosophical Publishing House
P. O. Box 270
Wheaton, IL 60189-0270

Library of Congress Cataloging-in-Publication Data

Mansfield, Victor.
Head and heart: a personal exploration of science and the sacred / Victor Mansfield.—1st Quest ed.
p.   cm.
ISBN 0-8356-0817-4
1. Religion and science.   2. Mansfield, Victor.   I. Title.

BL240.3 .M36 2002
291.1'75—dc21

2002024808

5   4   3   2   1   *   02   03   04   05   06   07

Printed in the United States of America

TABLE OF CONTENTS

Acknowledgments

For me, writing is a solitary passion. Nevertheless, my friends, teachers, and students have aided me in countless ways. The most unstinting help has come from my best friend, lover, intellectual companion, and wife of more than three decades, Elaine. She not only engaged me in intellectual discussion of ideas, but her comments on earlier drafts of this book also helped bring more warmth and clarity to my writing. Perhaps even more important, she takes so much time from her own writing to help pull me out of the psychological holes and emotional storms that I stumble into while writing. When intellectual discussion and psychology fail, she even cooks pasta just like my grandma did when I was a child! Thanks for all of it, Elaine.

I am deeply grateful to my friend Paul Cash, the editor and head of Larson Publications. His early advice, careful reading of an early draft, and many excellent suggestions helped me make this book stronger and more accessible and gave me more faith in the project. I also appreciate his help in proposing the manuscript to Quest Books. I wish to thank my editors at Quest, Sharron Dorr, and, especially, Jane Andrew. Their expertise, hard work, and patience helped make this a significantly more accessible and better written book. I thank my friends Timothy Smith, Karen Hamaker-Zondag, and Greg Bogart for reading and commenting on an early draft of chapter 3. I thank Erin Sullivan for her fine books and for teaching me some of the subtleties of astrology. My friend Richard Goldman, whose clarity and depth of thought have helped me in many parts of this book, deserves special thanks.

Over the past several years, I have been privileged to organize the Religion and Human Rights Speaker Series jointly sponsored by Wisdom's Goldenrod Center for Philosophic Studies (a nondenominational study and meditation community) and the Program in Religious Studies at Cornell University. Working on this series brought me into contact with many great people who stimulated my thinking and inspired my heart. Their influence pervades this book. I especially thank Rajiv Malhotra, whose Infinity Foundation financed the series. Through his generosity and vision, he encouraged us to think deeply and act boldly. I thank Professor Jane Marie Law of Cornell University for providing a context for the series by organizing a conference on religion and human rights. So many people from Goldenrod helped me organize the series that it is only possible to thank the event coordinators: Cindy Stillman, Martha Walsh-Cohen, and Elaine Mansfield. Jane Demakos deserves special thanks for directing the musical part of most of the programs and showing us how inspired music deepens and embodies clear thinking.

I thank the individual speakers in the series, whose lectures and workshops were the source of so much insight and inspiration. Dr. William Vendley, Secretary-General, World Conference on Religion and Peace/International, taught us how inner realization must issue in inspired action in the world. Rabbi Brian Walt led us into the depths of Judaism and taught how the moral burden of human rights can still be joyous. His effort was greatly aided by Cantor Robert Esformes, whose music brought us more into the heart of the tradition than I could have imagined. China Galland shared her work on fierce compassion and the neglected feminine. My deepest thanks go to Father Raimon Panikkar. He lit up our understanding with his brilliance, brought us into contact with the depths of soul, warmed us with his love, and offered me critical encouragement for this book. His benign influence is especially prominent in chapter 13.

Looking back on my scientific career, the list of influential teachers and helpful colleagues dwarfs my ability to do them justice. I can mention only those whose influence has been most profound. I thank Mr. William Gilmore, who taught me algebra and chemistry in high school with such verve and patience that the world of science became as interesting as the young women in my classes. (I sketch my relationship with him in chapter 5.) Scores of teacher-scholars at Dartmouth College deserve my gratitude, but I mention only Professor William Doyle, who was the first to initiate me into the beauties and depths of theoretical physics, and Professor Tomas Laspere, whose teaching, encouragement, and kindness both nourished me and set a high example.

From my days at Cornell University, my deep gratitude goes to Professor Yervant Terzian. His infectious and boundless love of science was matched only by his support of me and my crooked path through graduate school. I especially thank Professor Edwin Salpeter, who terrified me with his brilliant astrophysics and simultaneously taught me kindness. (More about his influence on me appears in chapter 5.) Professor Frank Drake deserves my gratitude for his unmatched teaching, inspiration in radio astronomy, and support of my graduate work. I thank Professor David Mermin not only for deepening my love of quantum mechanics and its many mysteries, but also for his virtuoso teaching and his lovely sense of humor.

I wish to express my gratitude to Colgate University for the privilege of being a professor. It still amazes me that they pay me for such delightful and satisfying work. They allow me to teach not only physics and astronomy but also many interdisciplinary courses in the General Education Program. This interdisciplinary experience has influenced me deeply and colors this entire book. I thank my colleagues in the Physics and Astronomy Department for their friendship and support of my unusual interests. I especially thank Professor Shimon Malin for being my research partner upon many occasions, for always drawing me more deeply into the mysteries of the natural world, and for providing helpful comments on an early draft.

After nearly thirty years of teaching, I am beginning to realize how deep my debt is to the many students who have passed through my classes at Colgate and Cornell. They have challenged me to think more deeply about physics and astronomy and about the interdisciplinary material in philosophy, psychology, and Buddhism that I have taught in Colgate's General Education Program. Their sincere desire to learn forced me to seek deeper understanding, taught me to articulate the material in fresh ways, and helped me appreciate my own shortcomings. Thank you for being my teachers.

Many people in the field of psychology, including professionals, friends, and the patients at the Agnew State Mental Hospital in San Jose, California, have helped me turn my theoretical understanding into living experience. I wish to single out the Jungian analysts Robert Bosnak, Marvin Spiegelman, and James Hall for special thanks. Each in his own way has helped me appreciate the extraordinary beauties and terrors of the psyche and make progress on my individuation.

My deepest debt is to my spiritual teachers. I offer sincere thanks to the late Paul Brunton. He asked me to write about the relationship between science and spirituality and taught me more than I could assimilate about mystical philosophy and the spiritual life. He also encouraged me to spend time with the late Sri Sankaracharya, the sixty-eighth holder of a title that goes back nearly eight centuries to the greatest Hindu philosopher and saint, Adi Sankara. Although we spoke few words, Sankaracharya initiated me into some of the depths of Indian spirituality and helped me appreciate something about the unity of soul and its moral implications. Two important experiences with Sankaracharya appear in this book. My profound thanks go to Tenzin

Gyatso, the fourteenth Dalai Lama. He too encouraged me to think deeply about the relationship of science to spirituality, brought me into the heart of Buddhist teaching and spirituality, and set an extraordinarily high example of wisdom and compassion. My deepest thanks go to my late teacher, Anthony Damiani. His benign influence appears in many chapters of this book, especially chapter 3. Through his personal example and patient instruction over seventeen years, his students learned to overcome cultural and linguistic barriers and approach the depths of many great world traditions of philosophy and religion. He taught us all this without limiting us to any one tradition, while igniting our passion for a personal realization of these great truths.

INTRODUCTION

The year is 1975. For two years, I have been teaching physics and astronomy at Colgate University and enjoying it immensely. Until this year, my research has been in theoretical astrophysics, but now I have accepted an invitation to try some hands-on experimental work. Today I am flying to Puerto Rico, where I will join a group that is using the world's largest single-dish radio telescope, located in Arecibo. Our team will study gaseous nebulae—huge, diffuse clouds left over from star formation—scattered throughout our galaxy.

It would have been difficult to refuse the invitation from my former thesis advisor, Professor Yervant Terzian of Cornell University. His sheer delight in doing science is utterly infectious. Besides, he has always been completely supportive—especially when I temporarily abandoned my Ph.D. dissertation in astrophysics for nearly two years while I immersed myself in various forms of psychology. His enthusiasm, my affection for him, my sense of indebtedness, and the opportunity for new research have brought me to this observational radio astronomy project. We hope that four days of observing will give our team useful data to make substantial progress on this project.

I usually enjoy flying, but this time, as I wait for the plane to take off from Ithaca, New York, I am invaded by an overpowering sense of dread. I am certain that death is near. Despite years of meditation training, my mind is embarrassingly wild. My biggest fear is that I will never see my wife and two young sons again. I consider just running off the plane and canceling the trip, but that would ruin the observing run for the rest of the team. It's very difficult to get observing time at the Arecibo telescope, so I force myself to stay on the plane.

I repeatedly try to reassure myself: "Don't be silly. The whole thing is a stupid joke. This isn't like you. Get a grip on yourself." Yet, images of my wife and sons repeatedly float into consciousness, along with a deep sense of inevitability and loss. There is no doubt. I am doomed. They will soon be a widow and fatherless boys. To end this obvious absurdity, I try to read Sri Aurobindo's *Life Divine*. It's no help. My mind races on: "So this is the way it ends? So much to do and love, and I'll never get off this plane alive. Why did I take this terrible window seat? I feel like an animal in a cage!" Torn between overwhelming dread and a voice telling me I am a hysterical fool, I am trapped, crushed, and powerless.

The plane lifts off and I wait for the inevitable crash or explosion. I have always feared death and here it is, hovering all around me—but am I not being ridiculous? However, my terror and sense of inevitability shout down that small calm voice. I can't take the tension any more. Out of pure exhaustion, I surrender my fate to that which is highest in me. I give up, let go, and pray for help in dying.

Gradually, the air in the cabin seems suffused with soft, golden light. My heart swells with devotion and gratitude and yet I am clearly aware of my unworthiness. Out of a deep sense of peace and joy, love radiates from me in all directions. Each person in the plane, and even the plane itself, vividly expresses divinity. I am as certain of the reality and presence of that sacred mystery as I am of my own body. I turn to the window to hide the tears of gratitude streaming down my face. As I gaze down on Cayuga Lake, embraced by the lovely emerald hills, my sense of reverence deepens even further. I put down *Life Divine*. There is nothing to do. This *is* the life divine.

We land without incident in New York City. The peace, devotion, and soft, golden hue extend to the tarmac and the terminal. It is disarmingly easy to see that all the people rushing around in the terminal are unique expressions of the sacred mystery. Although I have experienced moments of spiritual uplift before, they have always been fleeting. This state persists as I float onto the plane headed to San Juan, Puerto Rico.

By the time our plane approaches San Juan, darkness has descended, revealing pearl necklaces of lights strewn all over the tropical island. The director of the Arecibo Observatory meets me, and we fly in a light plane to the telescope at the other end of the island. More opalescent jewels of light float to me on the soft, moist air. Still feeling a great sense of devotion and peace, I find it impossible to summon any interest in astrophysical gossip or in shop talk about the telescope and my upcoming observations. I certainly cannot share my experiences on the plane out of Ithaca. We drive the last few miles from the airport over a tortuous, hilly road that twists its way into the valley that shelters the telescope. The warm air of the summer night caresses me and carries the gruesome sound of big frogs popping under the tires of our car. Even that is an expression of the great mystery.

At the observatory, my little room contains only the essentials and feels like a monk's cell. Entering it, I realize for the first time how isolating my new experience is.

It is unwise to talk about that which is most precious, most real, with those who have neither sympathy nor understanding for such things. Of course, there is also another danger: talking about spiritual experiences can be a great way to fatten your ego. At that time, less from humility and more from the fear of being misunderstood, I had for several years built a wall between my inner life and my scientific colleagues. The experience on the way to Arecibo put barbed wire on top of the wall. In fact, until this writing, I have told only my wife and my dearest teacher about it. Of course, walls not only protect but also isolate. Dismantling that wall through writing this book gives me opportunities for integrating my life as a scientist with my spiritual life, but it also creates the potential for misunderstanding—perhaps even ridicule.

Back in 1975, there was no question of taking down walls. I was concerned about whether I could get into the concentrated, high-energy mental state required to set up the telescope and take data. How could I make the transition from the depths of inner space to those of outer space? In those early years, I didn't even consider trying to integrate these two worlds—that seemed overwhelmingly difficult, if not impossible.

The next day, the golden light fell far into the background as I plunged into the frantic activity and high-intensity effort that characterizes big science. The day after that, I got into a nasty fight with another astronomer over rights to a certain time for observing. We even took our argument to the director's office. It was ugly. I learned a lesson repeated many times since then: one little glimpse of the higher self does not a saint make.

SCIENCE AND THE SACRED

The Arecibo radio telescope has a fixed dish, one thousand feet in diameter, anchored in a tropical valley. Pointing the telescope requires moving the signal-gathering feed, the apparatus shown in figure 1, in conjunction with the Earth's rotation. Even then, you can only scan part of the sky. Because of this, the objects we were observing during my 1975 visit could only be viewed in the middle of the night. My already delicate sleeping patterns were thoroughly disrupted, especially since construction was going on outside my room during the day. Instead of sleeping, I lay in my little room for hours reviewing my mysterious experience.

What did it mean? Was my glimpse of the sacred just the pathology of a neurotic who could not face his mortality and the realities of modern life? If not, where did that effulgent love for humanity go during the nasty fight over telescope time? How was I to balance my love for physics and astronomy with my love for

Fig. 1. Signal-gathering feed, Arecibo telescope (courtesy of Donald Campbell, National Astronomy and Ionosphere Center, Puerto Rico)

the sacred that expresses itself in so many ancient wisdom traditions? In other words, how was I to create harmony between my head and my heart?

It is difficult to conceive of objects more objective and independent of human concerns than those we were studying at Arecibo. On the one hand, I was concerned with radiation from galactic nebulae, while on the other, with the divine mystery radiating from my innermost self. *What are the essential differences between the scientific knowledge of galactic nebulae and the inner realization of soul?* This question has haunted me for years. Since high school, I have had a deep love of science and even before that I had a natural affinity for the sacred. I could never neglect one in favor of the other. They have an equal claim on me.

Nevertheless, following my own science instructors, I was teaching my students at Colgate University that the personal equation —the particular set of preferences, unique history, and individuality that characterizes each person—must be thoroughly removed from scientific investigation. This depersonalization is one of the pillars of modern science and has contributed to its great power. But what then is the status of feelings, which unite us with the object of experience rather than remove us from it, as in scientific objectivity? Do they have any access to truth? Does the private nature of the experience of the sacred diminish its value, make it less real or less true than a galactic nebulae that can be seen by anybody with a big enough telescope? What is the nature of the objectivity so prized in science? Can we bring the objective knowledge of science into harmony with the interior experience of spiritual truths as articulated in ancient wisdom traditions in both the East and the West?

These, then, are some of the questions I explore in this book. I do not try to answer them within the context of a relationship between science and any one particular religion, be it Christianity or Hinduism, old or new. My concern encompasses all religions, in that I am interested in the relationship between science and spirituality. By spirituality, I mean that set of ideas and experiences at the root of all major religions. Spiritual principles and experiences come in many forms, and no one religion has a monopoly on them. In spirituality, as I understand it, the emphasis is less on dogmatic formulation of truth and more on a personal experience of truth, and still more on appreciating how the light of the divine refracts through different traditions into a rainbow of meaning. Divinity expresses itself not only through a plurality of religious traditions, but also through the wondrous beauty and horror of the world.

Despite the tolerance built into this position, it does not mean that all expressions of divinity are equal. Nor does a genuine spiritual position shy away from the many intellectual challenges provided by the plurality of religious views. Instead, a spiritual position fully embraces direct personal experience and the demand for coherent understanding in the face of the multiplicity of religious forms and the obvious evils in the world. From this position, I address the complex question about the relationship between science and spirituality or, equivalently, science and the sacred.

I believe this question is not only personally pressing but also of great significance for our planetary culture. Ravi Ravindra, a physicist and professor of comparative religion, thinks it is *the* pressing problem for our generation:

> It is possible to hope that modern science and ancient spiritual traditions can be integrated in some higher synthesis. I would

even say that such a task is the most important of all that can be undertaken by contemporary intellectuals, for on such a synthesis depends not only the global survival of man but also the creation of the right environment, right both physically and metaphysically, for future generations.[1]

I fully agree with Ravindra that understanding the relationship between science and ancient spiritual traditions is of the utmost importance. However, I will argue that, given the nature of science and the sacred, a synthesis, in the sense of combining separate elements into one coherent whole, is impossible.

REALITY AND TRUTH

Over the years I have learned that reality, divinity, unity, or the absolute—whatever term you choose to describe the sacred mystery—cannot be limited either to the rationality and objectivity of science nor to the unity and subjectivity of spiritual seekers. This book tries to show that reality is both intrinsically rational and objective and, simultaneously, a superrational and subjective unity underlying diversity. In other words, reality cannot be reduced to the objective world of science nor to the subjective unity of the mystics. It intrinsically has both these seemingly incompatible aspects. Failure to embrace them both places artificial limits on reality and diminishes both our experience of reality and our sense of what it means to be human. Such lopsided views lead to extremism, despair, and moral paralysis.

Through the interplay of elegant theory and powerful instruments, our knowledge of the natural world has exploded in the last century. In the last decade, scientists have even made progress in unifying all the forces of nature (gravity, electromagnetism, and the strong and weak nuclear forces) into a grand unification, a "theory of everything." Such a theory would provide an explanation of all natural phenomena through a set of equations that could be written on one standard-sized piece of paper. Because of both the great success and future prospects of science, many believe that one great scientific truth, one theory of everything, encompasses all of reality.

Well before the advent of modern science, various religions offered their version of the one great truth that supports and explains all things in heaven and on earth. Unfortunately, the truths offered by the great religions are not in harmony with each other. For example, many speak of God, whether the God of the Judeo-Christian tradition, Allah of Islam, or Brahman of Hinduism. Yet, Buddhism denies the existence of any creator god, while the grand unification sought in physics encourages many to question even the need for a god.

Who then has the absolute truth? Is there one absolute truth? These are not merely academic questions. History clearly shows that when one group firmly believes that they have the one truth, all other groups are, by definition, in error and must be eliminated. Monotheism, or more properly "monotruthism," is always hostile to those not espousing the one great truth. Thus, clinging to the belief in one great truth, whether a "theory of everything" or the one true God, sets the stage for conflict, which modern technology makes more barbaric every year. As I will show, understanding the relationship between science and the sacred, between the head and the heart, sheds light on this issue of competing truths, whether among religions or between science and spirituality.

In elementary calculus, we must learn to differentiate before we can integrate. In a similar way, we must clearly differentiate scientific knowledge from sacred knowledge. Only then can we intelligently approach the problem of bringing some harmony between mathematically based sciences that provide only one clear answer to a problem and philosophical mysticism, astrology, depth psychology, and meditation. In other words, careful differentiation between the head and the heart must precede any possible harmony between them. However, harmony emphatically does *not* mean reducing one type of knowledge to the other.

Many of us seek a worldview that can accommodate both the latest vision of modern science and the many forms of traditional wisdom, a worldview solidly based upon reason that embraces the reality of quarks and the big bang alongside the sacred inner world. However, such a comprehensive postmodern view has not yet emerged, and its absence leaves us two alternatives, both unacceptable. We cannot revert to a premodern view that neglects the vast explosion of science and its handmaiden, technology. Nor can we stay on our present course, where modern science and technology make possible the savagery of modern warfare, unsustainable economic growth, ecological destruction, and life devoid of meaning.

My previous book, *Synchronicity, Science, and Soul-Making,*[2] addressed some of these issues via the psychological, scientific, and philosophical consequences of the Swiss psychologist Carl Jung's concept of synchronicity. Here my effort to understand modern science and its relationship to the sacred is both more personal and more general. It is more personal because I draw directly upon my own experiences of both science and the sacred. Greater generality comes from making use of many traditions, from depth psychology to Neoplatonism and philosophical Hinduism, yet relying exclusively on none of them. Instead, I build the discussion from first principles and analysis of personal experience.

I write about my experiences, such as the one that begins this chapter, with much trepidation. Speaking openly about our most intimate inner experiences can be a gross form of ego aggrandizement. Although spiritual effort should not seek to destroy the ego, that being neither possible nor desirable, the ego must become a servant of the higher self or soul. This shift is impossible if I boast about spiritual experiences. Nevertheless, I admit my ego's involvement and take the risk for four reasons. First, it allows me to embody abstract ideas in concrete experiences. Second, it makes the analysis more engaging and compelling. Third, I believe Ralph Waldo Emerson when he writes in his essay "The American Scholar":

> He then learns that in going down into the secrets of his own mind he has descended into the secrets of all minds. . . . The deeper he dives into his privatest, secretest presentiment, to his wonder he finds this is the most acceptable, most public, and universally true.[3]

Although this passage was written nearly a century before Jung's major works, in Jungian language we would say that in going deep enough into our personal material we reach a universal, archetypal level.

Fourth and finally, there is a philosophical reason for paying homage to the personal. There is a tradition, widely represented in both Eastern and Western thought, that exalts the impersonal over the personal. For example, many traditions encourage us to abandon, even destroy, the psychologically unique individual or ego in favor of the undivided, unitary soul or self. One of my heroes, Albert Einstein, expresses one variant of this approach. He tells us how his religious devotion to science allowed him to transcend the "merely personal," an existence "dominated by wishes, hopes, and primitive feelings."[4] I too have had some limited experience of the liberation that impersonal science affords from the merely personal. Nevertheless, I will argue that denying the personal turns the majestic unity of soul into a sham. How could soul be a true unity, an undivided whole, if it excludes me, an individual expression of both human folly and excellence? How does this lopsided emphasis on the impersonal fully express the unique miracle of Einstein as both a person and a scientist? For an example of how limited a view such impersonality gives, consider Einstein's autobiography, written at age sixty-seven. There we find no mention of his two wives and two sons, let alone his illegitimate daughter.

Rather than remove or denigrate the personal, I will argue for embracing both our timeless unity and the unique expression of that unity in daily life—you and me as transitory individuals in space and time. I am not elevating the ephemeral ego at the expense of the transcendent unity. Instead, I believe that our task is to experience the unity and simultaneously to appreciate plurality; that is, to appreciate soul as simultaneously an eternal, undivided unity and as a temporal, divided plurality. This approach allows us to cultivate life's intrinsic sacredness, including our personal expression of it in the empirical personality.

My approach to harmonizing science and the sacred involves a parallel appreciation that unity expresses itself in a plurality of religious, philosophical, and scientific views. Appreciating how unity expresses itself as plurality, both personally at the level of our own souls and universally through the diversity of religions, is my path to harmony between science and the sacred. Showing this path requires me to oscillate between intellectual analysis and personal narration, between the world of science and philosophy on one hand and that of psychological and spiritual experience on the other. Only by encompassing both experiences of the head and the heart can we get a glimpse of the fullness of reality and what it means to be human.

Part I

DIFFERENTIATING
SCIENCE AND THE SACRED

Chapter One

THE WEDDING OF SIR GAWAIN
AND DAME RAGNELLE

E veryone in the industrialized world, with or without formal scientific training, is deeply influenced by scientific materialism—
both by its view of nature and by its means of knowing. For
nearly all of us, the rational mind, conditioned by science, is our starting point for viewing the world and our relationship to it. Essential as
the rational mind is, experience has taught me that such a narrow focus is dangerously imbalanced and inadequate for grasping the whole
of the outer and inner worlds. Such an attempt at grasping the whole
of reality through the "keyhole" of the rational intellect will not help
us relate the head and the heart—here, science and the inner spiritual
world—either personally or as a culture. To begin broadening our perspective and preparing the ground for a more comprehensive view, I
begin with an engaging tale from the medieval Arthurian legends, "The
Wedding of Sir Gawain and Dame Ragnelle."[1]

Because myths, legends, and fairy tales are expressions of the
universal archetypes underlying human nature, they offer great insights
into our individual psychology. At the same time, if rightly understood,
they can also serve as a guide to questions facing the culture at large. In
both its personal and universal aspects, this ancient tale offers clues to
expanding our view of reality and bringing harmony between the head
and heart.

Long ago, before digital time, King Arthur was hunting a
hart [a mature male deer]. He ran the great deer into a fern thicket
and killed it there. Just after the king had tasted the meat, a powerful and heavily armed knight charged in and accused the king
of mistreating him for many years by giving his land away to
Arthur's favorite knight, Sir Gawain. In his rage, the formidable
knight, Sir Gromer Somer Joure, came close to killing the king

13

on the spot. However, Arthur skillfully convinced him that it would not be chivalrous, since Arthur was only in his light hunting gear rather than full armor.

Instead of killing Arthur, Sir Gromer gave him a riddle that he must answer, or die. After one year, Arthur was to return to that very spot and answer the question, "What is it that all women desire above all else?" The king was glad to have a one-year reprieve, but the question seemed impossible and his life uncertain. When the king returned to his castle, Gawain immediately noted his distress. After hearing the king's plight, the ever-enthusiastic Gawain suggested that they mount their horses and ride out in different directions to ask the question of every woman in the kingdom and record their answers in a great book. Surely that way they would find the right answer. Arthur was doubtful but saw no alternative. After almost a year of wandering and diligent questioning, their books were full of answers, but none of them seemed compelling.

Just before the appointed hour with Sir Gromer, while wandering in a deep woods, Arthur came upon a woman on an exquisitely beautiful horse that was embellished with gold and precious jewels. A fine lute hung from her shoulder. However, when she turned toward him, he saw she was horrifyingly ugly and misshapen. Snot dripped from her pig-like nose, one tusk turned up and one down, and her mouth was a gaping pit with loose, flapping lips. Dame Ragnelle immediately knew the king's plight and told him that she alone had the answer that could save his life. However, she would not give the answer unless she could marry the finest knight in the land: Sir Gawain.

"This is not a favor I can grant. It is Gawain's choice," said Arthur.

Upon returning to the castle from their separate journeys, Gawain again noticed the King's disturbed state and bade him explain. Without a moment's hesitation, Gawain offered to wed Dame Ragnelle. No price was too high for his beloved king's life.

At this point, pause a moment and ask yourself the question, "What is it that all women desire above all else?" Try to devise answers that are unique to women. For example, if you say, "All women desire above all else to be loved," that statement could just as well apply to men, so it is not really answering a question specifically about women. On the other hand, if you say all women want to be mothers, that does not apply to all women. Remember that this question is unlike a physics problem with one right answer and more like a dream with multiple levels of complementary meaning. Here is the answer the tale gives:

Arthur hastily returned to Ragnelle and told her of Gawain's acceptance. Ragnelle kept her end of the bargain. She told Arthur that, above all else, all women desire to be autonomous, to have sovereignty over their own lives. Elated, Arthur hastened to Sir Gromer and told him the answer. Gromer flew into a rage, not only because he had to let Arthur go, but also because he knew that the only person who could have told Arthur the lifesaving answer was Sir Gromer's own sister, Dame Ragnelle.

For her part, Ragnelle would not be a modest little bride. Unlike Gawain, she wanted a grand wedding in which the entire court participated. At the wedding feast, despite her fine raiment, everyone was aghast at her ugliness and extraordinarily ravenous appetite. She ate more food than six men, while Gawain looked on wanly.

On their wedding night, Ragnelle demanded a kiss of the reluctant Gawain. "Yett for Arthours sake kysse me att the leste." (Line 635) That momentous kiss transformed the world's ugliest hag into the most beautiful jewel of a woman. Gawain was initially frightened by the sudden transformation and feared she might be some evil spirit. "Who are you?" he asked.

"I am your loving wife." Then the most depressed of bridegrooms turned into the happiest of men. Amid the surprise and delight occasioned by her transformation, Dame Ragnelle explained that such was the curse on her that she could only be beautiful half the time. Gawain must choose whether he wished her beautiful in the night with him or during the day at court. The rest of the time, Ragnelle must revert to her hideous self. After carefully considering the question, Gawain told Ragnelle that the decision must be hers.

With Ragnelle granted full autonomy by Gawain, the spell was completely broken. Ragnelle could be beautiful all the time. There followed hours of rejoicing and lovemaking. In the meantime, the court, ignorant of this immense transformation, feared for Gawain's well-being. They worried that Ragnelle was some sort of predator, too wily and fierce even for Arthur's best knight. When the wedding chamber was thrown open, all rejoiced in the realization of Ragnelle's inherent beauty. The celebration brought the king and queen together with Gawain and Ragnelle, who even pleaded for indulgence toward Sir Gromer.

We can view this tale as a powerful, dreamlike expression of the collective psyche, a symbolic articulation of its primordial structures. Such tales erupt into collective consciousness and capture our imagination for centuries. They are the collective psyche's reaction to some sort of imbalance or misalignment in our attitudes and behavior. From this standpoint, these tales are understood as symbolic representations of forces seeking our personal and collective psychological transformation. Just like major dreams, such tales can be interpreted from many complementary points of view without any one view negating another. The following depth psychological interpretation stays close to the original text and is in harmony with the best literary and historical scholarship,[2] which demonstrates that Gawain is the courteous champion of the great mother goddess, often known as Sovereignty.

The tale begins with King Arthur, the symbolic embodiment of collective consciousness, hunting a hart, often the symbol of our higher individuality. Arthur has offended Sir Gromer by giving Gomer's land to the hero Sir Gawain, and this conflict within the masculine principle sets the story in motion.

Note that a conflict within the masculine results in a puzzle about the feminine. Only through solving the puzzle about the feminine can the male principle be saved. Aggression and heroism cannot gain this truth. Out of the deadly passion of masculine strife comes the question, "What is it that all women desire above all else?" Despite the heroic and obviously naïve efforts of Gawain, the conscious and willful approach to the question is unproductive. It is a psychological law that whatever is rejected and feared turns ugly and even more troublesome, whether it is a personal problem or a conflict in global politics. Although we need not always fully embrace the rejected, we certainly need to stay aware of it and in touch with it. Surprisingly, that which we reject, that which we fear, often contains exactly what we need for our health and wholeness, whether personal or collective. Our tale represents this profound truth through the image of the grotesque Dame Ragnelle, made ugly by men's rejection and fear. Only she holds the answer, which she will reveal only in exchange for love from the hero. Here, men are out of harmony, fighting over land and prestige, and only the rejected, and therefore ugly, woman holds the redeeming truth. Gawain shows that his extraordinary loyalty and self-sacrifice are the lifegiving balm. Sometimes the greatest hero is one who gives up personal desires and aversions in the name of loyalty and idealism.

Autonomy or sovereignty over one's own life is what all women desire above all else. Realization of this truth rescues the masculine and, when fully achieved as Gawain grants his wife the choice of when to be beautiful, transforms Ragnelle from ugly hag to radiant princess. The story concludes with the royal *quaternio*: the king and queen on one side and Gawain and Ragnelle on the other. The quaternio (a traditional symbol of wholeness examined at length by Jung[3]) can encompass even the dark rage of Sir Gromer.

Initially it made me uneasy that Gawain grants Ragnelle full autonomy by allowing her to choose which half of the day she will be beautiful. If she is *given* autonomy, rather than claiming it as her birthright, can't the gift be taken back? What kind of autonomy is that? I propose both a philosophical and psychological answer.

Philosophically, I draw inspiration from the Buddhist principle of emptiness, the very heart of that great tradition. Emptiness means that all phenomena, from our deepest sense of self to the most distant galaxies, lack independent or inherent existence. Their true reality is not their apparent independence, but their deep relatedness and mutual dependence. Therefore, from a Buddhist perspective, even autonomy lacks independent existence. Even independence of action or self-determination depends vitally upon one's relationship to others, in this case, the relationship of Ragnelle to Gawain. Thus, the feminine is dependent upon the masculine for its autonomy, yet Arthur's very life depends upon the feminine. Nothing independently or inherently exists, whether it is the notion of autonomy or the life of a king.

Psychologically, it is clear that the masculine *can* deny autonomy to the feminine. In a patriarchal society, it is assumed that the masculine has that authority. More personally, I think of the many times that I have inappropriately denied my feminine aspect its necessary expression. Yet the unconscious, the feminine ground of my being, grants me life both psychologically and physically. Another psychological dimension of the problem forces itself upon me in the form of the question, "Why is the autonomy of the feminine so fragile, so dependent upon the masculine?" A partial answer comes from realizing that because the feminine gives birth in the broadest sense of the term, whether to physical life or to creative thoughts and urges, its very function often puts it second. Whether as the servant of nature in the maternity ward or as the creative matrix out of which our psychic life is born, the feminine, by its very nature, must give precedence not to itself but to what is being born. As many mothers learn, having a child can crush their autonomy. This self-sacrifice of the feminine in favor of whatever is born thus makes her autonomy fragile and in need of support from the masculine.

To understand this tale more deeply, we need a better appreciation of the feminine principle and what its autonomy or sovereignty actually means. Surely, it is not simply that women should exercise their personal will in all things at all times. Such a one-sided view could not be the secret of wholeness and completion. Perhaps the place to start is to ask what the feminine symbolizes. Here I cannot follow many modern feminists who assert that femininity is just cultural conditioning. Yes, cultural conditioning surely affects our view of the feminine and its expression. However, the obvious biological differences between the genders must express themselves psychologically, even if culture inevitably modifies this expression. In other words, the continuity between mind and body, so evident in modern biology and medicine, demands that the biological differences between genders must have a psychological expression. Gender differences are more than social conditioning.

For at least two reasons, it is a daunting task to understand the feminine principle. First, the feminine is unappreciated, even denigrated, in our culture. Second, thanks to feminists and others, it is simultaneously being redefined. The very notion of "the feminine" is a moving target cloaked in layers of cultural overlay. Even Jung, who championed the feminine well before it was popular to do so, was a victim of the prejudices of his times. While his work clearly articulates and advocates feminine aspects of the psyche, several passages about the feminine are embarrassingly offensive to modern sensibilities.

In an attempt to get beyond the culturally defined stereotypes of female and male, let's consider the ancient Chinese doctrine of *yin* and *yang*, the fundamental and equally important principles generating the entire universe, as it is presented in the *I Ching* or *Book of Changes*.[4] This step does not merely exchange one set of cultural prejudices for another because the treatment of yin and yang in the *I Ching* is so much more profound and balanced than typical Western discussions of gender differences. It is a good place to start.

As a leading Chinese scholar, Wing-Tsit Chan, tells us, "The yin-yang doctrine is very simple, but its influence has been extensive. No aspect of Chinese civilization—whether metaphysics, medicine, government, or art—has escaped its imprint. In simple terms, the doctrine teaches that all things and events are products of two elements, forces, or principles: yin and yang."[5] The traditional diagram in figure 2 concisely depicts the yin-yang theory. The circle is the totality, all things in heaven and on earth, and is composed of or generated by the yin (dark) and the yang (light). Figure 2 clearly shows that yin and yang are distinct principles on an equal footing. Neither is inherently superior to the other, nor can one be reduced to the other. Their dynamic

Fig. 2. Yin-yang symbol

interplay accounts for the entire universe and its kaleidoscopic transformations. They are interdependent and, in a sense, define each other. The small dark disk within the light and the small light disk within the dark show that the opposites always contain each other. Even the most yin phenomenon has some yang in it, and vice versa.

In the first complete translation of the *I Ching*, by Rudolf Ritsema and Stephen Karcher, we find the following definitions, where the word "struction" means "to construct":

> Yin, **struction**, is the shadowy, structive aspect of phenomena. It refers to: build, make concrete, establish; limited, bound, given specific being; consolidating, conserving, structuring something. By consolidating the present, yin stops forward motion, drive, or purpose. The yin aspect of phenomena is the result of contraction and concentration; it is their positive (from *ponere*, to place, to put) mode of existence. It is diverse, adaptable extension in space, and an open system where all things are categorically discontinuous.
>
> Yang, **action**, is the light, active aspect of all phenomena. It refers to movement, dynamic development, thrust, stimulus, drive; focusing on a goal, giving direction to something. By creating the future, yang destroys the present, negating anything that exists in a positive or consolidated sense. The yang aspect of phenomena is their dynamic mode of becoming: arousal, transformation, and dissolution. It is united, continuous, unidirectional, a closed system where all things are categorically equal.[6]

Ritsema and Karcher supplement these definitions with a list of qualities that I've adapted for Table 1. Unpacking these definitions, we can say that the yin principle is the dark, cool, moist, receptive womb of the universe. It creates by receiving forms and giving them concrete expression. Through embodiment, the forms become explicit and complete. Because manifestation requires that only certain possibilities among many be realized, yin contains an aspect of contraction and limitation.

Table 1. QUALITIES OF YIN AND YANG

Yin/Struction applies to...	Yang/Action applies to...
The shady, cool southern bank of a river	The bright, warm northern bank of a river
The shady, cool northern slope of a mountain	The bright, warm southern slope of a mountain
Water	Fire
Moon	Sun
Lower	Upper
Interior	Exterior
Dark	Bright
Moist	Dry
Soft	Hard
Obscure	Manifest
Contracting	Expanding
Reaction	Stimulus
Incoming	Outgoing
Completing	Beginning
Receiving	Initiating
To be	To do

Realizing the yin principle in an individual psyche generates the feminine, lunar consciousness, with light reflected rather than intrinsic to it. Constantly involved in creation and dissolution, the dark interior world of feminine consciousness is ever in motion. With its inherently open appreciation of diversity, the feminine principle takes on an aspect of relatedness, without compromising its inward aspects of contraction and concentration. Although fecund, its creativity is not intellectual, but rather operates in the shadowy realm of body or instinct and is therefore not penetrable by the light of intellect. This darkness can seem mysterious or even threatening to yang consciousness.

The yang principle is light, hot, dry, active, and expansive. Its arousal gives direction, discipline, and focus. Its single-mindedness makes it a closed system unrelated to what comes before or after it. Realizing this principle in an individual psyche generates the masculine, solar consciousness, whose effulgent light and heat are intrinsic to its dynamism. Its dynamic, outward, thrusting aspect is symbolized by the hero and warrior, while its focus on goals and direction gives it a limitation and structure characteristic of the light of intellect.

Yin and yang are thus closely akin to what I call the realms of the heart and head. The heart (yin) is ruled not by reason but by obscure and shifting feelings, desires, and aversions. Yet, out of this creative matrix, impenetrable by the light of reason, comes every form of psychic life, from sublime spiritual intuitions to monstrous passions. Just as a mother instinctively loves the child born from her womb and immediately sees its beauty, the heart loves its productions indiscriminately. This love gives the entire world its value and beauty.

The head (yang) illuminates all in its white, energizing heat, brushing aside the messy realm of obscure feelings in its creation of intellectual structure and order. Without the heart's investment in its productions, the head can easily abandon one scheme or structure for another. The head's very dedication to ideal order and form blind it to relationship— and to the vagaries and shifting boundaries attendant on that mode of being.

These principles are a primal duality of life, and without some harmony between them, we careen from one excess to another and fail to achieve the true unity that is our birthright. In recorded history, at least in the West, the masculine has been favored over the feminine. "The Wedding of Sir Gawain and Dame Ragnelle" tells us that the deadly strife within the male principle can be halted and the neglected, and thus monstrously distorted, female principle can be rescued only by giving autonomy to the feminine. In other words, yang must let go of some of its focus on action, intellect, order, and structure and grant autonomy to the obscure and irrational, yet creative, forces of yin. (Here it would be appropriate to replace the word "irrational" with "superrational," that knowledge not encompassed within conventional notions of rationality.) From this choice ensues a synergy and dynamism that results in the wholeness symbolized by the royal quaternio with which the tale ends.

But how does an individual apply these ideas? Because the qualities of yin also accurately describe the collective and personal unconscious, the first step is simply to pay attention to the productions of those realms. Thus, the world of dream, vision, and fantasy, of sudden eruptions of feelings and intuitions, must be appreciated and given autonomy to express itself. This does not mean acting out every impulse springing from the unconscious, letting yin give explicit form to every urge. However, it does require that the so-called irrational (more properly, superrational) be given a seat of honor alongside the rational. Since the images flowing from the unconscious, and their meanings, are unique to each person, this step of allowing the feminine autonomy must be taken with full regard for individual differences. Here we take our lead from the heart and resist domination by the head's premature intellectual formulations, which minimize the individual in favor of the universal.

Let me give a concrete example of giving autonomy to the feminine. Examples could be taken from any field, from the sciences to art in the broadest sense. I draw this one from psychological experience, because that realm is familiar to everyone.

Consider working with a dream. Notice that I did not say "dream interpretation." Simply using that verbal formulation already makes the psyche, in its yin mode of giving birth and form to all images, subservient to yang's thrust for intellectual order and structure. The shadowy, shifting, mysterious, evanescent, ambiguous, interpenetrating, and seemingly irrational realm of dream is a beautiful expression of yin consciousness. One of the common mistakes in working with a dream is the tendency immediately to seek some rational understanding, some clear interpretation—to shine hastily the light of reason into the dream's murky depths before allowing the dream to speak in its own style and language. You might ask, "What's wrong with getting some clear understanding of a dream?" I would answer, "Nothing." I am certainly in favor of clearly understanding psychological experience. The type or school of dream interpretation is not the issue here. Rather, the problem lies in *immediately* shifting attention away from the detailed sensations, feelings, particularity, and general mystery of the dream and toward intellectual formulation of its meaning or purpose. This reaction is an example of the masculine denying autonomy to the feminine, of the intellect's tendency quickly to drag the dark yin mystery of dream into the light of reason, neat explanation, and categorization. It is the masculine intellect saying to the form-giving feminine, "Don't speak to me symbolically, woman! *I'll* tell you what you're saying."

It is important here to recall Jung's view of dreams as primarily unconscious compensation. For Jung, the vast intelligence symbolized by the unconscious relates to consciousness primarily by providing compensations, corrections, and new insights. Through dreams, the unconscious uses imagery to transform us by revealing hidden sides of our personality or new views of old problems or sometimes entirely new avenues for development. Thus, each major dream is an expression of the intentionality or purposiveness of the psyche, and it tells us something new or shows us a different way of seeing. In other words, if the dream seems to be telling us something we already know, we have missed the point.

If we immediately try to discern a rational structure in the dream, in almost all cases we are just restating the conscious ego's views, which the dream is trying to change. The intended transformation is therefore blocked, and we simply spin around within the same old structures of consciousness. If the intellect is good at denying the new input of the unconscious, of denying autonomy to the feminine, then nightmares as ugly as the early Dame Ragnelle will erupt.

What then is the proper approach to dreams? How can we give appropriate autonomy to the feminine unconscious? A detailed examination of these important questions would lead us too far afield, but a few brief suggestions are necessary. First, it is important to enter the dream space with humility. Entering the dream space means attempting to get back into the dream, to relive it in all its vivid detail, particularity, and mood. Of course, this can sometimes be a painful exercise. The ability to enter that dream space humbly comes from a deep appreciation that the dream holds wisdom not encompassed by the rational intellect nor by its structures and language. We must believe that there is something of deep value in the dream symbolism that cannot be approached like a physics problem.

As we enter that space, we attempt to set aside our preconceptions, pet theories, and tendency to reason our way through the dream and, instead, enter into the feelings and mystery of the dream—not as conquering heroes, but as sincere students. Such exploration of the sensual and emotional details of the dream requires a balance between two competing forces. We need to focus sharply on the dream images and simultaneously cultivate a diffuse awareness of our emotional reactions, associations, and intuitions to the various aspects of the dream.

The head's laserlike focus on the dream's detailed images, mood, and structure must be combined with the heart's response to the shifting depths of meaning.

Only after we have done our best to live our way back into the dream—experienced it in all its fullness, allowed it to evoke images and feeling responses without straying too far from the details of the dream—should we be analytical. Only after the feminine has spoken in her own language and we have been receptive to her particular symbolism is it appropriate to supplement her voice through our favorite scheme of dream interpretation. It may be appropriate to take many days or weeks of living with the dream images before proceeding to analytical judgments and interpretations. Giving autonomy to the dream world is challenging, but if done with sincerity and patience, the ugliest and most violent of nightmares can turn into a blazing display of feminine beauty and wisdom—just as in our tale of Gawain and Ragnelle.

Looking back on my experience during my trip to Puerto Rico, discussed in the preceding chapter, I notice connections to Gawain and Ragnelle's story, a tale I discovered decades after the original experience. These parallels stand out clearly if we consider each element in the myth as though it were a dream image symbolizing an aspect of my own psyche. The hero archetype has always appealed deeply to me, so I can easily identify with King Arthur, that paragon of masculine power and wisdom, and Gawain, his heroic and idealistic knight. On my trip to Puerto Rico, like Arthur, I was hunting—galactic nebulae rather than stags, true, but both quarries require definite skills. During the course of our hunting trips, we both confronted our mortality. Arthur and Gawain tried to solve their problem using the virtues characteristic of the hero. I too tried to control my fear and anxiety through the application of will and reason, the standard approach of yang consciousness.

Just as Gawain had to surrender to the insistence of the fearfully ugly Dame Ragnelle, I too eventually surrendered to my mortality, my recognition that the yin world of the body inevitably dies and transforms. In India, Kali, the goddess of death and sustenance, is believed to come for us when we die. I was convinced her hot breath was on me. Curiously, Arthur's salvation came not from heroism, but through yielding to the desires of the monstrous feminine, just as mine issued from the yin approach of surrender—of granting autonomy to the feminine. Out of this yielding, this abandonment of yang consciousness, issued an experience of the sublime aspect of yin. Allowing the feminine to express itself transformed my fear of death into spiritual rebirth, just as allowing autonomy to Ragnelle transformed impending death and hideousness into life and stunning beauty.

Granting autonomy to the feminine means that the scientific and rational approach, for which the West has been famous, must allow for an autonomous expression of the nonscientific and irrational (or superrational). Within the clockwork universe of Newton, we need room for the synchronistic universe of meaning. Within the universe of quantum field equations, human genome research, and nuclear weapons, we need a place of honor for spiritual experience and personal transformation. Within the universe of ordered doing, we need space for disordered being. The intellect must humbly accept that the heart's meaning, which transforms both itself and the intellect, cannot be completely comprehended by the head. Equal honor goes to the scientist with her separative and rational view of the universe and to the mystic with his unitive and feeling connection to the cosmos. Reality in all its fullness, pluralism, and splendor cannot be comprehended by either the head or the heart alone. Attempting to do so is like trying to walk on one leg—barely possible and full of danger.

Chapter Two

LESSONS FROM RADIO ASTRONOMY ABOUT OBJECTIVITY

I n my first year at Dartmouth College, as I study in Baker Library, I
am mesmerized by the Orozco frescoes covering the library walls.
Often my eyes are pulled away from my textbook up to them. Loom-
ing over me are oversized images of a man being flayed while tied upside
down, soldiers marching into death, Aztec priests ripping out a victim's
heart, early Native Americans being fed into a great machine, modern
gods of war—these and many other gruesome images emerge boldly
from the burning colors of those walls. Although I am anxious about
whether I can do the work demanded of a first-year student, I find the
Orozco frescoes so much more captivating than my text.

Those epic frescoes representing Pre- and Post-Colombian civilization frequently drew me from my immediate concerns and into some
of the finest experiences of my undergraduate years. The portion of the
fresco shown in figure 3 is as captivating for me today as it was nearly
forty years ago. Stillborn knowledge issues from a skeleton mother, who
is balanced precariously on a stack of ponderous tomes. Academic gowns
adorn the obstetrician and the dead figures in attendance. The most
compelling image for me is that of the homunculi sealed into bell jars
(fig. 4). I always imagined them to be professors hermetically sealed
into their own little worlds. I now understand that they are confined
by their overreliance on the intellect and an often too-literal belief in
one great truth, whether it be scientific materialism or the latest version of literary deconstruction. As a student, I kept coming back to
those homunculi; even today, when I reflect on the Orozco frescoes,
that image floats first and most vividly to mind as an early, if dimly
understood, image of the limitations of a narrowly intellectual approach.

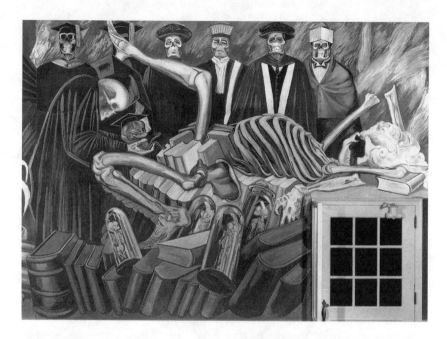

Fig. 3. Panel from Orozco fresco (with permission of Baker Library, Dartmouth College)

Fig. 4. "Professor" in a bell jar (detail from fig. 3)

As an undergraduate, I sensed only dimly the great dangers of dead knowledge and the isolation of academics from the great world beyond books. Today, my interest in those sealed-in professors is more personal and more pressing. Although I am concerned in general about the dangers of isolation, irrelevancy, and deadness in the academic world, I am more concerned about the risk of becoming one of those professors myself, of personally embodying those deadly qualities.

It seems that the more powerful the intellect and its knowledge, the greater its tendency for hubris. In that state, we falsely believe that all problems can at least be understood, if not solved, through the functioning of the intellect. Thus, transcendent knowledge, which demands as a precondition for its arrival the shutting down of the mind, becomes inaccessible to one devoted to the intellect. The great Christian mystic and philosopher Meister Eckhart forcefully expresses this well-known idea. He says that knowledge of the sacred can occur only "in the purest element of the soul, in the soul's most exalted place, in the core, yes, in the essence of the soul. The central silence is there, where no creature may enter, nor any idea, and there the soul neither thinks nor acts, nor entertains any idea, either of itself or of anything else."[1] The prerequisite of complete inner silence makes attaining high realizations of the sacred difficult for anyone, but even more difficult for those wedded exclusively to the intellect.

A story from the Zen tradition, reflecting Zen's intense focus on a direct, nonconceptual experience of the transcendent, expresses a similar example of how professors have special problems when approaching spiritual experience.

> Nan-in, a Japanese master during the Meiji era (1868-1912), received a university professor who came to inquire about Zen.
> Nan-in served tea. He poured his visitor's cup full, and then kept on pouring.
> The professor watched the overflow until he no longer could restrain himself. "It is overfull. No more will go in!"
> "Like this cup," Nan-in said, "you are full of your own opinions and speculations. How can I show you Zen unless you first empty your cup?"[2]

Eckhart and Nan-in are not saying that transcendent knowledge is anti-intellectual, but that the head and the heart are two broad approaches to knowledge—a theme I return to throughout this book. These two approaches to knowledge are approximately complementary, like waves and particles in quantum mechanics. Whether these approaches are revealing different faces of the same truth or are actually different truths is a crucial point addressed in detail in chapter 13. However, as I reflect on it, this complementarity generates tension in me. The part of me who is a devotee of theoretical astrophysics, who revels in using the intellect to penetrate into outer nature, denigrates the part of me who is a mystic longing for a direct intuitive grasp of the essence of being.

That skeptical astrophysicist considers inner events, such as those that occurred during my flight to Arecibo, as merely subjective or personal. In other words, such experiences have no objective basis in the world of scientific fact. They may be psychologically satisfying, but they are not "real," not building blocks for a modern scientific view of the world. This commonly held view shows the reverence we have for science and objective knowledge. Yes, science yields extraordinary knowledge through its emphasis on objectivity. The modern love affair with science has brought great benefits to us all, even if in the last few decades we have begun to understand how severe the ecological and social costs have been.

However, we rarely appreciate how our veneration of science and its objectivity has shriveled our inner life and demoted its value and significance. So many of the personal and public crises of modern society can be traced to this lack of reverence for the inner world. However, science is actually less objective than is usually understood, and, despite its many virtues, it can never grasp some vital aspects of reality. Thus, it is important to understand precisely *how* science is objective. With this in mind, we will now make a little excursion into a central idea in radio astronomy, the concept of convolution and deconvolution of radio signals. This example gives us an opportunity to examine the nature of scientific objectivity in a fresh way.

This example is also one of several instances where I use scientific ideas to illuminate psychological, philosophical, or spiritual ideas. This approach has its dangers, but it is also an important way of relating science and the sacred and can sometimes lead to a deeper and richer understanding of both. Strangely enough, this approach also connects back to the fresco I have found so fascinating all these years. Take another look at figure 3, and notice the door in the lower right corner. That's a real door; Orozco just painted the fresco around it. The scientist in me says, "So what?" However, the lover of symbolism in me says that perhaps my door to deeper truth lies under and through the dead intellectualism represented above it. Let's see if we can walk through together.

CONVOLUTION AND DECONVOLUTION

In radio astronomy, each telescope can observe some parts of the sky and some frequencies better than others. For example, the Arecibo telescope is less sensitive to objects near the horizon. In addition, because of its geometry and the details of its electronic receivers, the telescope is more sensitive to some frequencies than others. These varying sensitivities are mathematically described by *response functions*. The measured signal from a particular astronomical object is then a combination of the signal actually emitted by the astronomical object (called the intrinsic signal) and the response function of the telescope.

Let's clarify this with a more familiar example. The human eye is only sensitive to visible light, a limited part of the electromagnetic spectrum. Our eyes cannot see the radio waves studied at Arecibo. Even within the visible part of the spectrum, the eye responds more strongly to some frequencies (that is, colors) than others. In addition, the eye can see objects directly ahead better than those at the periphery of its field of view. This variation in sensitivity depending on frequency and position, along with many other attributes, makes up the response function of the eye, which is completely analogous to the response function of a radio telescope. The actual image we perceive is thus a combination of the light actually emitted by the object and the response function of the eye.

As part of the calibration of a radio telescope (a procedure that helps ensure that measurements are accurate), astronomers carefully measure the response function and give it a detailed mathematical description. In radio astronomy language, we say that the intrinsic signal from the astronomical object is *convolved* with the response function to give the measured signal. That is, we can never directly measure the intrinsic signal from any astronomical object. What we do measure is always a combination or convolution of the intrinsic signal with the peculiarities of the particular telescope. Fortunately, there are well-defined mathematical methods called *deconvolution* that permit a radio astronomer to remove the effect of the response function and thereby retrieve the intrinsic signal. Figure 5 summarizes this relationship.

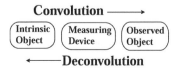

Fig. 5. Convolution/deconvolution

Returning to the example of human vision, we acknowledge that our actual experienced image depends on the eye's contribution when we say, "This print looks blurry; it must be my weak eyes." However, since the human eye is much more complex than a radio telescope, deconvolution (that is, removing the contribution of the eye's response function) is much more difficult, but possible in principle. Similar ideas apply to any measuring device, whether it be a little hand-held voltmeter or a nuclear magnetic resonance machine used in medical imaging. In the latter case, deconvolution is essential so that doctors can be confident that they are seeing an accurate picture of a medical condition and not the result of some peculiarity of the machine's functioning.

The following box gives a more precise description of convolution and deconvolution. If you don't have a taste for such mildly technical discussions, you can skip this explanation without any loss in continuity. On the other hand, you might find the graphical examples helpful.

A Graphical Example of Convolution and Deconvolution

Let's imagine that some intelligent civilization is broadcasting a signal that looks like the graph in figure 6. The horizontal axis displays time increasing to the right, and the vertical axis plots the intrinsic signal strength. In fact, if we ever saw such a signal, we might guess from its sharp edges and uniform positive and negative values that it was some sort of digital broadcast.

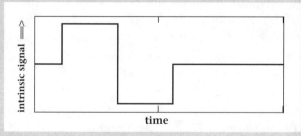

Fig 6. Intrinsic signal

Next, imagine that we are observing this intrinsic signal with a primitive radio telescope whose simplified response function looks like the graph in figure 7. Time is again plotted increasing to the right. This response function tells us how a measuring device responds to a very sharply peaked pulse, that is, an intense burst of electrical energy of very short duration—a sort of flashbulb pop. The graph shows that the telescope gradually "wakes up," or registers that the pulse is present. This is the left part of the plot, where the curve is increasing. From the right side of the plot we can tell that the telescope takes some time to "fall back to sleep," to return to the quiescent condition it was in before the electrical impulse occurred. This is just what happens in the human eye. It takes time for the eye to register that the flashbulb has gone off, and it also takes time for the afterimage to fade.

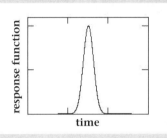

Fig. 7. Simplified response function

Figure 8 shows the signal the telescope would record. It is the result of convolving, or combining, the intrinsic signal (fig. 6) with the response function (fig. 7). This measured signal clearly displays similarities to the intrinsic signal, but the slow response (limited time resolution) of the telescope, embodied in its response function, has smeared or spread out the intrinsic signal. In other words, this response function makes individual events appear to last longer than they actually do. The once-blocky intrinsic signal now appears more like a smooth sine wave. Fortunately, the mathematical process of deconvolution allows us to retrieve the intrinsic signal if we know both the measured signal and the response function. On the other hand, if we don't know the details of the response function, we can only guess at the intrinsic signal.

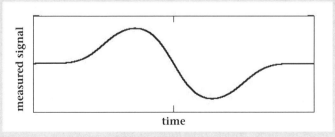

Fig 8. Measured signal

Deconvolution is a mathematical way of attempting to achieve the scientific ideal: to apprehend the world without the interference or influence of the subject. As I have discussed elsewhere,[3] both the theory of relativity and quantum mechanics place some limits on this ideal. Nevertheless, deconvolution precisely expresses the desire to remove any influence of the measuring device, including the structure of our mind-body complex, from our view of nature. Can this ideal be realized?

To answer this question, let's make a leap in abstraction and generality by thinking of our entire mind-body complex as the measuring apparatus. Include all the properties of the senses, nervous system, and brain (the hardware). Include all the psychological processes and all the philosophical, linguistic, scientific, and cultural presuppositions (the software). All these properties, processes, and presuppositions, taken together, are a *metaresponse function*. Of course, such a metaresponse function would be unimaginably complex. The most difficult point is that many aspects of this metaresponse function are unconscious. In other words, many unknown aspects of our mind-body complex (especially our psychological, philosophical, linguistic, and cultural presuppositions) make a significant contribution to our metaresponse function. For example, our attitudes toward gender can significantly modify our view of the world:

> While we all have the experience of not seeing things that are before our eyes, it still may be difficult for most nonscientists (or scientists) to believe that scientists' values, beliefs, and expectations can influence what they are actually able to *see* or *hear* with their perfectly functioning senses. For example, leading microscopists of the 17th and 18th centuries, including the great van Leeuwenhoek, claimed they had seen "exceedingly minute forms of men with arms, heads and legs complete inside sperm" under the microscope. Their observations were constrained not by the limited resolving power of the microscopes of the time, but rather by the 2,000-year-old concept, dating from the time of Aristotle, that women, as totally passive beings, contribute nothing to conception but the womb as incubator.[4]

Since many of our attitudes and presuppositions are unconscious, they cannot be included in any metaresponse function that we might try to fashion for humans.

Our experience, in the broadest sense of the term, is thus a convolution of the intrinsically given (that is, what nature actually provides) with our metaresponse function. Unfortunately, in this case, deconvolution is impossible in principle, for two reasons. First, we cannot know all the aspects of our metaresponse function, since that would require full knowledge of our hardware and software—including the unconscious aspects, which are intrinsically unknowable. Second, even if we could attain such superknowledge of the metaresponse function (including all the unconscious components), there would be insurmountable computational difficulties with applying it. Therefore, unlike radio astronomy, we cannot retrieve the actual given input to our experience. Our knowledge is always a convolution of our metaresponse function with what is actually given, and there is no way to separate them fully.

Communicating with Extraterrestrials

At about the time I was learning about convolution and deconvolution while taking two radio astronomy courses from Frank Drake at Cornell, he and the astronomer Carl Sagan were designing a message plaque for the Pioneer 10 space probe (fig. 9). Pioneer 10 was launched on March 2, 1972, and is now nearly seven billion miles from the Sun. In June 1983, it passed the orbit of Pluto and thus became our first material artifact to leave the solar system. Depending upon your point of view, it is

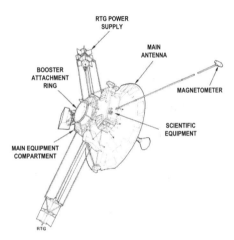

Fig. 9. Pioneer 10 space probe (courtesy of National Space Agency, Pioneer Project, Ames Research Center)

either the leading edge of our species' journey to the stars or our first material pollution outside our solar system. (Of course, we have been broadcasting TV signals into the galaxy for decades.) Knowing that any civilization that might encounter the plaque would not share our linguistic conventions, Sagan and Drake decided to use the structure of the physical world as the medium of communication. The feature they settled on was the 21-centimeter radiation from neutral hydrogen (see box). Because this radiation is so strong and hydrogen is so common, Sagan and Drake reasoned that it would be a good length scale to use for communicating with an advanced civilization.

The Hydrogen Line

Ninety percent of the atoms in the universe are hydrogen. When hydrogen is unionized, or neutral, it generates a powerful and specific narrow band of energy, called line radiation, with a wavelength of 21 centimeters (8.3 inches). This line is produced by the following processes. Quantum mechanics dictates that the spins of the electron and the proton in the hydrogen atom can have two configurations: the spins are either aligned or anti-aligned (that is, oriented in opposite directions). Although atomic spin is a quantum mechanical property without a classical analogue, it often helps to picture particles as little spinning tops. The arrows in figure 10 indicate the different directions of the spins.

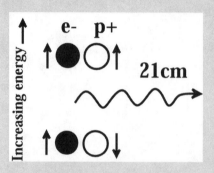

Fig. 10. Spin orientations and energy levels for 21-centimeter radiation

When the spins are aligned, the atom is in a higher energy state. When hydrogen atoms collide because of their random thermal motions, these collisions tend to populate the higher energy level, or excited, state. The excited atom then spontaneously drops into the lower energy state, in which the spins are anti-aligned, and emits a photon with a wavelength of 21 centimeters. The energy of this photon is exactly the difference between the energies of the high and low states. Figure 10 shows a spin flip leading to emission of a photon (or photoemission).

The 21-centimeter line is one of the most easily observed features of neutral hydrogen and is often used in radio astronomy. For example, in my project at the Arecibo telescope, mentioned in the Introduction, we were using this line to study neutral hydrogen in gaseous nebulae in our galaxy.

On the Pioneer plaque (fig. 11) are sketches of a man and a woman drawn to scale standing next to a line silhouette of the spacecraft.[†]

[†]A couple of years after the spacecraft was launched, Sagan told us that several people had complained about showing the humans naked. Perhaps they were concerned about offending the good taste of some alien civilization, or perhaps they simply did not want taxpayers' money supporting what they thought was pornographic graffiti. In any case, their comments show that everyone has a different metaresponse function.

Between the bracketing bars on the far right (near the woman's left hand) is the binary representation of the number eight. The unit of measurement is indicated in the upper left by a diagram denoting the 21-centimeter spin-flip transition of a hydrogen atom. Therefore, the woman is 8 x 21 centimeters tall (168 centimeters, or about 5'6").

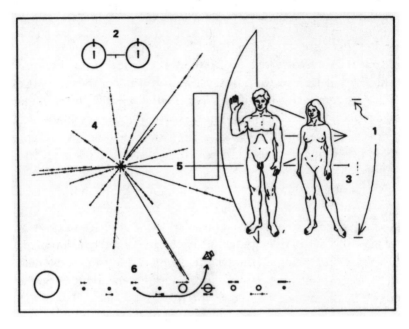

Fig. 11. Pioneer 10 plaque (courtesy of National Space Agency, Pioneer Project, Ames Research Center)

The path the spacecraft used to escape the solar system is shown schematically at the bottom of the plaque. If this spacecraft is ever picked up, it is likely to be very far from our solar system. Therefore, a radial pattern etched on the plaque represents the position of our Sun relative to fourteen nearby pulsars (rapidly rotating neutron stars). There is also a horizontal line depicting the direction to the center of our galaxy—this message-in-a-bottle thrown into the galactic ocean has a return address! The hope is that perhaps in the distant future, even billions of years from now, Pioneer may wander into a stellar neighborhood possessing an advanced civilization that can decode the plaque.

Let's focus on the presuppositions of Sagan and Drake in designing the plaque. They, and most of the scientific community along with them, assume that all technically sophisticated alien civilizations will agree on the structure of the hydrogen atom, even though their perceptual apparatus is likely to be different from ours. Their way of doing science may also be different, but if they are at least as sophisticated scientifically as we are, then they will surely recognize the internal structure and behavior of the most common atom in the universe. In fact, since we are relative newcomers in our galaxy, an alien civilization is likely to be much older and more advanced than we are. The assumption is that the structure of the universe they observe will be essentially identical to ours.

But this assumption is a huge leap of faith. I stressed earlier that we cannot deconvolve our metaresponse function from the known world. By that I mean we can never remove the contribution of our mind-body complex, with all its psychological, philosophical, linguistic, scientific, and cultural components. We don't know if aliens can get direct knowledge of the given world (without some metaresponse function), although it seems unlikely. In any case, it is really an article of faith, and nothing more, that another civilization will see essentially the same world we do. I certainly want to grant that there is an intrinsically given world, the bedrock input for our experience, but what that world is *in itself* we can never know. Yes, our scientific knowledge may improve in its empirical adequacy, its comprehension of more and deeper phenomena. However, it is impossible to observe nature independent of our metaresponse function, independent of our subjectivity in the broadest sense of the term. Nor can we be sure that another intelligent creature with a different metaresponse function will arrive at a description of nature that is equivalent to ours. If we accept that fact, what then happens to the cherished belief in the objectivity of science?

In fact, the objectivity of science is not located in the object, but in the scientists investigating the object.[5] Objectivity in the scientific sense is actually intersubjective agreement among competent observers—that is, agreement among persons who already agree on the psychological, philosophical, linguistic, scientific, and cultural components of the metaresponse function.

Thomas Kuhn, in his famous book *The Structure of Scientific Revolutions,* has used other arguments to question the objectivity of science. Responding to the concerns of Kuhn and many others, Sheldon Glashow, the Nobel Prize–winning physicist, gave his "cosmic catechism" at the twenty-fifth Nobel conference:

> We believe that the world is knowable, that there are simple rules
> governing the behavior of matter and the evolution of the uni-

verse . . . [and that] [a]ny intelligent alien anywhere would have come upon the same logical system as we have to explain the structure of protons and the nature of supernovae. This statement I cannot prove, this statement I cannot justify. This is my faith.[6]

This is a lovely profession of scientific fundamentalism; it would take only a few word substitutions to make it sound like any variety of religious fundamentalism. As we will see in later chapters, fundamentalism, whether in religion or science, becomes the confining bell jar of Orozco's fresco. Not only does fundamentalism separate us from reality in its many forms, but it is also the breeding ground for conflict and hatred.

However, faith in the objectivity of science is hardly the same as science being genuinely objective. At the very least, science should be more modest in its claims about objective knowledge. The preceding discussion shows that all science always includes a large, unknowable, and inextricable contribution of our subjectivity. This circumstance does not diminish the real accomplishments of science nor its great value, but it does take much of the force out of the argument that some scientists make about the lack of objectivity in inner experiences.

As important as it is to appreciate that science can never be fully objective, it is equally important to appreciate that reality, the fullness of what actually is, can never be fully objective either. Why? Because reality includes you and me and our subjectivity. We must appreciate that true subjectivity, by its very nature, cannot be turned into an object for scientific investigation. If you believe that subjectivity will eventually be turned into an object for scientific study, as is claimed in the well-known book *Consciousness Explained*,[7] then I respectfully submit you are considering only a superficial level of subjectivity, not what I am calling true subjectivity. This misapprehension stems from confusing the contents of consciousness with the subjective principle of consciousness itself, or equivalently, from conflating the contents of awareness with awareness in its purity.

Clearly, different levels of objectivity and subjectivity exist. Any sighted person looking out my office window as I write this could see a cardinal at the bird feeder, while the woman sitting next to me on the plane to Arecibo probably had no contact with my inner experience. However, it is not possible to stand on a Himalayan peak of scientific objectivity and criticize inner experiences as merely subjective. There is no such peak. Clinging to some pure notion of scientific objectivity and neglecting the subjective aspect of reality seals the bell jar, entombing the professor within.

Chapter Three

A SPECIAL KIND OF KNOWLEDGE

Tibetan Buddhist master Sogyal Rinpoche[1] tells an old Tibetan story of a frog who lived in a well who was visited by a frog from the ocean. The ocean frog explains that he lives in a big body of water. The frog in the well asks, "Is the ocean as big as my well?"

"No, it is much bigger."

"Is it twice as big as my well?"

"No it is much, much bigger."

The frog in the well just cannot comprehend what the ocean frog is talking about, so he accepts the other frog's invitation to visit the ocean. After a long and arduous journey, he finally comes to the ocean.

It is such a shock that his head explodes.

Of course, this story has nothing to do with bodies of water of different size or other external objects. As Sogyal Rinpoche makes clear, it is about the kind of self-knowledge that can transform our being at the deepest levels, or make our head explode. We must distinguish knowledge of objective facts, such as the size of the ocean or ideas in science, from a kind of knowledge that I'll call *transformative self-knowledge*. I begin by describing a personal example of such knowledge. In later chapters, I'll argue that it is wrong to apply the logic and presuppositions of science to such knowledge. Such an approach dishonors this nonscientific knowledge and is a destructive form of scientism—that is, an attempt to apply science and its methods where they do not belong. On the other hand, clearly distinguishing scientific knowledge and transformative self-knowledge allows for a deeper understanding of both and prepares the way for some degree of harmony between them.

On a cold, gray day in January 1968, some friends and I are on the way to a local Chinese restaurant in Ithaca, New York. We come upon something new—the American Brahman Bookstore. Its window is dominated by a big, seated Buddha statue nestled among an assortment of books on Eastern thought, mysticism, and astrology. Finding it irresistible, we enter.

The air is dense with a mixture of sandalwood incense and the sharp sting of cigarette smoke. The well-worn store is filled with classical music, but the bookshelves are mostly empty except for a few photographs and the temperature is only a few degrees warmer than the street. The cigarette smoke comes from a handsome man in his mid-forties with longish black hair and an equally black goatee. He is standing on a circular heating grate, trying to get warm. He greets us with a thick Brooklyn accent, throws his cigarette butt down the grate, and starts another. I drift to the shelves and look over a few books. I quickly realize that they are part of the personal collection of the bookstore owner, who soon engages us in a philosophical conversation. His long, graceful hands sculpt the air during our animated discussion. Although his accent is reminiscent of a New York City cab driver, he speaks with great clarity and authority on a wide range of topics that could be broadly classified as philosophic mysticism. In the midst of making a philosophical point, he walks over to a shelf and pulls down texts ranging from *Plato's Dialogues* to the Buddhist *Heart Sutra*. He seems to know the exact pages of the quotations he wants.

He is a powerful and magnetic presence, utterly without pretense. In the course of our far-ranging conversation, he offers to cast our horoscopes. I agree and give him my time and place of birth. My friends and I eventually make our way to the Chinese restaurant where, between gulps of won ton soup and egg rolls, we share our amazement about this extraordinary man.

FINDING THE TEACHER

The bookstore owner was Anthony Damiani (fig. 12). I later learned that Anthony had never finished college but had spent many years as a longshoreman, subway token collector, headwaiter, and bookstore manager before becoming a toll collector on the New York State Thru-way. Following an inner prompting and with the help of his oldest son, Steven, he opened a metaphysical bookstore in downtown Ithaca, New York, in November 1967. He built the bookstore's collection and attracted a large following, while at the same time working on the Thru-way and raising six sons.

At the time, I was a graduate student in theoretical astrophysics at Cornell. I was an agnostic who believed that love and peace were much more valuable than reli-gious doctrine, which had often been the cause of more suffering than good. Al-though for years I had loved and struggled with the Catholic Church, it had been nearly a decade since I had thought of my-self as a Christian. My religious urge expressed itself through social activism, pri-marily civil rights work and resistance to the Vietnam War. Like many in that era, I also experimented with powerful psyche-delic drugs, which exploded my inner world

Fig. 12. Anthony Damiani
(courtesy of Jan Hollien)

and gave me intimations of the truth of some of the great mystical and philosophical traditions—what many call the perennial philosophy. Largely because of these experiences, I had a growing interest in East-ern thought, primarily Buddhism and Hinduism.

A week or so after the initial conversation at the bookstore, I was walking past the store again, this time with my girlfriend (who later became my wife), on the way to the same Chinese restaurant. As we went by, Anthony stuck his head out the door and offered to interpret the horoscope he had cast. In that conversation, my view of astrology was transformed. This unusual man, who had his feet firmly planted on the ground, an active family life, and intimate knowledge of many of the world's great religious and philosophical traditions, showed me how astrology could be used as an x-ray machine for the psyche. How-ever, I saw no way to bring astrology into a compatible relationship with the scientific world of my profession. That day marked the begin-ning of my struggle to harmonize the ancient wisdom of astrology with modern science—a struggle that informs parts of this book.

Those were turbulent years. As much as I loved theoretical astro-physics, I felt a deep restlessness that I could neither identify nor satisfy.

In between my involvement with civil rights activism and war protests, I road-raced motorcycles (fig. 13). Fortunately, the exhilaration of roaring into a sharp turn at more than 120 miles per hour waned before I killed myself. Of course, none of this fully answered my soul's demands, and my graduate career wound through many twists and turns, including taking more than a year off to go to California. There I pursued an eclectic mix of psychological training, work in a mental hospital, and research in astrophysics at Stanford University. The astrophysics provided a much-needed rational haven, an island of logical order in a sea of enormous eruptions of the unconscious caused by the psychological study, mental hospital work, and psychedelics. After answering my need for something beyond a science education, I returned to Ithaca and, supported by Anthony's encouragement, eventually earned my Ph.D. from Cornell.

Fig. 13. Vic preparing for road-racing

About three years after first meeting Anthony and after several visits to his home— where we were treated by his wife, Ella May, to great Italian food and family warmth—I realized that he had become my guru, although it happened gradually and neither of us ever used that term. He was not looking for disciples. I was not looking for a guru. Nor did he fit my "image" of a proper guru; yet, he has had the most benign influence on my life of any person I have known.

While I developed my research and teaching in physics and astrophysics at Cornell and Colgate universities, through Anthony's instruction I became deeply involved in meditation and the study of mystical philosophy, astrology, and depth psychology. Under his influence, I also stopped using all psychedelics and became a vegetarian. For seventeen years, Anthony taught a group of dedicated students to think deeply, meditate, and listen to classical music with such loving concentration that it became a genuine spiritual experience. His great passion was to get beneath the linguistic differences among such widely varying traditions as Advaita Vedānta (philosophical Hinduism), Buddhism, Neoplatonism, and Jungian psychology. He combined great personal warmth and charm with a fierce desire to understand the philosophical underpinnings of astrology and these diverse traditions. Some of this work has been published.[2] Perhaps most important, he enkindled our desire to seek a personal realization of the great truths buried in these traditions.

In the late sixties and early seventies, we attended weekly classes and meditations at Anthony's bookstore. At 5:30 P.M., I would leave the hill on which Cornell is perched and descend into downtown Ithaca to meditate with Anthony and scores of his students. Learning to meditate was a struggle. We could hear the TV from the diner next door. Passersby on the street would often peer in the store window, gawk at us, and speculate on what might be taking place. If my body was not protesting from having to sit still in a proper meditation posture, my mind was swimming with thoughts. I distinctly recall trying to still my mind and having it be flooded instead with the equations I had been working on that afternoon. Despite both external and internal distractions, Anthony inspired us and we all pushed ahead.

Fig. 14. Handyman's special

Fig. 15. Building a log house at Wisdom's Goldenrod

In the summer of 1972, my wife and I bought an old farmhouse on sixty-six acres. It was a classic handyman's special (fig. 14). I had to work furiously on that house just to make it livable. However, it had the great virtue of being near Anthony's home and the land that he donated to our group. We had outgrown the bookstore and were constructing a log building for classes and meditation on Anthony's donated land (fig. 15). I spent a good deal of time working on that building and the three that followed, while also doing postdoctoral work at Cornell. It was interstellar medium calculations by day and carpentry and study with Anthony by night and on weekends. During it all, I was finding great joy in my marriage and being a father to our two-year-old son.

A GLIMPSE BEYOND THE EGO

Despite all this frenzy of mental and physical activity, meditation got a little easier. Although I had no dramatic breakthroughs, there seemed to be fewer equations and thoughts running around in my head when I tried to meditate. One day after meditation, before I could get back into normal consciousness, Anthony came up to me and said, "In a little while you will have an experience like an inner orgasm." He then abruptly walked away. I was startled and left without a clue as to what he meant. He would sometimes make these strange pronouncements to me and refuse to say more about them. Many years later, he told me that he spontaneously got these intuitions and could offer neither explanation nor amplification for them.

To get some concentrated time alone, a break from my frenzied activity, and more time for meditation, I had arranged to spend a couple of days in retreat at a local Benedictine monastery. The arrangements had been made weeks before Anthony gave me that cryptic prophecy. At the monastery, I easily fell into the monks' rhythm of silent meals and repeated periods of community prayer. I supplemented this routine with long walks, reading, hatha yoga, and several hours a day of meditation. I loved being alone in my tiny, white-walled cell, which, I realize now, was not too different from the room I occupied three years later at the Arecibo Observatory. Because my inner struggles with the Catholic Church more than a decade earlier had been so painful, it was particularly healing to enjoy the monastery; to again be inspired by Christian prayer, scripture, and iconography; and to reawaken warm childhood memories of religious life.

While meditating late one morning, I felt an unusual amount of energy at the base of my spine, in the perineum. I tried to ignore it and push steadily ahead. The last ordinary thing I recall was birds making a terrific racket just below my open window. Perhaps they were encouraging their young to fly from a nest in the ivy growing there. Suddenly, an intense heat flashed up from the bottom of my spine and roared to the top of my head. My entire body, right out to the ends of my limbs, was flooded with an extraordinary ecstasy. Along with this powerful feeling, my mind exploded with intense white light. A profound bliss of devotion, love, tenderness, and gratitude accompanied the bodily and mental sensations. Initially, it seemed like effulgent love without an object, gratitude without limit. Then I recalled Anthony's prediction, and the words "He is the hand of God" spontaneously formed in my mind. With this, Anthony was enveloped in that love without boundaries.

After I had luxuriated in this state for perhaps fifteen minutes, the chapel bells started ringing, as I had never heard them before. They seemed to peal on endlessly with one melody flowing seamlessly into another. I eventually got up and went to lunch in a completely altered state of consciousness, still feeling the tingling ecstasy right out to my fingertips and toes. I was late and noticed that they were serving an unusually opulent meal. The monks were even having small glasses of wine. I refused the wine and, I am ashamed to say, felt morally superior in doing so. It was clear that something special was going on both outwardly and inwardly. I was so grateful that I did not have to make small talk at the table. What wisdom the Benedictine Rule embodies! At every meal, a monk reads from scripture or a religious text. From the reading that day, I learned it was the Feast of the Assumption of the Virgin Mary into Heaven. Every August 15, Catholics celebrate the assumption of the Virgin's body and soul into heaven. It seemed synchronistic to me that on that particular feast day, in a Catholic monastery, the feminine spiritual energy called *Shakti* or *kundalini* in the East was elevated, giving me a glimpse of heaven.

In the language of chapter 1, we could say that initially I was aware of that feminine yin consciousness as sexual energy, as my personal expression of the ravenous side of Dame Ragnelle. Then that expression of yin, independent of my will, transformed from fearsome sexual power into a genuine spiritual awakening.

The next day I returned to the bookstore and told Anthony about the experience. I was too embarrassed to tell him of my overblown intuition that he was "the hand of God." Nevertheless, I hoped he would help me understand the experience. He just said, "Now you know what sex is about," then abruptly spun on his heel and walked away. I was flabbergasted. I wanted him to tell me that I was soon to become the next Buddha and how such ecstasies and illuminations would be my constant companions. In retrospect, all this is embarrassing. A little kundalini experience suddenly made me think I was a spiritual giant, superior to those wine-drinking monks and never again subject to the sorrows of earthly life.

By now, I have learned that such experiences always entail a primitive ego inflation and that Anthony was trying to minimize it by his curt response. In addition, it is well known that arousal of kundalini can generate bodily or psychological problems, but I am happy to say that, other than inflation, I never suffered any such problems. Despite the inflation, I had a genuine experience of something transcendent to normal ego consciousness and yet more intimate than my own breath.

Many years later, I read the following quotation from Anthony's teacher, Paul Brunton:

> Either at acceptance or later, the disciple experiences an ecstatic reverie of communion with the teacher's soul. There is a sensation of space filled with light, of self liberated from bondage, of peace being the law of life. The disciple will understand that this is the real initiation from the hands of the teacher rather than the formal one. The disciple will probably be so carried away by the experience as to wish it to happen every day. But this cannot be. It can happen only at long intervals. It is rather to be taken as a sign of the wonderful relation which has sprung up between them and as a token of eventual attainment. [3]

This statement echoes Anthony's refusal to be involved in any ritual of outward initiation and his insistence over the years that the real spiritual initiation occurs in the depths of our own hearts.The quotation leaves open the question of what "the real initiation from the hands of the teacher" actually means. How much of an intervention did Anthony make? I simply don't know. He always insisted that he only "threw the switch" and the light came from our own souls.

LESSONS ABOUT THE OUTER AND INNER WORLDS

It is difficult to discuss experiences such as this and the one described in the introduction. On one hand, others can easily misunderstand them; on the other hand, I can fatten my ego with them. Nevertheless, these pivotal experiences shaped my understanding of both the outer and inner worlds. For that reason, I take the risk of reporting them. I cannot claim to fully understand the kundalini experience, but some lessons from it seem clear.

OUTER WORLD. Despite my immediate attraction to Anthony, I still had a healthy reserve toward him until the kundalini experience. However, that experience taught me that Anthony was my teacher in the highest sense of the word: an important, although still mysterious, link to what is best and most authentic in me. For those who have never had such a relationship, it is difficult to appreciate its depth, beauty, potential for abuse (which did not happen to me), and the difficulty and importance of learning to walk on your own. In a recent paper, I have examined the psychological and spiritual dimensions of the guru-disciple relationship and how we can work from it toward independence.[4]

My direct experience of an immaterial, transcendental principle— something not included in a scientific materialist's view of the world—dramatically demonstrated that normal science could not explain this unrepeatable experience. Nor could science explain what it implied about my relationship to the cosmos. The experience destroyed any lingering allegiance I might have had to a narrow scientific materialism. After it, I realized life was too precious to devote myself excessively to career or sacrifice the inner life for outer achievement.

The physician and educator Rachael Naomi Remen, M.D., expresses this idea very beautifully:

> Science has cast a deep shadow over our ideas about life. We may even have allowed science to define life for us, but life is larger than science. Life is process, and process has Mystery woven into it.
>
> Things happen that science can't explain, important things that cannot be measured but can be observed, witnessed, known. These things are not replicable. They are impervious to even the best designed research.
>
> All life has in it the dimension of the Unknown; it is a thing forever unfolding. It seems important to consider the possibility that science may have defined life too small. If we define life too small, we will define ourselves too small as well.[5]

INNER WORLD. So much of what I had studied in various traditions, both East and West, became more direct and vivid for me after that experience. I could no longer doubt that there are nonmaterial principles that can benevolently intervene in our life to further our psychological and spiritual evolution. Of course, this view flies in the face of the modern scientific view of a world where there is no purpose or teleology. But on that day, the soul, self, higher mind, subtle consciousness—or whatever term you prefer—became for me a living and active reality. My little taste of it changed me forever.

It helped me appreciate that sexuality and spirituality need not be mortal enemies, as my early Catholic upbringing had taught me. The body is not naturally antagonistic to spirit. It was a major realization to appreciate that the energy invested in sexuality could be a power for spiritual transformation. I also realized that the event was more than a blissful expression of something transcending my ego. The event also contained within it the appreciation that it was only a minor mystical experience, despite my initial inflation. Furthermore, the experience came with a demand for sustained effort to deepen my commitment to the spiritual path, to intensify and extend my efforts at self-realization.

CHARACTERIZING TRANSFORMATIVE SELF-KNOWLEDGE

The kundalini experience was one of my earliest instructions in distinguishing the head from the heart. Through it, I began to distinguish between scientific knowledge, such as the astrophysical research I was working on at the time, and what I am formulating here as transformative self-knowledge. Scientific knowledge, with its emphasis on objectivity and separation from the observer, repeatability, and precise use of mathematics and abstraction, contrasts sharply with knowledge through identity. By knowledge through identity I mean an event that obliterates the dividing line between content and knower while the heart gropes in the dark to formulate its subjective experience of principles superior to itself. A powerful insight, aesthetic experience, dream, vision, mystical experience, synchronicity experience, or some combination of these could also be an instance of transformative self-knowledge. However, any example of such knowledge must embody the following seven qualities.

1. Although elements of this knowledge are external to me, it is primarily an *interior intuition*, one welling up from my deepest subjectivity. A research physiologist measuring the effects on the nervous system of that kundalini experience would get exterior knowledge of the event. I experienced it from the inside, subjectively. This is a sufficiently critical point that another example seems in order. Imagine a person with a wide range of eating experiences and a sophisticated ability to discriminate various tastes. However, this imaginary person has never tasted chocolate or anything like it. No matter how you describe the minute details of eating chocolate, either by comparison with other foods or from a biochemical viewpoint, you cannot deliver the experience of eating chocolate to this person. Analogously, no matter how much you describe an experience of transformative self-knowledge, either from a phe-

nomenological or psychosomatic point of view, your description is only exterior knowledge and thus is qualitatively different from the actual interior experience.

2. It is *holistic knowledge*, connecting to all aspects of my life and me. Transformative self-knowledge includes the whole of a person: the body, mind, and spirit. It can never be restricted to one part of life but must include all aspects of the person and his or her activity.

3. Despite its universal elements (untold numbers of people have had similar experiences), this knowledge is *particular* to me and my specific path of psychological and spiritual development, my journey to becoming fully human. As in any example of transformative self-knowledge, the one I've described had a unique and specific effect upon me and answered the special needs of my development at that moment. This in no way denies that archetypal or universal themes shape the experience. It is just that these universal themes must weave together with the particular historical details of the person's life in a way that is unique to the soul's needs at that moment.

4. Although in some sense every piece of knowledge changes us, the primary value of transformative self-knowledge is its profound *transforming effect* on the person having it. Although we change from day to day, even from hour to hour, the knowledge I gained in that moment produced significant changes in my view of the world, Anthony, and myself. Of course, it is still possible to pervert or deny the experience. Wasn't I, within minutes of my little taste of this knowledge, looking down my nose at men who had committed their entire life to religious practice? Religious history shows that such backsliding is possible at even an advanced level: even the Apostle Peter denied Christ three times before the cock crowed—not that I compare myself to Peter. Nevertheless, transformative knowledge causes major turning points in life.

5. Because of the particular transforming nature of such experiences, they are *unrepeatable*. No psychological or spiritual experience can be truly repeated. Yes, you can see the same motion picture more than once, but each time the experience is different because you are different. Not only do you know the plot and anticipate the scenes, but your psyche has also changed since the last viewing and thus your response to the film must be different each time.

6. Since such experiences always display a deep purpose, intent, or goal, they are *teleological*. Our soul seems to have a "vision" of our deepest identity, and it draws us toward what we are meant to be. Many Eastern traditions claim that we are already liberated and that all spiritual development merely attempts to do is discover and bring this fact fully into actuality. To believe that the future may be drawing us toward it, that teleology even exists, is difficult for those reared in a scientific culture that claims today's conditions are caused only by previous conditions.

7. Finally, whether because of all these attributes or because of its intrinsic nature, this knowledge carries a great *sacredness*. Although I had had different sorts of religious experiences previously, the word *sacred* took on a much deeper significance through that event. It was no longer an adjective, but a living experience.

In summary, transformative self-knowledge is primarily *an interior intuition that is holistic, unique to the individual, transforming, unrepeatable, teleological, and sacred*. Of course, such characteristics cover a broad spectrum of experiences, from powerful psychological and aesthetic experiences to mystical experiences of a much higher order than the kundalini experience described here. Despite the broad range of such experiences, the knowledge they yield is not ineffable, as these seven characteristics show. Yet, by their very nature, they defy complete description. In more advanced experiences, this quality becomes accentuated. Nevertheless, they have a distinctive character that can be contrasted with scientific knowledge, as later chapters will show.

Chapter Four

A Cosmological Analogy for the Nature of Soul

We are a weird-looking foursome, walking down the main street of a dusty little town in South India. My good friends Michael and Harriet Eisman and my wife Elaine and I are the only non-Indians in Kanchi Puram, a town of about 100,000 known for its silk, ancient temples, and the reason for our being there: Sri Sankaracharya. He is the sixty-eighth holder of a title that goes back to the eighth century C.E., when the famous Adi Sankara systematized and reformed Hinduism.

Our weirdness is not merely that we are not natives. Michael and I look truly bizarre. The airlines left our luggage behind in London, and we arrived in winter clothes appropriate for upstate New York. The temperature in Kanchi is around ninety degrees Fahrenheit with high humidity. The next London-Madras flight will not be for another week, so we have to buy clothes. However, the Tamils in this part of India are tiny by American standards. We cannot find pants with a thirty-six-inch waist. Michael and I keep asking for the next size. The exasperated clerk turns his hands palm up, shrugs his shoulders, and announces, "Final size. Final size." In desperation, I boldly suggest that we wear dhotis, those white cloths wrapped around the waist that drape to the top of the feet. All the other adult males in town wear them, so why not us?

The clerks are shocked, begin to laugh, scurry around us with new energy, and eventually show us how to wrap and tuck them in the traditional manner. But dhotis are not easy to wear. At any moment they could fall to the ground and leave us standing in our underwear in the middle of the street. So we hitch them up higher and give them an unconventional and ugly roll at the waist. Instead of the dhoti barely revealing graceful, sandaled feet, Michael's hairy legs hang out, revealing his Nike running shoes. I nickname him Swami Nike. Myself, I opt for a pair of Indian sandals that torture my feet but seem much more stylish.

While we wait for our luggage, we learn to live with our dhotis and the kind but uncomprehending stares of the Indians. One real advantage of dhotis is their comfort for meditation, which we discover during the hours we spend meditating among Sankaracharya's devotees at the *mutt* (Hindu temple). I have had the good fortune to be in the presence of many evolved beings, but Sankaracharya's presence is surely the most overpowering and yet loving of any. Meditating so many hours in his presence allows us to go deeper in meditation than any of us have ever gone. We get into a daily routine of walking back and forth to the mutt from our very modest hotel, meditating, eating, and sleeping restlessly through the warm tropical nights.

After we have been in India for a week, our luggage arrives in Madras, and Michael and I go to the airport to claim it. Although the airport is only a couple of hours' ride from Kanchi, we know it will take all day to retrieve our luggage. Everything is unimaginably inefficient in India, but we are in such a state of grace that we believe we can work through it without frustration. After much rigmarole with betel-nut-chewing bureaucrats, the procedure stops abruptly: everybody is breaking for a long lunch. While we wait for the two-hour lunch period to end, I watch several women in saris doing construction work in an adjacent part of the airport. In India, the women do most of the heavy construction work for less than a U.S. dollar a day. Having worked in construction for many years as a youth, I take a keen interest in the innumerable Indian work sites. I am

Fig. 16. Women laborers in India (photo by author)

amazed no wheelbarrows are used. Instead, the women, with their beautiful saris, gracefully carry everything in huge bowls, often on their heads (fig. 16). It amazes me that they can do such hard, dirty work and not get their saris filthy. At home, I can barely pump gasoline without needing a complete change of clothes.

At the construction site, I notice a little girl about three or four years of age. She is playing near her mother, who glides back and forth with loads of bricks on her head. I catch the little girl's eye and wave to her. Suddenly the mother sweeps up the child in her arms and bursts through the glass doors into the lobby area where Michael and I are sitting. She repeatedly gestures for me to take the child with me on my flight. The child's eyes are wide and she wraps her little brown legs more tightly around her mother's waist and clings to her left side. I am thoroughly confused. I am from America, where all mothers fear for their young daughters' safety and don't want strange men even talking to their children. I ask Michael, "Is this woman really trying to give me her little girl?"

"No doubt about it," he answers. "You see the guy coming through the door? He wants some money for her."

I can tell the woman is asking her daughter if she wants to go with me. The little child is filled with wide-eyed anxiety and clings even more tightly to her mother. My legs are shaking as I communicate through gestures that I cannot take her child.

The mother leaves in frustration, while the child seems relieved. I sit down weakly since my legs will barely hold me up. My legs have not shaken like this since somebody tried to cut up my face with a beer can opener in a street fight when I was fifteen. Michael is an experienced medical doctor and, unlike me, deals with the underprivileged

Fig. 17. A mother's love (photo by author)

in our part of Appalachia every day. Nevertheless, he too is shaken by it all.

I cannot believe she wanted to give me her child. Every day I see from simple body language how devoted Indians are to their children. For example, in Kanchi I had photographed the mother love between a different mother and a child about the same age as the little girl in the airport (fig. 17).

However, there is no doubt: the mother in the airport wanted me to take her little three- or four-year-old daughter. As we drive back to Kanchi, I cannot get the incident out of my mind.

What could the mother have been thinking? Was she convinced that the little girl would have a better life with me than with her? Perhaps she reasoned that she could never build the dowry required for a good marriage. The little girl would be doomed to the same lifelong drudgery her mother was living—or maybe worse. Perhaps nobody at home could take care of the little girl and the mother had to take her along to work. Did she believe that the highest expression of her love was to give the girl away to a rich American? Or was she just dumping her child?

It was some time before I could make any sense of the experience, especially my physical reaction, but now I see it in terms of my understanding of the nature of soul. As I will discuss in more detail later in this chapter, soul has two very different aspects. On one hand, soul is a finite, divisible, and changing intelligence at the center of our psychological and spiritual experience. On the other hand, it is simultaneously an infinite, indivisible, and unvarying intelligence linking us to each other and the cosmos. Because of its indivisibility, soul intimately connects me to that desperate woman and her wide-eyed child and gives me—a complete stranger from the other side of the world—some responsibility for their well-being.

INVISIBLE MASS AND UNCONSCIOUS COMPENSATION

To help unpack this profound view of soul, we need to leave rural India, planet Earth, our solar system, and even our galaxy. We need to take the largest possible view of the universe, the one routinely employed in modern cosmology. In so doing, we will find that concepts from modern science can help illuminate ancient wisdom regarding the soul's nature—one instance of the synergy occasionally possible between science and the sacred.

Over the course of the last half-century, astronomers have developed the big bang model for the birth, evolution, and death of the universe. In standard big bang cosmology, the universe began about fourteen billion years ago as an unimaginably hot and dense sea of elementary particles. This sea of particles expanded, cooling in the process, and formed galaxies that still recede from each other today. This model, the cornerstone of modern cosmology, has been developed through the interplay between Einstein's elegant theory of general relativity and observations from a variety of dazzling modern telescopes.

Early in the twentieth century, astronomers learned that the average mass density of the universe (its mass per unit volume) was the critical parameter determining the ultimate fate of the universe. If the average density is smaller than a defined critical value, found by a combination of theory and experiment, then the universe will expand forever. Then all galaxies will recede endlessly from each other, their stars eventually cooling into dead cinders. On the other hand, if the density is greater than the critical value, the recession will stop and reverse.[1] The galaxies will then someday fall back together at ever-increasing velocities and converge into a cosmic inferno, the "big crunch."

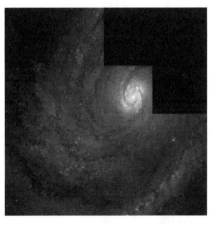

Thus, the average density of the universe determines whether it ends with a whimper or a bang—that is, with a diffuse, deathly cold stillness or a fiery, cataclysmic big crunch.

In the last couple of decades, it has become firmly established that the visible universe—everything seen by employing the entire electromagnetic spectrum, from radio wavelengths to gamma rays—represents less than five percent of the total mass of the universe. For ex-

Fig. 18. Spiral galaxy M100 (courtesy of National Space Agency, Hubble Space Telescope Institute)

ample, the spiral galaxy shown in figure 18 is overwhelmingly composed of unseen or nonradiating matter. The visible universe, of consuming interest to us since our Neanderthal ancestors gazed heavenward, is truly like the tip of an iceberg. A galaxy typically has one hundred billion stars, and there are about ten billion galaxies in the visible universe. Vast as these numbers sound, all the galaxies, stars, and gas clouds seen in all parts of the electromagnetic spectrum still make up less than five percent of the total mass of the universe. As a result, the average density of the universe, and thus its evolution and eventual fate, is

largely determined by the remaining ninety-five percent of the mass—
the great, invisible bulk of the universe.

If so much of the universe is invisible, how do we know it is
present? The evidence comes from gravitational effects. If invisible,
nonradiating matter is present, its mass will affect the motion of visible matter in very specific ways that are predicted by gravitational
theory. For example, gravitational effects observed in the motions of
galaxies and clusters of galaxies imply the presence of enormous
amounts of invisible matter. Even the details of the rotation of our
galaxy imply that enormous quantities of unseen matter exist right in
our own stellar neighborhood.

Likewise, just as the universe is composed of visible and invisible
matter, the human personality is composed of conscious and unconscious aspects. Consciousness, the realm of the visible, of sensory images,
known contents, feelings, thoughts, desires, and activities—this is our
familiar, everyday mental state. If somebody asks, "What kind of person are you?" you will probably make your list largely from the conscious
side of your personality. You might say, "I am kind, honest, inept mathematically, and I love cats, doing needlepoint, and practicing Olympic
weight lifting."

Yet, important as it is, consciousness is only a fraction of the whole.
Like the luminous galaxies in the universe, consciousness is enveloped
and permeated by a more extensive invisible component—the unconscious. In contrast to consciousness, the invisible unconscious is not
directly knowable. We cannot make an explicit and detailed list of the
structure of our unconscious as we could for our conscious personality.

Just as the cosmologists infer the nature of the invisible matter by
studying the detailed behavior of the visible matter, depth psychologists infer the nature of the unconscious by carefully observing its effects
upon consciousness. Our slips of the tongue, surprising intuitions, sudden impulses, dreams, spontaneous fantasies, compulsions, and visions
that break into consciousness with a will of their own all express the
mysterious intelligence generating them—the unconscious.

In cosmology, gravitation accounts for the interplay between visible and invisible matter, while in Jungian psychology, the interaction
between consciousness and the unconscious is largely governed by
unconscious compensation. That is, the unconscious, through its compensatory function, seeks to transform our lopsided attitudes or distorted
beliefs about ourselves and our actions in the world. For example, if it

is important for our development, the unconscious might show through a series of dreams that the claim "I am kind and honest" is not entirely accurate. By taking the dreams seriously, we might confront some unpleasant aspects of our personality. Experience shows that the various expressions of the unconscious have a transformational purpose or intent. Jung tells us that this compensatory function of the unconscious is "the self-regulation of the psyche":

> As a rule, the unconscious content contrasts strikingly with the conscious material, particularly when the conscious attitude tends too exclusively in a direction that would threaten the vital needs of the individual. The more one-sided his conscious attitude is, and the further it deviates from the optimum, the greater becomes the possibility that vivid dreams with a strongly contrasting but purposive content will appear as an expression of the self-regulation of the psyche.[2]

Jung often uses a biological analogy in describing unconscious compensation, saying that it is the psychological equivalent of the body's self-correcting tendency, like a fever or the swelling of an infected wound. Within our cosmological analogy, unconscious compensation is analogous to the pull of gravity of the invisible on the visible matter. Just as these gravitational forces affect the evolution of the universe, the "pulls" from unconscious compensations affect our psychological evolution. However, this compensatory principle is much more than a striving for psychological equilibrium, which would be a recipe for boredom and stagnation, not evolution. Instead, Jung found by examining long series of dreams that he could clearly discern an overall pattern, a purposive guidance, playing itself out in the life of the dreamer. The unconscious, through a series of specific compensations, like carefully directed rocket bursts, guides each of us along a particular trajectory, unique to our needs. Unlike the universe, which has only two possible endpoints, the unconscious directs a human personality to its *unique* expression of wholeness and completion. This lifelong process of becoming who we are truly meant to be Jung calls the process of *individuation*:

> This phenomenon is a kind of developmental process in the personality itself. At first, it seems that each compensation is a momentary adjustment of one-sidedness or an equalization of a disturbed balance. But with deeper insight and experience, these apparently separate acts of compensation arrange themselves into a kind of plan. They seem to hang together and in the deepest

sense to be subordinated to a common goal, so that a long dream-series no longer appears as a senseless string of incoherent and isolated happenings, but resembles the successive steps in a planned and orderly process of development. I have called this unconscious process spontaneously expressing itself in the symbolism of a long dream-series the individuation process.[3]

Individuation is a natural process of psychological maturation. Although powered by a complex series of unconscious compensations, it requires the aid and cooperation of the conscious personality. Not only must we attend to the messages and guidance of the unconscious, we must also consciously actualize these realizations in our daily life. Along the way, individuation demands that we learn about the heights and depths of our personality. It is a long and sometimes painful journey, but it gives meaning to our lives.

Just as in cosmology, where invisible matter dominates the process of evolution, the invisible aspect of the personality, the unconscious, dominates our psychological evolution. In the first paragraph of his autobiography Jung writes, "My life is a story of the self-realization of the unconscious. Everything in the unconscious seeks outward manifestation, and the personality too desires to evolve out of its unconscious conditions and to experience itself as a whole."[4]

In modern cosmology, the underlying laws of physics are the ultimate guiding principles for the evolution of the universe. In Jungian thought, the intelligence or ultimate organizing principle, the hidden "orchestra leader" for the symphony of our psychological and spiritual evolution, is the archetype of the *self*. The self, the intelligence expressed in the individuation process, is primarily the archetype of meaning, and its meaning is usually infused with powerful feelings. Consciously actualizing and expressing the self's intent in life is the process of individuation. Table 2 summarizes this analogy between modern big bang cosmology and Jungian psychology.

In *Anima*,[5] James Hillman has carefully discussed the many subtleties and ways of using the terms self, soul, anima, and psyche. Here I use self and soul interchangeably as both the totality of the psyche (analogous to the sum of the seen and unseen components of the universe) and as a union of opposites, as when Jung says, "I have defined the self as the totality of the conscious and unconscious psyche . . ."[6] and as "a perfect *coincidentia oppositorum* expressing the divine nature of the self."[7]

Table 2. The Universe and the Psyche—An Analogy

Modern Cosmology	Jungian Psychology
Visible matter	Conscious aspect of personality
Invisible matter	Unconscious aspect of personality
Invisible matter known by its influence on visible matter	Unconscious known by its influence on consciousness
Gravity governs interaction between visible and invisible	Unconscious compensation governs interaction between consciousness and unconscious
Universe evolves to one of two different endpoints	Each individuation is a unique expression of wholeness
Organized by laws of physics	Organized by archetype of the self

The cultivation of an ongoing relationship with this guiding intelligence superior to our ego is one of the greatest joys of the inner life. Through such a relationship, we come to appreciate that the true center of personality is the self or soul, and not the ego. It is both a relief and a cause for thanksgiving to realize that a wisdom superior to that of our ego guides our evolution. This shift in perspective is the psychological equivalent of the Copernican revolution—the intellectual upheaval that placed the Sun, not the Earth, at the center of the solar system. However, this analogy to Copernican cosmology is problematic because the relationship between the ego and the self is not like that between two bodies in space and time, such as the Sun and the Earth. While the ego is located in space and time because of its intimate relationship to our bodies, the self is neither visible nor localized in space or time. Therefore, while the analogy correctly captures the shift in perspective, the visible, localized Sun is not an accurate parallel to the invisible, nonlocalized self that guides consciousness toward individuation.

The analogy of the invisible mass that pervades the entire universe and guides its evolution is a better image than the Copernican Sun for the self's dynamic compensations guiding our evolution. Although the invisible mass analogy is an improvement over the Copernican analogy, it too has a significant shortcoming. The difficulty springs from the image of a pervasive, invisible matter, which misleadingly implies that this intelligence, the self or soul, spreads out uniformly in space like a gas. Despite our tendency to see everything in material terms, the soul is not in space or time.

However, we can turn to big bang cosmology again for a third analogy, which is more apt than either the Copernican revolution or invisible mass. In general relativity, matter generates a *curvature* to the spacetime geometry of the universe. This idea of the curved spacetime of the universe provides a powerful analogy for soul and its activity. Using it, we can better understand the relation between the invisible, nonlocalized soul and the finite center of consciousness that goes through the individuation process.

COSMOLOGICAL EXPANSION AND CURVED SPACETIME

Shortly after Einstein developed the theory of general relativity in 1916, astronomers discovered that the stars first seen through Galileo's telescope are located only in our own galaxy, which is merely one undistinguished member among billions in the universe. American astronomer Edwin Hubble then discovered that distant galaxies recede from us with velocities that are proportional to their distance from us (fig. 19). He found that in all directions, the farther away the galaxy is, the faster it flees from us. For example, if a galaxy at a distance D recedes from us with a velocity V, then a galaxy at a distance of $2 \times D$ recedes at a velocity of $2 \times V$. This special motion is known as Hubble's expansion.

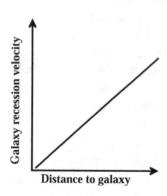

Fig. 19. Hubble expansion: The more distant the object, the more rapidly it recedes

A little reflection on Hubble's discovery might prompt us to ask, "Does this mean that we are at the center of the big bang expansion? Have we overthrown the idea that Earth is the center of the solar system, only to find that we are at the center of cosmic expansion?" Einstein's general relativity elegantly answers these questions by showing that the four-dimensional spacetime geometry of the universe is curved by its total mass distribution. The implications of this answer are revealed by another analogy.

Although we cannot visualize four-dimensional spacetime, we can work with a two-dimensional analogue frequently used in introductory discussions of cosmology. From this analogue, we can draw three critical conclusions about the spacetime geometry of the universe. First, every cosmic observer sees the *same Hubble expansion* regardless of where she is in the universe. Second, the overall cosmic expansion has *no geometric center*. Third, the universe has *no edge* or limiting boundary.

As the first step toward these conclusions, consider a balloon with pennies glued to its surface (representing observers) as shown in figure 20. Now blow up the balloon continuously and consider yourself a *two-dimensional creature confined strictly to the spherical surface of the balloon*. Provided you can maintain the viewpoint of that two-dimensional creature and resist the temptation to jump above or below the two-dimensional surface, the expanding spherical surface is a good two-dimensional analogy for the curved four-dimensional space-time of modern cosmology.

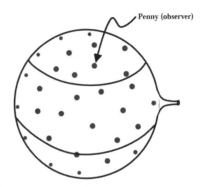

Fig. 20. Balloon analogy for Hubble expansion

To make this analogy more useful, we need to add two refinements. First, the universe is not as homogeneous as the balloon analogy leads us to believe. The cosmic neighborhood of each observer is unique to that observer's region of spacetime. The detailed distribution of galaxies, stars, and gases varies markedly from one point to the next. In our analogy, this variation would correspond to little wrinkles, imperfections, and a varying density of pennies across the surface of the balloon. The surface is not perfectly spherical; each part inflates at a slightly different rate, and so forth.

Second, despite these local variations, the universe has well-defined average properties. In our analogy, over a distance that covers a significant fraction of the balloon's surface, it has a well-defined curvature, rate of inflation, density of pennies (observers), and so on. Our analogy must reflect not only the well-established observational fact that locally each observer sees a slightly different picture, but also that, when viewed on a large enough scale, the universe is exceedingly homogeneous or smooth. In short, we need to account for local differences and global homogeneity.

Those with a taste for algebra can easily show that, while the balloon is blowing up, each two-dimensional observer stationed on a penny sees all other pennies expanding away from it with the same Hubble expansion. That is, each penny sees the others receding from it with a velocity that increases with the two-dimensional distance between the pennies, just as in figure 20. (Remember that we measure distances only on the curved surface of the balloon.) In cosmology, once observers reach out beyond their neighborhood with its local peculiarities, they all see the same Hubble expansion. Since this is true for all pennies, it shows that no observer is the true center of cosmic expansion. Aside from local variations, modern cosmology removes all privilege, all uniqueness, from our position in the universe. It has truly completed the Copernican revolution. Now we are no more central or privileged than any other cosmic observer. Equivalently, each observer can rightly claim to be at the center of the universe.

The balloon analogy also shows that the universe (the two-dimensional surface) is not exploding from a geometric center like the bomb dropped over Hiroshima. *Each point in the two-dimensional space (not just the locations of the pennies) is the center of its own expansion.* You may object that the balloon's expansion does have a center—the geometric center of the balloon. But we are supposed to be two-dimensional creatures who can't jump off the spherical surface! Notice that if we stay on the two-dimensional curved surface of the balloon, it has no edges, no places where this space ends. Future astronauts need not fear an edge to spacetime like Christopher Columbus' crew feared the edge of the Earth. The curved four-dimensional spacetime of our universe contains all there is in both space and time—a cosmic ouroboros† with neither edge nor center.

SOME PSYCHOLOGICAL CONCLUSIONS

Let me draw some conclusions from the cosmological analogies. Begin with modern cosmology, with its equality of all observers and its lack of a center or an edge to the spacetime geometry. In this analogy, I equate the ego with an individual cosmic observer (a penny on a balloon) and the self with the entire balloon and its overall expansion that generates the individual Hubble expansions seen by each observer. From a psychological perspective, the cosmological equality of all observers reflects our modern culture's growing appreciation of diversity and pluralism at all levels. No particular gender, race, culture, religion, or political orientation is inherently privileged. Yes, by historical accident, vast inequalities have arisen, but these do not spring from any

---

†An ancient symbol depicting a serpent swallowing its own tail that trepresents the cycles of nature, the eternity of the world, and the infinite order of life.

intrinsic privilege built into gender, race, culture, or religion. Of course, it is a great challenge to honor diversity without degenerating into lack of judgment and moral relativity—especially because of our complete fascination with one observer, our ego, and our innate belief that it does have privilege.

We cannot deny the psychological truth that each of us experiences ourself as the center of our psychological drama. We relate all our experience to our ego, our center of empirical consciousness. Yet, coming to wholeness, or the process of individuation, implies that the ego is not the true subject, not the true director of psychological life. Unconscious compensation, for example, could not occur if the ego were the true intelligence guiding our evolution. In fact, the ego requires unconscious compensation and is subject to the corrections, guidance, and inspiration of a nonlocalized intelligence—the self or soul. The psychological experience of the ego's centrality finds its analogue in every cosmic observer (each penny on the balloon) seeing herself as the center of a Hubble expansion. In truth, she is only one of an infinite number of equivalent focal points generated by an unimaginably larger motion. Analogously, we believe that our ego is the center of psychological movement when in fact it is only a limited reflection of the soul's indefinitely larger motion.

Turning to the Copernican revolution analogy, we can see that the awareness of being the center of our own experience, of relating all thoughts, feelings, and outer and inner adventures to our ego, was merely being projected into geocentric or Earth-centered cosmology. We unconsciously transformed egocentric psychology into geocentric cosmology. In contrast, the heliocentric or Sun-centered view implies that the *perceived* motions of the Sun, stars, and planets across the sky are actually due to our Earth's movement, to our rotation and revolution about the Sun. The Earth's motion, rather than that of the heavenly bodies, causes the illusion of a setting sun or a rising moon.

When we appreciate this Copernican revolution psychologically and realize how our unconscious psychological motions condition and distort our experience, how our projections shape the world, then we begin to break out of the egocentric position. When we learn the power of our psychological complexes to project their own contents unconsciously, then we make the first tentative steps toward the psychological equivalent of the Copernican revolution.

While that is an important advance for the psyche, the Copernican revolution presents difficulties as a psychological analogy, as mentioned earlier. The overall expansion of curved spacetime described in modern cosmology provides a better image. It simultaneously accounts for both the effects of Hubble's Law seen by local observers and the uniqueness of each observer (analogous to our egocentrism) and yet has neither a center for the expansion nor an edge to the spacetime. Although the ego falsely believes itself to be the center of experience, we are actually a small aspect of a greater motion, a motion without a center or whose center is not in our spacetime.

In psychological terms, the true and inclusive subject, the intelligence guiding our life, is the self or soul that includes the ego and *all else* within it. We can easily fail to appreciate that nothing exists outside the soul, because in our analogy we instinctively embed the two-dimensional curved surface of the balloon in our familiar three-dimensional space. This three-dimensional perspective gives the illusion that there is an outside, an edge, and an inside to the curved two-dimensional space. However, that is not true when you use the analogy properly and restrict yourself to the curved surface. Perhaps we can gain some additional understanding of this inclusiveness from a dream analogy that Anthony Damiani often used.[8]

For this analogy, don't consider dreams as symbolic windows into the psyche, but rather as epistemological lessons in how we know and what we know. If we try, while in the dream, to imagine a time before the dream or a space outside it, we automatically bring them within the dream as another dream content. In this way, the dreaming mind has no edge in either space or time, just as the cosmological analogy implies that the soul has no edge, that no place and no time exist where soul is not. Yet, because the dream protagonist and all else in the dream are created and animated by the larger dreaming mind, just as the individual observer's Hubble expansion is created by the larger motion of the curved space, the ego or individual observer is contained within the larger whole. Appreciating this relationship gives the ego its place without taking it as the center of life.

PLOTINUS ON THE ESSENCE OF SOUL

Now our task is to build upon this Jungian view of self or soul and develop the idea of the double nature of soul. So far, we have only considered the soul's divisible or finite aspect, but it also has an indivisible and infinite aspect. Understanding this double nature will reveal the full majesty of soul.

The most profound thinking on this double nature can be found in the writings of Plotinus, the greatest developer of Plato's ideas in the school of philosophy known as Neoplatonism. Plotinus, who lived from 205 to 270 C.E., was born in Egypt, studied philosophy in Alexandria, and then moved to Rome, where his school gained a wide following. Despite Plotinus' rejection of Christianity, his writings, collected in *The Enneads*, had a significant influence on early Christian thinkers.

Although many of Plotinus' writings concern soul, none is more central to his vision than *Ennead* IV, tractates 1 and 2, entitled "On the Essence of the Soul (I and II)."[9] In both parts I and II, he draws inspiration from the famous section in Plato's *Timaeus* that discusses the double nature of soul. For Plotinus, the soul's undivided or unified nature is a consequence of its origin in the Supreme, in the Intellectual-Principle or realm of Authentic Essence. There, all principles are fully united and eternally unvaried. Yet, soul even at its summit has a nature lending itself to divided existence, to multiplicity and change. For Plotinus, the essence of soul consists in always having both of these contrary natures at every level. In IV.1.1 Plotinus says:

> The Intellectual-Principle is forever repugnant to distinction and to partition. Soul, there without distinction and partition, has yet a nature lending itself to divisional existence: its secession, entry into body. . . .
>
> "Formed from the undivided essence and the essence divided among bodies": this description of Soul must therefore mean that it has phases above and below, that it is attached to the Supreme and yet reaches down to this sphere, like a radius from a centre.
>
> Thus it is that, entering this realm, it possesses still the vision inherent to that superior phase in virtue of which it unchangingly maintains its integral nature. Even here it is not exclusively the partible soul: it is still the impartible as well: what in it knows partition is parted without partibility; undivided as giving itself to the entire body, a whole to a whole, it is divided as being effective in every part.

Let's unpack this a little. In the Plotinian view, the soul at its highest in the Intellectual-Principle, where all is unity and eternality, "has a nature lending itself to divisional existence." Thus, the very summit of soul, its most exalted, integral nature is "attached to the Supreme and yet reaches down to this sphere." While being immortal and unchanging, soul intrinsically partakes of the world of change and limitation. These seemingly disparate qualities—of indivisibility, infiniteness, and eternality on one hand and divisibility, finiteness, and temporality on the other—define the essence of soul. It always partakes of both the infinite and finite; its very nature blends the unified and eternal with the multiple and ephemeral. However, it "is parted without partibility," because no matter how fully soul seems to divide itself among the transient multiplicities, its eternal unity is never sundered. The soul can appear to fragment and yet never lose "the vision inherent to that superior phase."

Plotinus often uses geometric analogies to help the reader grasp these complementary aspects of soul, for example, " . . . attached to the Supreme and yet reaches down to this sphere, like a radius from a centre." A little later, he uses the same geometrical analogy when he characterizes the indivisible nature of soul by telling us:

> . . . it is an essence eternally unvaried: it is common to all that follows upon it: it is like the circle's centre to which all the radii are attached while leaving it unbrokenly in possession of itself, the starting point of their course and of their essential being, the ground in which they all participate: thus the indivisible is the principle of these divided existences and in their very outgoing they remain enduringly in contact with that stationary essence. (IV.2.1)

To take this circle analogy further, consider a turning chariot wheel, like those that rolled through the streets of second-century Alexandria. The center of the rolling circle is analogous to the undivided essence or unity of soul that remains intact and motionless. Its radii reach down to the rotating circumference of the wheel, to our moving sphere of sense and division. The difficulty with both the original geometric analogy and my expansion of it is that, although the center has a different nature than a radius, they are both visible objects sharing the same nature inherent in all such objects in Euclidean geometry. Although my image of the wheel has the virtue of bringing rotation into the picture and thereby distinguishing more fully the still center from its moving radii and circumference, in fact both center and radii move as the wheel rolls by a stationary observer.

Once again, the cosmological analogy of the expanding universe can help us get beyond the limitations of such images. Previously I used this universe-as-expanding-balloon analogy to discuss the relationship between the ego (analogous to the pennies as observers) and the Jungian notion of self (analogous to the curved space and its overall expansion). That discussion applied to soul in its finite or divisible aspect, what Jung calls the self. Now I want to use the same analogy at a higher level to discuss the relationship between the divisible and indivisible aspects of soul. Here the divisible and finite aspect of soul is analogous to the pennies as individual observers, while the indivisible and infinite aspect of soul is analogous to the curved space and its overall expansion.

To return to the analogy, consider an observer who is always strictly confined to the balloon's surface. Then each individual observer—each unique center of observation—is a limited or divided expression of an indivisible motion of the whole, of the expansion of the entire sphere. In other words, the overall or indivisible expansion of four-dimensional spacetime, which is invisible to us as localized observers, generates our limited perspective, our Hubble expansion. Inherent in each individual observer and her perceived Hubble expansion is the generating expansion of the sphere, the intrinsic expansion of each point in spacetime, which the limited observer is always expressing and with which she is always in contact. Or as Plotinus says in more abstract terms, "The indivisible is the principle of these divided existences and in their very outgoing they remain enduringly in contact with that stationary essence."

Yet, from the point of view of a particular observer, the larger generating motion of the expanding sphere is not visible, not part of her observations. In a similar way, although the indivisible aspect of soul is always present and makes the divisible possible, by its very nature the indivisible is not apprehended by the divisible. Although the expansion of the sphere inheres within each particular center of expansion and generates its particular Hubble expansion, the limited perspective of a single observer cannot directly comprehend the larger generating motion.

The divisible nature of soul can never be separated from the indivisible. As Plotinus says, "Even here it is not exclusively the partible soul: it is still the impartible as well: what in it knows partition is parted without partibility; undivided as giving itself to the entire body, a whole to a whole, it is divided as being effective in every part." So, whether we participate in mystic union with the ineffable Supreme or the most banal everyday task, both the unity and plurality of the soul are present in every experience.

In our cosmological analogy, the balloon's expansion is made divisible because a particular observer identifies with a unique viewpoint.

However, the larger generating motion is in no way broken up or made "partible," despite its generating a particular Hubble expansion. The larger motion divides by "being effective in every part." Recall that each point in the two-dimensional spacetime is the center of its own expansion, and yet the center of the larger generating motion does not lie in that curved two-dimension space.

Finally, let me squeeze a little more out of this analogy, before turning to another way of attempting to grasp symbolically this dual nature of soul. Plotinus says:

> The nature, at once divisible and indivisible, which we affirm to be soul, has not the unity of an extended thing; it does not consist of separate sections; its divisibility lies in its presence at every point of the recipient, but it is indivisible as dwelling entire in the total and entire in any part.
>
> To have penetrated this idea is to know the greatness of the Soul and its power, the divinity and wonder of its being, as a nature transcending the sphere of Things.

At every point of the surface of the balloon, the overall expansion creates a Hubble expansion, analogous to "the recipient," the limited observer. Herein lies soul's divisibility. Just as local peculiarities, history, and contingencies guarantee the uniqueness of each cosmic observer, so too our biological and psychological peculiarities, history, and contingencies guarantee the uniqueness of each divisible soul. Yet, the overall expansion of the curved surface is in no way surrendered or splintered into many separate motions by creating such limited perspectives. Similarly, the indivisible aspect of soul does not become divisible or change its fundamental nature, since "it is indivisible as dwelling entire in the total and entire in any part."

With ideas this profound, no analogy is adequate. Nevertheless, let me try another. This analogy is neither geometric like that of Plotinus nor cosmological like mine, but relies instead upon Damiani's epistemological use of dreams. From this perspective, each element of the dream—the sky, trees, animals, feelings, actions, and so on—are productions of the dreamer's mind. In this analogy, before expressing itself in a panoply of images unfolding in space and time, the dreamer's mind is unified and indivisible. Yet, this mind has a "nature lending itself to divisional existence" expressed in the dream as particular images. However, each element of the dream, whether a tree stump or a fluttering heart, has the entire dream mind present and invested in it. Whether a mountain or a microbe, the dream mind is fully present in each of its

varied productions. In this way, the dream mind is divisible and, simultaneously, the dream mind's unity and integrity are in no way
compromised by its production of images, its divisible outflow. No
matter how many dream images are produced, no matter how fully
present the mind is in each image, its native unity is not sundered.
This property follows because the image occurs as an expression of
mind, rather than mind occurring within image. Plotinus concludes:

> There is, therefore, no escape: soul is, in the degree indi-
> cated, one and many, parted and impartible. We cannot question
> the possibility of a thing being at once a unity and multi-present,
> since to deny this would be to abolish the principle which sus-
> tains and administers the universe . . . (IV.2.2)

SOME CONCLUSIONS ABOUT THE NATURE OF SOUL

How do we connect this double nature of soul to the concerns of depth
psychology? When the indivisible and eternal aspect of soul reaches
into the psyche and works through its forms and life processes, this
interaction generates the self or soul (in the Jungian sense in which I
used the term earlier). The only aspect of soul we can know empiri-
cally, through images or actions in the psyche, is the divisible soul,
that being which partially reveals itself through the rich phenomena
of our inner life. We may *infer* the indivisible or unitary aspect of soul,
but Plotinus tells us that it cannot be grasped in a divisible form, in an
image. The indivisible summit of soul must be approached through
the *via negativa*, the path that eschews all images, negates all ideas about
the formless truth. For example, in the Mundaka Upanishad, where
the term self is equivalent to indivisible soul, we read:

> Self is everywhere, shining forth from all beings,
> vaster than the vast, subtler than the most subtle,
> unreachable, yet nearer than breath, than heartbeat.
> Eye cannot see it, ear cannot hear it nor tongue
> utter it; only in deep absorption can the mind,
> grown pure and silent, merge with the formless truth. [10]

This indivisible aspect of soul is "everywhere" and yet "unreach-
able" through normal consciousness. Rather, "only in deep absorption
can the mind, grown pure and silent, merge with the formless truth."
Thus, the indivisible aspect of soul, by its very nature, is difficult to
know, since we can only "know" it by becoming it, by uniting with it.
In this knowing, we can no longer proceed by image, but by becoming

it in the silence. This idea of the via negativa has influenced me deeply and, as we will see, plays a critical role in my experience with the mother and child in India. Nevertheless, despite our inability to grasp this level of soul through images of any kind, its immanence in every expression of the divisible soul guarantees its presence in even the least expression of the psyche. Whether we embrace the fecundity of images springing from the imagination's boundless creativity or tread the via negativa, we are always within the cosmos of soul.

Many consequences follow from this double nature of soul. I'll conclude by mentioning one that particularly troubles me; it relates to my experience with the mother and child in the Madras airport.

To reach any significant realization of divisible soul, we must enter the inner realm of thought, image, and meditation. Unless we can see the archetypal dimensions of our inner life—that Aphrodite and Mercurius dance through our dreams, that Mother Kali and Krishna are as alive in us as in the poor Indian villager—then our inner life is barren and soulless. The soul radiates through each inner image, as more than aesthetic, but as the very outpouring of the divine.

But what about the smog and crime-choked inner cites of the world. Is soul there, too? Am I to experience soul in the fear of inner-city violence, the barbarity of modern terrorism and ethnic warfare? *If soul is truly indivisible, then it cannot be divided between the inner and outer realms. It must be as present in the outer world as in the inner.* If I accept the indivisibility of soul, then I must deify the outer world, too: I must see Aphrodite and Mercurius, Kali and Krishna not only in the "mountain's purple majesty" but equally in the ugliness of the mall parking lot.

But such deification of the world is actually the easy part. The more difficult task is this: just as my soul journey requires me to tend to my interior expressions of the shadow, anima, and the entire bestiary of archetypal forces, it also demands that I tend to these forces in the outer world. It is not enough to minister only to the shadow within me. The realization of the indivisible nature of soul demands that I also minister to the evil in the outer world, work with it, attempt to heal it, integrate it into the whole. It is not enough to nourish just the neglected feminine and its offspring within me. The indivisible nature of soul demands that I somehow nourish, care for, and embrace the neglected feminine in the world, wherever I find it, whether in South India or upstate New York. Indivisible soul must be realized in both our own body and in the body of the world.

This is a terrifying realization for me. In light of it, I now understand my experience in the Madras airport. At some largely unconscious level, I understood then that I had some responsibility for that desperate mother and her frightened child. At the time, I could not intellectually formulate this responsibility, but my body registered my terror in the uncontrollable trembling of my legs. In the airport, my head could not formulate the reasons for the trembling, but my heart understood the responsibility and how helpless I felt in being unable to act on it. Afterwards, I was sorry I had not given all the money in my wallet to that woman. I tried to assuage my guilt by saying that it is madness to distribute money to the poor in India. The few times I tried resulted in gruesome stampedes of relentless beggars. I kept telling myself, "It does no lasting good." Despite my rationalizations, my head's attempts at saving me from the heart's pain, the memory still troubles me today. I now understand that the unity and bliss I was seeking in meditation with Sankaracharya had a hidden moral obligation that could not be discharged by merely emptying my wallet.

Those meditations in the presence of Sankaracharya were a continuous attempt to reduce the stream of imagery, of divisible productions of mind, so that I might become one with the indivisible and thereby experience its joy, peace, and eternity. I was attempting to follow the instruction in the Mundaka Upanishad that says, "Only in deep absorption can the mind, grown pure and silent, merge with the formless truth." Although the din from frenzied devotees buzzed continuously at the periphery of my awareness, I still had some small successes: I can still vividly recall the occasional touches of the hem of the undivided mind and the feeling of its majesty, ecstasy, and peace. However, the mother and child in the airport shattered my too-fragile peace and powerfully reminded me of the outer world that bleeds with pains and miseries unknown to a privileged rich man like me. What is more, the indivisible nature of soul implies that the transcendent reality I so keenly desired to experience inwardly also expressed itself outwardly in the pain and desperation of that mother. Can I embrace only the inner expression and neglect the outer, or seek the bliss and run from the pain? How then would soul be indivisible if grasped only as inner experience?

Sankaracharya, who has since died, was one of India's greatest proponents of nondualism in the twentieth century. No doubt, he helped prepare me for my encounter with that woman and her child. However, in trying to give her child to me, the mother herself directly taught me that unity, indivisibility, nonduality, and all these terms for the ineffable whole known as soul imply heavy obligations toward the outer expression of the divine. It seems simple, but I have fought this realization for a long time. However, I have no doubt that transformative self-knowledge, which teaches us about both the divisible and indivisible aspects of soul, has daunting moral demands.

These reflections make me acutely aware that my theoretical knowledge races far ahead of my personal realization. The problems of the world, along with the persistence of my innate selfishness, seem too great, too overwhelming for me. The practical reality is that the needs in the world and its wounded body are endless. They are far beyond the capacity of any individual to heal. Given this, how can I embrace and cultivate my realization of the indivisible soul in both its inner and outer expressions?

Perhaps the ecological activists can offer guidance. In the face of daunting global ecological problems, they advise us to "think globally, act locally." Following their counsel, I try to cling to the double nature of soul and simultaneously respond, in the present, to the person in front of me and to the problems in the world that spontaneously appear in my life. When I succeed, it seems that small ripples of compassionate action gradually flow beyond my little circle of family and close friends. My hope is to extend my concern out in ever-widening radii, until it encompasses more and more of the great suffering body of humanity. This effort is rarely easy, but the indivisible nature of soul demands that I continue trying.

Chapter Five

SCIENTIFIC KNOWLEDGE

You cannot mistake the sound of breaking glass or the smell of rotten eggs.

"Do I hear people buying? Remember, you break it, you buy it," says my high school chemistry teacher, Mr. Gilmore. His gold teeth flash through his broad smile. His black, bald head glistens under the classroom lights as he glides like a panther across the room to get his account book. "Let's see, a graduated cylinder . . . another dollar on Mr. Granger's account."

I am giggling with the young woman next to me about Granger's clumsiness. He has just broken his graduated cylinder and spilled hydrogen sulfide, making us all acutely aware of the smell of rotten eggs.

"What do you find so funny, Mr. Mansfield?"

"Ah, nothin'."

"You better get concentrated or I'll be adding to your purchasing list too. While you're at it, spit out your chewing gum and report to afternoon detention. I have already warned all of you about my gum-chewing policy."

"Damn!" I mutter under my breath. "Detention for just chewing gum!"

Fig. 21. Mr. Gilmore in the classroom (courtesy of William Gilmore)

Although I chafed under his strict classroom discipline, I was more inspired by Mr. Gilmore (figs. 21 and 22) than by any other high school teacher. Everything about him was quick. He talked fast, moved fast, and poured chemicals from one test tube to another at lightning speed. He could calculate on a slide rule so swiftly that it seemed miraculous. Although I never heard any student making racial slurs about him, I'll bet he had to be quick to navigate around the racial bigotry that flourished in Norwalk, Connecticut, in the late 1950s.

I had already loved his teaching in ninth-grade algebra, where I first experienced his iron rule. No talking in class, no gum chewing, no excuses for late work. Nevertheless, he really wanted us to understand. When he was straining to answer a student's question, he would wipe his head with his left hand while he wrote on the blackboard with his right. It seemed to help him concentrate. Despite his speediness, he would work with you until you got it straight—even if it took the best

part of a class period. Such an extraordinarily beautiful smile, replete with flashing gold, would break out when a student finally understood, when "the lights went on." As a teacher, I know the joy of those experiences, but Mr. Gilmore first showed me the student's joy in them. There were other dedicated teachers in my high

Fig. 22. Mr. Gilmore being heroic (courtesy of William Gilmore)

school, but none as demanding and inspiring as Gilmore. He taught me a style of thinking, an approach to teaching and learning, that I still cherish.

After the spring of my first year at Dartmouth College, my high school was still in session and I went to visit Mr. Gilmore. The halls echoed with student laughter and the banging of locker doors. As I approached his room, there seemed to be a faint odor of hydrogen sulfide—perhaps it was only a memory. I wanted to pay homage to him, to tell him how important his class and whole approach to science had been to me. Maybe I would even find some time to brag a bit about my good grades at college. However, he had to run to his next class and we only had time for a warm handshake, smile, and brief thanks. It was short and a bit awkward, but he got the point. I never saw him again.

A few years ago, I was walking through a dormitory at Colgate University dedicated to students of color. On a big white board there was a sign asking us to write about any person of color who had a beneficial influence on us. People had written all sorts of testimonials to everybody from rap stars and athletes to Jesse Jackson and Nelson Mandela. I had the distinct pleasure of writing, "If it were not for Mr. Gilmore, my high school chemistry teacher, I would not have become a scientist." I signed it more formally than usual: "Vic Mansfield, professor of physics and astronomy."

Even more recently, I called my high school to get a picture of Mr. Gilmore for this book. I was delighted to find that he was still alive. The school office told me to call him at home. I called Mr. Gilmore, identified myself, and told him I wanted a picture of him for my book because he was such an inspiration for me. He said he remembered me, and we had the sweetest conversation catching up on the nearly forty years since we had seen each other. Toward the end of the conversation he said, "What a blessing this has been."

Fig. 23. Ed Salpeter (courtesy of Edwin Salpeter)

At Dartmouth, I met many other inspiring teachers, both in the sciences and the humanities, who initiated me into the life of the mind. They provided an extraordinary intellectual opening for me, not just in science, but in the liberal arts. However, I want to skip from the foothills to the Himalayan heights and recall my interactions with Professor Edwin Salpeter of Cornell University (fig. 23), a member of my Ph.D. committee and my postdoctoral advisor. I'll begin with a typical interaction that occurred about the same time as the kundalini experience described in chapter 3.

Ed Salpeter and I are in his office discussing my latest calculations on supernovae. Besides the big bang, supernovae are the largest explosions in the universe. They liberate more energy in a few seconds than all the solar energy that could fall on the entire Earth's surface in 10^{20} years.[†] (The universe is only about 10^{10} years old.) The supernova explosion directly produces a beautiful filamentary structure (fig. 24), which results when the outer layers of the massive star are ejected and plow into the interstellar medium, the mixture of gas and dust left over after star formation. There is much interesting physics in all this, and Ed and I are working hard to understand how the supernova's ejected material interacts with the interstellar medium.

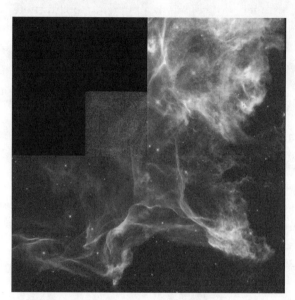

Fig. 24. A portion of the Cygnus Loop nebula (courtesy of National Space Agency, Hubble Space Telescope Institute)

Ed is a towering figure in astrophysics, and he is surely one of the kindest men at Cornell. However, working with him for an hour is the intellectual equivalent of running at absolute top speed for ten miles. A telephone call interrupts our discussion, and I am glad that somebody is asking for his advice, so I can breathe for a moment. I need to collect my thoughts, go over what we just talked about, and get myself ready for the next part of our discussion.

He holds the telephone to his ear, stares out the window with a distracted look, and paces around his small office. He fiddles nervously with some pencils in a jar on his windowsill, listens intently, asks questions, runs a hand through his long mane of brown hair, and offers suggestions. After twenty minutes or so he hangs up the telephone and resumes our conversation as though he had only taken a breath. "As we were saying, the cooling mechanisms in that shocked region are critical. If we don't get it right, we won't have any faith in those calculations."

[†] In scientific notation, 10^{20} means 1 followed by 20 zeros.

Ed had not seen the details of my calculation, but he had an almost supernatural ability to go right to the heart of the matter and smell out mistakes I never dreamed were there. More than once I had done some elaborate calculation and gone to discuss it with him. He would say something like, "That's strange, I thought it would go inversely with the density. Are you sure it's right?" I would try to convince him I was right. More often than not, I would get that sinking feel that he smelled a rat and it was probably a big ugly one. Working with Ed not only exposed me to the functioning of a great mind, but it also brought out the best in me. As one of his famous coworkers once said to me, "There are many bright stars in the scientific heavens, but Ed's star is the brightest."

Many of those astrophysical stars came together for a couple of days in the fall of 1997 to honor Ed on his retirement. There were two hundred guests or so, nearly all of whom were either his former graduate students or coworkers. Several elegant papers related to Ed's work were presented, and we were reminded of the many honors he had received over the years. The highlight was supposed to be a "roast"—one of those events where different people poke fun at the guest of honor. Those things, despite being well intentioned, can be brutal, but Ed's roast turned into a lovefest. Nobody seemed able to poke fun, but instead one speaker after another praised the depth and breadth of his contributions to astrophysics and, even more, the extraordinary kindness and generosity he showed to everybody who crossed his path.

I'll end my own homage to Ed by telling a brief tale of how he not only taught me to think deeply about astrophysics, but also how to embody tolerance and kindness—traits in short supply in all fields. This experience occurred when I was a graduate student trying to find a way to have some fun on spring break, a couple of years before the kundalini experience discussed earlier.

After months of hard study, problem assignments, and research in the cold, dark Ithaca winter, I and my roommate David Hollenbach [also a Salpeter student and now a famous astrophysicist] decide we need some sun. We find that for a mere ninety dollars we can get a round-trip ticket from Ithaca to San Juan, Puerto Rico. We can stay for free in a little loft in San Juan belonging to some radio astronomer friends of ours. They will be observing at the Arecibo Observatory during our spring break, so for a couple of hundred bucks we can live the good life in the sun.

There is only one impediment to bikini bliss . . . Ed Salpeter. He expects us to carry on with our research projects over spring break. We decide on a slimy strategy: we make up a story, telling Ed we have heavy obligations that require us to be out of town for the whole spring break. A few days later, we're in San Juan. Warm sun, friendly people, beautiful beaches, the intoxicating smell of suntan lotion, and, yes, many lovely, bikini-clad women. We enjoy the beaches, but the most interesting places are the poolside bars and cabanas of the big hotels. There we can enjoy good swimming, drink *Cuba Libres* (rum and Coke) in the shade, and attempt to meet some of the lovelies. Nobody can tell that we are not guests in the hotel, so we act as if we own the place, believing that the best defense against being found out is a good offense. Things are going well. My roommate and I have managed to strike up a conversation with a couple of attractive women, and we go to the poolside bar to buy some drinks.

While we are waiting for our drinks at the bar, someone walks up behind us and says hello. It's Ed Salpeter.

I want to jump in the pool and just swim right down the drain. Ed explains that he is providing some theoretical astrophysics expertise at the Arecibo Observatory and is staying for a night at this hotel. We mumble something and get out of there as quickly as we can, leaving the lovely women with their fresh *Cuba Libres*.

On one hand, it doesn't seem like a big deal, a major moral lapse. On the other hand, some uncomfortable questions keep circling in my mind like hungry buzzards. Why did I engage in such a stupid piece of petty dishonesty? Why didn't I just tell Ed that I wanted to get some sun and not work on my research project? Why didn't I have the guts to say something honest right at the bar? I blew it. He now knows what a dishonest and useless turd I really am. It surely won't help in any future recommendations he writes for me. The whole thing is much more painful because of Ed's kindness. How could I do that to such a fine man? The weather is beautiful for the rest of my spring break, but even with sunshine, alcohol, and charming women, I can't quite shake the dark cloud that follows me around.

Back at Cornell, I dread the next meeting with Ed. How can he resist making some remark about my bald-faced lie? What will I say?

What can I say? To my surprise and relief, he never mentions a word about it. We go on as though he had never seen us at the poolside bar in Puerto Rico.

I was so relieved and grateful for Ed's kindness. If I had been in his place, the temptation to make the offender squirm would have been irresistible. By his kindness, which contrasted so sharply with my shabby behavior, he taught me so much more about honesty and tolerance of the weaknesses of others than if he had given me a long, painful lecture about it.

In the next section, I use my experience of lying to Ed as a springboard to discuss a paradox about the nature of time. The resolution of this paradox is a lovely piece of astrophysics that will help us understand the nature of scientific knowledge and contrast it with transformative self-knowledge.

A PUZZLE ABOUT THE NATURE OF TIME

My moral lapse in the Puerto Rico escapade, whether small or large, cannot be undone. Whatever learning, confessing, or reinterpreting is done, it cannot change the fact that I lied. There is no going back. Let's hope recalling it will help me in the future, where there is some chance that I can improve.

We all appreciate this qualitative difference between the past and the future. The events in the past have a fixity that contrasts sharply with the more malleable future, where we can still influence events.

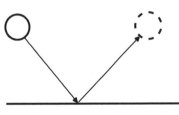

Fig. 25. Time reversal of bouncing ball

For these reasons, time is said to have directionality. The metaphorical "arrow of time" points from the past, through the present, and into the future. In contrast, such directionality does not occur for space: the space to my left is qualitatively the same as the space to my right.

All this seems natural and obvious. The puzzle comes when we look at the nature of time in physics. Let's take the simple experiment of bouncing a ball off the floor at an angle, as shown in figure 25. Let the ball be thrown from the left (the solid sphere), bounce off the floor at an angle, and end up on the right (the dashed sphere). Choose a lively superball that loses almost no energy in the actual collision. If a movie of this little experiment is run backwards, then the ball starts on the right and ends up on the left. This time-reversed motion obeys all the laws of physics and nothing seems strange about it. In fact, if you don't know the movie is running backwards, you have no way to tell, just from looking at the ball, that the motion is reversed.

Take a more complex example. Our Sun revolves around the center of our galaxy in an approximately circular orbit. It takes about one hundred million years to complete one full orbit. At the same time, the planets revolve around the Sun, with each planet simultaneously rotating on its axis. Imagine a movie of this complex motion being run backwards. Everything would be reversed: the planets rotating around each axis, the planets revolving around the Sun, and the Sun orbiting around the center of the galaxy. However, all these time-reversed motions would obey all the laws of Newtonian mechanics and nothing in the backward-running movie would seem strange. All this can be summarized by saying that the laws of mechanics are time-reversible. For this reason, whether we are considering a bouncing ball or the solar system's motion around the center of our galaxy, the time evolution of the system can run either forward or backward and still obey all the appropriate laws of physics.

The situation is the same in a quantum mechanical system. Consider the energy levels of atomic hydrogen used in the radio astronomy study of neutral hydrogen, as mentioned in chapter 2. The hydrogen atom has its lowest energy state with the spins of the proton and electron anti-aligned and a higher energy state with the spins aligned. When the atom drops from the higher to the lower energy state, the difference in energy is carried off by a photon. This photon emission generates radiation with a wavelength of 21 centimeters. This process can go in the reverse direction: a low-energy hydrogen atom can absorb a 21-centimeter photon and end in the higher energy state. Such photon absorption is merely the time-reversed evolution of the photon emission. All this is possible because the laws of quantum mechanics are also time-reversible, as are all the laws in physics.[1]

But there is a paradox here. Consider an egg sitting on a tilted table. Soon the egg rolls off the edge and splatters on the floor. If we film this egg breaking and run the film backward, it will look very strange. Nobody sees eggs that are spread out on the floor suddenly reassemble themselves and hop up on a table! That process is certainly not time-reversible or time-symmetric. Nor have we ever seen rotten fruit gradually return to its fresh state, nor old bodies or rotten teeth become whole again. So our puzzle is that the fundamental underlying laws of physics are time-reversible, but there are clearly time-irreversible events that we experience, whether the breaking of an egg or the breaking of our moral standards.

THE PHYSICS OF TIME

> Time is the substance I am made of. Time is a river which sweeps me along, but I am the river; it is a tiger that devours me, but I am the tiger; it is a fire that consumes me, but I am the fire.
>
> —Jorge Luis Borges[2]

In this passage, the poet Borges has captured some very complex ideas in just a few words. In this section, I will develop those ideas by building upon some earlier work[3] regarding the physics of time. As it turns out, understanding something about time in modern physics deepens our sense of how time is "the substance I am made of" and how we are both the devouring tiger and the consuming fire.

Our inevitable ride down the river of time is full of irreversible transformations, leading to death, the one we fear most. Innumerable experiences of such irreversibility demand that we understand, within the time symmetry of the fundamental physical interactions, how nature generates asymmetric and irreversible processes. As we will see, such an understanding provides deep lessons about our relationship to the universe.

TIME AND RELATIVITY. The few decades that we have to live may seem criminally short, yet time may also seem to crawl unendurably in our final days. However, in this digital age most believe, despite such subjective experiences, that time is absolute. For example, we believe that ten years is a well-defined interval that all observers can agree on, despite their subjective biases. How accurate is this view? Let me proceed by way of example.

The carrots I plant in my garden take 70 days to reach harvest time. Our belief in the absoluteness of time or its independent existence is evident in our view that this time interval is something intrinsic to the carrot. As long as the growing conditions are normal, it does not matter how this time is measured or who measures it. It has an independent or absolute nature; that is, its nature is independent of the point of view from which measurements are made—the reference frame.

However, suppose an astronaut takes the same seeds and grows them in a spaceship traveling at ninety percent of the speed of light, relative to the Earth. Then the theory of special relativity tells us that the days to harvest (as measured by an Earth-based observer) would be 161 days.[4] Figure 26 shows the days to harvest, as observed on Earth, plotted against the velocity of the spaceship relative to Earth, v, divided by the speed of light, c. So, for example, when $v/c = 0.9$, we move straight upward from that point on the horizontal axis and intersect the curve at 161 days. Only when there is no relative motion between the growing carrots and the observer (in the rest frame) is the time to harvest 70 days.

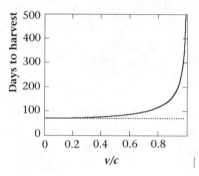

Fig. 26. Relativity of time

Relativity emphatically states that no value of the days to harvest time is any more real or intrinsic than any other. For example, if the astronaut looked back at the carrots in my garden, she would correctly measure their time to harvest as 161 days. Since time intervals depend directly upon the relative velocity between the object and the observer, they are essentially relational. *We cannot consider time intervals independent of a particular point of view or reference frame.* Time intervals lack independent existence, and they only make sense relative to a particular observer. If the seed manufacturers were devotees of relativity, they would state on the package, "The time to harvest is 70 days only in the rest frame. For other reference frames, consult figure 1." We can attempt to evade this relational nature of time by saying that humans never travel at any significant fraction of the speed of light, and so this is just an academic consideration. This evasion denies the conceptual import of relativity's view of time and the thousands of experiments done all over the planet every day that rely on it.

The implications of this discussion extend to our ideas of "the present." The essentially relational nature of time intervals, whether decades or microseconds, is complemented by a thoroughgoing relativity of the present. Let us first clarify the idea of the present moment. Take the reasonable notion that all the simultaneous events for an observer at one time define that present moment. Let's say I plant my carrots at exactly 11:00 A.M. on a given day and at that moment a friend in Australia boards a plane, while my son enters a classroom in a distant city. Relativity teaches that those simultaneous events defining the moment of carrot planting are only simultaneous in my garden's reference frame. If our farmer-astronaut, moving at ninety percent of the speed of light, passes directly over my garden at 11:00 A.M., she observes a different set of simultaneous events and thus her present moment differs from mine. Another astronaut, traveling at a different velocity over my garden at 11:00 A.M., finds yet a third set of simultaneous events and thus a different present from mine or that of the first astronaut.

Therefore, relativity makes both time intervals and individual moments relative to a given reference frame, leaving our old absolute view of time far behind. Similar things can be said about other primary qualities of objects, such as their length and mass. A still more interesting and profound quality of time can be appreciated by understanding the qualitative difference between past and future, the question we turn to next.

TIME ASYMMETRY OUT OF SYMMETRIC INTERACTIONS. Suppose I store my carrots in the cellar, where there is a cool, even temperature. However, even there, they rot after four to six months. We have never seen rotten food return to its fresh state. Rotting, whether of vegetables, teeth, or our entire bodies, is an irreversible process. Given that the quantum mechanical laws that govern the chemical changes of rotting are time-symmetric, as discussed earlier, this irreversibility is mysterious. The great Austrian physicist Ludwig Boltzmann made the first significant progress in understanding this mystery. He realized that irreversibility comes from reversible underlying laws only when you have large numbers of particles in the system.

Boltzmann started by considering a simple box containing many gas particles governed by Newton's laws. In analyzing this system, he assumed that it was totally isolated from the rest of the universe. The universe had no influence on the box and its contents, or vice versa. In other words, the box was energetically isolated from the rest of the universe, so that no energy moved from the box to the rest of the universe, or vice versa. Boltzmann then imagined a partition in the middle of the box, with all the particles located in just one half of the box and the other half totally empty.

To proceed further we need to understand the concept of *entropy*, a measure of disorder. The more disorder in the system—or, stated differently, the less we know about the details of the system—the higher the entropy. Consider my desk as an example. When I am working hard, my papers, books, journals, writing tools, computer disks, and so forth all pile up, increasing the general disorder or entropy of my desk. When I can't stand the disordered or high-entropy state any longer, mostly because it is so difficult to find anything, I spend some time and energy setting it in order and thereby decreasing its entropy.

Returning to Boltzmann's box, we next consider what happens when the partition separating the gas particles is removed. The gases will reach a new equilibrium condition, and the overwhelmingly most probable configuration of this equilibrium involves the gas being distributed evenly throughout the box. In principle, it is possible, although exceedingly unlikely, for the gas particles to bunch up in only one corner of the box. However, it is overwhelmingly more probable that the gas will attain a new equilibrium configuration in which it is diffused evenly throughout the box. Such equilibrium states have maximum entropy. This is an example of how a disturbed system moves toward a new equilibrium with higher entropy.

Consider a more familiar example. Imagine a completely ordered deck of cards with all the cards of a particular suite collected together and arranged starting with two, three, and four and going on up to the jack, queen, king, and ace. This completely ordered deck is in a state of very low entropy. It is also in a low-probability state, because out of the huge number of possible states of the cards, only one corresponds to the ordered state. When all states are equally likely, as in a shuffled deck, that single, perfectly ordered state is very unlikely to occur. Now imagine continuously shuffling the cards for a full ten minutes. At the end of that time, it is overwhelmingly likely that the cards will end in a state of much greater disorder or entropy. That is the normal reason for shuffling the cards in the first place. Although it is possible that, after ten minutes of shuffling, the cards could end up completely ordered again, this outcome is exceedingly unlikely. Here again, as with Boltzmann's box, we see that systems evolve to states of high probability corresponding to increased entropy.

Through this line of reasoning, Boltzmann proved the famous Second Law of Thermodynamics, which says that the entropy of any isolated system must either stay the same or increase. Therefore, when the partition in the box ruptures, the gas is overwhelmingly likely to go to a state of greater entropy. What is more, the increase in entropy defines the direction of the arrow of time. *Time advances in the same direction in which entropy increases—what we call the future.* This conclusion does not deny that there are local decreases in entropy, such as the growth of a child, but the global entropy relentlessly increases with time.

For several years, I taught Colgate University's junior-senior level course on statistical physics. We used the standard textbook and followed Boltzmann's derivation of the Second Law of Thermodynamics, with the appropriate level of mathematical sophistication. However, I found that there were arguments from as far back as 1877 showing that this derivation has serious problems. I have reviewed some of these issues in nontechnical language elsewhere.[5] Here, I take a different approach and follow an elegant and simple argument by the eminent physicist P. C. W. Davies,[6] which can be skipped without undo loss of continuity. As we will shortly see, entropy does increase, but not in the way Boltzmann thought.

Isolated Systems Are Always Reversible

The basic difficulty with Boltzmann's derivation of the Second Law of Thermodynamics, which can be seen in several independent ways, is this: a completely isolated system, like the box of gas, cannot generate time directionality because the laws governing the system are time-symmetric. Figure 27 displays the equilibrium entropy, S, of an isolated box of gas plotted versus time, t. It shows that the random gas motions give occasional deviations below the maximum. Although unlikely, the random motions spontaneously generate states of greater order or lower entropy, which are then brought back to maximum disorder by the same randomization. This process is like the shuffling of playing cards that, on very rare occasions, puts them into states of greater order, with continued shuffling returning them to disorder.

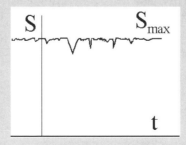

Fig. 27. Entropy versus time

Now imagine the experiment illustrated in figure 28. We patiently monitor the system until its entropy spontaneously drops to the value S_1 (or below) at a time t_1. Since we choose a low value for S_1, this could take a long time. The virtue of choosing a low value of S_1 is that once it occurs, we know we are very likely to be near the bottom of a dip in the entropy curve, rather than partway down a larger dip. This is true simply because the dip to S_1 is already unlikely, so a larger dip is even more unlikely. The low-entropy state, S_1, occurs at time t_1. At that point, the system is very likely at the minimum of a dip, so entropy increases either before or after t_1. More explicitly, at time $t_1 + \varepsilon$, where ε is some small time interval, the entropy increases. From the point of view of t_1, the time $t_1 + \varepsilon$ is in the future. However, the entropy was also greater in the past, at $t_1 - \varepsilon$. Therefore, the symmetry of the underlying laws of physics gives no directionality to entropy increase or time. In this way, we can see that Boltzmann's analysis is fatally flawed. An equilibrium system isolated from the rest of the universe cannot distinguish the future from the past.

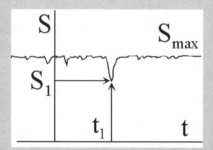

Fig. 28. Time symmetry of entropy

As Thomas Gold, one of my professors at Cornell, showed many years ago, the main problem lies in assuming we have a totally isolated system independent of interaction with the universe. Gold showed that we must always account for interactions between thermodynamic systems and the universe. For example, how did Boltzmann's box get into the low-entropy state of having all particles in just one half? This state did not result from just waiting a long time for random motions to throw the gas all to one side, but from Boltzmann evacuating one half and placing gas in the other. However, all the procedures that put the box in a low-entropy state must generate more entropy elsewhere in the universe. For example, Boltzmann consumed calories from lunch and then radiated energy from his body that eventually went into deep space. In other words, processes outside the box put it into a low-entropy condition, but at the expense of an entropy increase elsewhere in the universe.

Let me give another example from my garden. I walk in the garden to check whether mice have eaten the carrots. My footprints in the soft soil give it more order and structure, thus lowering its entropy. However, this lower entropy comes from a much greater generation of entropy from my metabolic processes, which eventually degrade to heat radiated to the universe.

As physicists now realize, this process of emitting energy into deep space from our activities is only possible in an expanding universe. The reasoning behind this conclusion runs as follows. Consider being in a large forest on level ground. Although there is plenty of space between the trees, when you look deeply into the forest, your line of sight will eventually fall on a tree trunk. In every direction, at eye level, you see brown tree trunks. On the other hand, imagine that each tree has picked up its roots and is moving away from the other trees. In such a forest, in which the distance between every tree is constantly increasing with time, not every line of sight will fall on a tree trunk.

Analogously, in a static or nonexpanding universe, any line of sight away from the Earth, when extended far enough, would land on a star surface. In this case, rather than seeing tree trunks in every direction we would see stars filling all space. In actuality, because the universe is expanding, we see plenty of dark sky. Since light also travels toward the Earth on the same lines of sight, in a nonexpanding universe the effective temperature of deep space would be that of the surface of stars, which is typically 6,000 degrees Kelvin; instead, the actual temperature of deep space is 3 degrees Kelvin. In a nonexpanding universe, because the sphere of the sky above Earth would be hotter than the Earth itself, the simple process of radiating our body's energy into space would be blocked. There would be no way to radiate our waste heat away. Neither Boltzmann nor his entropy-changing box could exist.

All systems that organize themselves (i.e., decrease their entropy), whether a growing carrot, a snowflake, or a child, cause a decrease in entropy in one location that must be accompanied by generation of greater entropy in another. All this exchange would be blocked in a static universe. Therefore, the first point to appreciate is that the expansion of the universe is essential for entropy to increase—and thus for time to have an arrow.

Finally, what caused the Sun and other stars to be in a low-entropy condition in the first place? The answer lies in the first three minutes of the big bang, when the expansion rate of the universe was faster than the rate at which nuclear reactions generated complex nuclei from simple particles. Toward the end of the first three minutes, when nearly all the helium (about twenty-five percent of the total mass of the universe) had formed, the continuing expansion cooled the particles below the temperature needed for nuclear reactions, thereby stopping further nuclear synthesis. If the expansion and associated cooling had been much slower, then all the matter in the universe would have been processed into iron-56, a very stable isotope of iron. The result would have been an inert and high-entropy condition with no differentiation into elements. The stars would not shine; there would be no great entropy gradients in the universe, no time asymmetry, and, of course, no life as we know it. Therefore, for entropy to increase in the normal way and for time to have an arrow, two conditions are necessary. First, the universe must be expanding on the largest possible scales. Second, the initial cosmic expansion had to happen faster than the nuclear reaction rates in order to produce low-entropy stars. *Therefore, local time asymmetry, such as the decay of any biological system, from carrots to our own bodies, must be accounted for by connecting it to the overall expansion of the universe and its earliest evolution.*

The full explanation of this extraordinarily beautiful result has many technical twists and turns. However, the central idea is clear: increasing entropy and time asymmetry owe their existence to the largest and earliest processes in the universe, to its rapid early expansion and continued expansion thereafter. This scenario is a long way from the isolated and noninteracting system initially assumed by Boltzmann. Consider this: when you put cold milk into your coffee and the mixture comes to the same temperature and a higher entropy than when the fluids were separated, you are profiting from the universe's present expansion and its earliest development. Similarly, that we must all face the irreversible process of death, with its massive entropy increase, is traceable to the largest and earliest processes in the universe. In other words, the impermanence and decay found all around us are connected to processes utterly remote in space and time.

On a more positive note, irreversible processes are also essential to life. If metabolic processes did not irreversibly transform my lunch, not only would I get indigestion, I could not live. There are innumerable other irreversible processes in biology, from the growth and repair of cells to the secretion of hormones. That which sustains me also destroys me. Indeed, as Borges says, time "is a fire that consumes me, but I am the fire."

TRANSFORMATIVE SELF-KNOWLEDGE VERSUS SCIENTIFIC KNOWLEDGE

I chose this lovely piece of astrophysics about time because, unlike a more specialized or technical piece of scientific knowledge, it has broad implications for our relationship with nature. It thus makes for a richer comparison to the instance of transformative self-knowledge considered in chapter 3. To differentiate these two types of knowledge, I will apply the seven characteristics of transformative self-knowledge to the above example of scientific knowledge. As we will see, some of the seven characteristics are more compatible with science and its methods than others.

1. *Scientific knowledge is not an interior intuition.* In stark contrast to transformative self-knowledge, all scientific knowledge must be objective, something we can articulate, usually in mathematical form. It must be public knowledge, something readily reproducible by a scientist with the requisite theoretical or experimental training. For example, Boltzmann's argument about why entropy increases, whether it is right or wrong, must be reproducible by anybody with the requisite training in thermodynamics. However, as I argued in chapter 2, the objectivity so valued in science has limits. Feelings, intuitions, and other forms of subjective experience can be scientifically studied only if they can be objectified, that is, turned into an object that can be dealt with in a laboratory or mathematically analyzed. In science, we know by separating ourselves from the object of knowledge. In contrast, consider the principle of awareness—not a content within awareness, but the actual intrinsic "light" of the mind, that by which all else can be known. Can this be objective? No. If you could objectify it, then there must be some deeper or more encompassing awareness that illuminates the version claimed to be objective. In fact, only contents of awareness, not awareness per se, can be objective. I consider the issue of objectivity in more detail in chapter 9, in connection with possible measurements of synchronicity.

2. *Scientific knowledge is not holistic.* Although any genuine piece of transformative self-knowledge must involve the whole of the person, every aspect of their being, this need not be so for scientific knowledge. As beautiful and far-reaching as a piece of science might be, it is possible to partition it off from the rest of your life. For example, I tried to give a sense of how the very growth and decay of our own bodies connects us to the largest scales and earliest minutes of the universe. This point may be interesting, but hardly life-transforming. Some, of course, might be deeply moved by it, both in their sense of self and their relationship to the universe. Then the distinction between transformative self-knowledge and science would be blurred. However, this must surely be an exception.

    For another example, getting a Ph.D. in physics requires no moral or psychological transformations. Yes, you have to have stamina, the ability to take orders, and at least some talent for physics, but in general, being a scientist requires no moral preconditions, nor does it necessarily generate any moral transformations. Therefore, scientific knowledge is compartmentalized knowledge of the material and energetic universe that need not affect the whole of the person.

3. *Scientific knowledge is not unique to the individual.* In contrast to transformative self-knowledge, all scientific knowledge must be free from individual subjective bias. This could be considered an aspect of the objectivity of science, but it is worth treating it separately. Conclusions cannot depend upon who does the investigation— on their racial characteristics, religious beliefs, cultural background, or psychological peculiarities. (Of course, all these individual peculiarities can and do affect the form of transformative self-knowledge.) Anyone who has mastered the technical material and can do the calculations or measurements properly must get the same results, independently of subjective bias or presuppositions.

    Reviewing a dark hour in the history of physics will bring this point into sharper focus. In the 1920s, some well-known scientists were much taken by Nazi ideology. Because of this, they claimed that Einstein's work on relativity was "Jewish physics." This stunning piece of stupidity from otherwise capable physicists shows that racism can easily overrule rationality. Special relativity is a particularly elegant piece of physics that is mathematically deduced from just two initial axioms, which can be written down in a few sentences. There is not the slightest thing Jewish about these axioms, but with them, all of special relativity can be mathematically deduced. For example, we could generate all the physics needed for the earlier discussion about different perceptions of the time to harvest for carrots. It does not matter if you are a Nazi, Jew, or African college student; the physics is the same.

In this sense, scientific knowledge is free from individual subjective bias, but science does have its own values, such as elegance and economy of ideas. These and many other values pervade the practice of science. Nevertheless, it is free from *individual* psychological, philosophical, and cultural bias. In other words, science is done within all sorts of background assumptions, values, and conventions, but individual bias does not enter the picture. Of course, great individuals such as Einstein can influence both the content and intellectual style of physics, but Einstein's contributions could have been made by others. In contrast, although transformative self-knowledge usually has universal or archetypal elements, it is deeply structured by and dependent upon the uniqueness of the individual.

4. *Scientific knowledge is not necessarily transforming.* Scientific knowledge is generally not transformative. Yes, it changed my life to learn science and its methods and values, and I have had truly rapturous delights in doing physics, but these experiences have generally not been transformative in a deep sense. However, for some people the rationality expressed in science is such a valued feature of the universe that it really becomes their god, the center of their religious worship. Einstein expresses this view with exceptional clarity:

> It is quite clear to me that the religious paradise of youth, which was thus lost, was a first attempt to free myself from the chains of the "merely personal," from an existence which is dominated by wishes, hopes, and primitive feelings. Out yonder there was this huge world, which exists independently of us human beings and which stands before us like a great, eternal riddle, at least partially accessible to our inspection and thinking. The contemplation of this world beckoned like a liberation, and I soon noticed that many a man whom I had learned to esteem and to admire had found inner freedom and security in devoted occupation with it. The mental grasp of this extrapersonal (*ausserpersonlichen*) world within the frame of the given possibilities swam as highest aim half consciously and half unconsciously before my mind's eye.[7]

A liberation from the "merely personal" through a contemplation and profound apprehension of the "extrapersonal" world is a spiritual experience. I have had experiences in science like this, and I affirm this point of convergence between transformative self-knowledge and science. However, this aspect of *doing* science is generally accidental to its value as a *piece* of science. Such spiritual experiences can, but need not, occur in the doing of science.

However, I believe Einstein had a lopsided emphasis on the impersonal, the universal, the realm that excludes the "wishes, hopes, and primitive feelings" of a unique human being. Holding such an incomplete view denigrates the greater part of the life we actually live. In contrast, in the preceding chapter, I discussed the double nature of soul, which embraces simultaneously the personal and the impersonal, the transient and the eternal. This view provides a foundation for making all experience sacred, including science.

5. *Scientific knowledge must be repeatable.* One of the hallmarks of science is that the results must be publicly repeatable. Whether it be a powerful piece of theoretical physics, such as special relativity, or a measurement of the cosmic background radiation left over from the big bang, independent scientists must be able to duplicate the calculation or measurement. Public repeatability is one of the reasons that people have so much faith in science. Even during the height of the Cold War, we did not dismiss bold claims by Soviet scientists as propaganda, because the scientific community has this safeguard of public repeatability. Of course, this requirement strongly contrasts with the unrepeatability of transformative self-knowledge.

6. *Scientific knowledge denies teleology.* Ever since the founding of modern science in the sixteenth century by Galileo and others, teleology or final purpose has been ruled out as an explanatory principle. Because matter, whether a subatomic particle or a star, has no interiority, no will of its own, science holds that all physical process are due to the action of external forces. These forces are also insentient and have neither interiority nor will. As the great Nobel Prize winner Steven Weinberg says, "The more the universe seems comprehensible, the more it also seems pointless."

7. *Scientific knowledge can be sacred.* In the quotation above, Einstein beautifully expresses the sacredness of doing science. Moments of

genuine spiritual uplift are possible through science. However, if we divide reality between the head and the heart, between objective knowledge and transformative self-knowledge, then science is almost entirely in the head realm and thus not normally sacred.

The five chapters of Part I have differentiated science and the sacred. I have discussed how science is not as objective as most generally believe: all observations are modified at many levels by the response function of the observing instrument, whether a telescope or a human being. In the analysis of my kundalini experience, I then discussed another type of knowledge, called transformative self-knowledge, which is an equally important part of reality. The key to understanding that type of knowledge is the notion of soul. With the help of an analogy drawn from cosmology, I explored the mystery of the simultaneously finite and infinite nature of soul. Part I ended with a scientific discussion about the nature of time and entropy and their relation to the origin of the universe, which further differentiated between the two kinds of knowledge.

In the next four chapters, Part II, I will explore some of the tensions that arise when these two ways of knowing confront each other. As a particularly vexing example of these interactions, I discuss the case of astrology. I first show how the tensions between science and astrology reveal the great dangers in an uncritical identification with the idea that one great truth encompasses all reality. I then review Jung's idea of individuation. This provides a framework for understanding synchronicity and astrology. Part II culminates with a discussion of the possibility of scientifically testing synchronicity and astrology, which further clarifies the differences between science and the sacred.

Part II

SOME INTERACTIONS OF SCIENCE AND THE SACRED

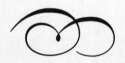

Chapter Six

THE DARK SIDE OF MONOTHEISM

The choirmaster, Mr. Bugler, nods to me and begins playing the pipe organ in his usual theatrical style as I sing my solo of *Ave Maria*. Looking down from the choir loft, I can see that Saint Mary's Catholic Church is filled to capacity for the High Mass. People are just starting to walk up to the altar to receive communion. I gaze directly into the tabernacle as I sing and feel carried along by devotional feelings. Despite my natural and easy devotion, especially toward the Virgin, I am mystified by the idea that Christ's flesh somehow resides in that dry little white communion wafer that usually sticks to the roof of my mouth. Those receiving communion look up at me as they walk back to their seats, and I bask in their awareness of my singing.

The next day, back in class, my fifth-grade teacher, Sister Bertil, praises my performance. I luxuriate in her compliments on my singing—especially since she usually focuses on my sinning. A few minutes later, I am talking in class as usual, when Sister Bertil slips up behind me, bellows some indistinct words, and slaps me sharply on the right side of my face. I am totally surprised, humiliated, and angry. The entire right side of my face stings and my ear rings loudly. Despite the pain, I am not going to give her or anyone the satisfaction of seeing me cry. I take no comfort from noticing that Sister Bertil's false teeth have skidded up underneath the desk in front of me. I bolt out of the room. Once out, I decide to walk home. Since my mother is still at work, nobody will know I got home early.

Sister Bertil must have been embarrassed about losing her patience (and her teeth). She did not report me for leaving school and never spoke about the incident again. I don't remember much of what Sister Bertil tried so hard to teach me, but I do recall how often she preached to us about the two greatest commandments. She exhorted us to love God with our whole heart and soul and our neighbor as ourself. I tried to embody these ideals, but it was never easy. Even in elementary school, I was beset by conflicts between my ideals and my actions, between what I vowed to do and what I was able to put fully into action. Taking Catholicism seriously made those conflicts severe. However, they got worse when they broadened to encompass doctrinal issues. In a few years, I would be struggling with questions such as, "How could a lustful thought, which floats so naturally into my mind, be a mortal sin and condemn me to eternal suffering?" Or, "How could wine that looks no different from what my grandfather drinks turn into the blood of Christ?" The nuns and priests confused and mystified me by answering, "No, the transubstantiation is not symbolic; it is real."

At age eleven, I wondered how a Sister of Mercy, a bride of Christ, who taught me to love God and my neighbor, could strike me like that—especially over just talking in class. Now it is easy to understand. She was, despite being a good nun, also human, and I was the class troublemaker.

Fig. 29. Vic and Sister Bertil

The photograph here shows Sister Bertil and me three years later at my eighth-grade graduation (fig. 29). By then, I was no longer a boy soprano and my days in the choir had ended. Although unintended, one of her most lasting lessons was about the frequency of conflicts between ideals and actions, between the gospel of love and the failings of humans. As we will see in the rest of this chapter, such conflicts are intrinsic to the usual narrow and rigidly held view of any "-ism," whether Christian monotheism, scientific materialism, or astrological fundamentalism. These conflicts also generate rancor between astrology and science.

Monotheism: The Darkness behind the Ideal

Deuteronomy, the culmination of the first five books of the Old Testament, contains the Shema, the most famous prayer in Judaism, recited daily by the devotee: "Hear O Israel: The Lord our God is one Lord: And thou shall love the Lord thy God with all thine heart, and with all thy soul, and with all thy might" (6.4–6). This soaring expression of monotheism has been placed reverently in innumerable tephillin or phylacteries, posted at the entry to the homes of the religious, and enriched over the millennia by the daily repetition of countless Jews.

Jesus considered the Shema the first and greatest commandment. In Mark 12.29–31 we read:

> The first of all the commandments is, Hear, O Israel; The Lord our God is one Lord. And thou shalt love the Lord thy God with all thy heart, and with all thy soul, and with all thy mind, and with all thy strength: this is the first commandment. And the second is like, namely this, Thou shalt love thy neighbour as thy self. There is none other commandment greater than these.[1]

The continuity on this point between the Old and the New Testament, and thus between Judaism and Christianity, is even more apparent when we realize that Jesus quotes Deuteronomy more than any other book of the Old Testament.[2] These exhortations to monotheism and love of others have inspired me, ever since the Sisters of Mercy taught them to me in grammar school. However, I did not appreciate then that the monotheism celebrated in these commandments also has a dark side. Although Deuteronomy has a broad humanitarian spirit, with its concern for strangers, women, and the poor, it also tells us that if anybody, including our spouse or children, tries to induce us to worship other gods, then they should be exterminated. For example, a few paragraphs after the Shema we read:

> Thou shalt not consent unto him [the unbeliever], nor hearken unto him; neither shall thine eye pity him, neither shalt thou spare, neither shalt thou conceal him: But thou shalt surely kill him; thine hand shall be first upon him to put him to death, and afterward the hand of all the people. (13.8–11)

Nor is it enough to kill the nonbelieving tempter. We must seek him out and mercilessly destroy him, his cities, and all his goods so that he cannot rebuild:

Then shalt thou inquire, and make search, and ask diligently; and, behold, if it be truth, and the thing certain, that such abomination is wrought among you; Thou shalt surely smite the inhabitants of that city with the edge of the sword, destroying it utterly, and all that is therein, and the cattle thereof, with the edge of the sword. And thou shalt gather all the spoil of it into the midst of the street thereof, and shalt burn with fire the city, and all the spoil thereof every whit, for the Lord thy God: and it shall be a heap for ever; it shall not be built again. (13.14–16)

This attitude is hardly consistent with the second of the two greatest commandments, to "love thy neighbor as thy self." Despite my great appreciation for the Judeo-Christian tradition that nourished my inner life as a youth, it is clear that powerful injunctions such as these fueled the Crusades and the Inquisitions. It is also sobering to recall these passages while today so many in the West condemn the Islamic extremists for their interpretation of the Koran, which they claim supports *jihad* or holy war. Whether a religion invokes Deuteronomy or says, "There is no God but Allah" or "only science leads to truth," a fanatical clinging to one God or one truth inevitably leads to intolerance and inhumanity.

Such tension between ideals and actions is thus not only a personal one—as in the contradictions that troubled me about the incident with Sister Bertil and my own attempts to live with Catholic doctrine—but also a tension within the history of monotheisms in general. The next section shows that such inconsistency also occurs in scientific monotheism.

SCIENTIFIC MONOTHEISM

In our day, scientific materialism is the reigning arbiter of what is real and true. I am not claiming that a particular scientific content or idea is a form of monotheism. Rather, I am suggesting that the so-called scientific method and the set of assumptions, values, attitudes, and approaches to knowledge that go along with it constitute a form of monotheism. "Science is the one true path to knowledge" replaces "The Lord our God is one Lord."

For example, for a modern person who is trying to answer the question, "Who am I?" the view of science, while perhaps not conclusive, is certainly crucial. Am I merely an exceedingly complex tangle of atoms and molecules choreographed by the laws of physics? Is there room for soul in the scientific worldview? Just the phrasing of the question ("is there room") implies that for knowledge to be legitimate, it must find a place under the scientific umbrella. But can science help "save" my soul, or at least help give my life meaning?

Answering that question was formerly the job of clerics or medicine men, but since science has become the dominant religion, that role has been taken over by scientific "medicine" men. Modern medicine has an extraordinary claim on our bodies from cradle to grave. In the United States, the money spent on scientific medical care is one-seventh of the gross national product. The revenues of traditional religious organizations surely fall well short of that expression of value.

Because science and religion have had such a strained relationship in the West, it may seem strange to claim that science is a religion or can be understood as one. To show that science can indeed be considered a form of religion, let me turn to the definition of religion given by the internationally recognized expert in comparative religion, Raimon Panikkar:

> By religion, I mean the set of symbols, myths, and practices people believe gives ultimate meaning to their lives. I stress the believing factor, for religion is never just an objective set of values. Religion is always personal and necessarily includes the belief of the person. . . .
>
> . . .Religions can only be true or false inasmuch as they speak to our mind and our mind reflects upon them. In this sense, a true religion has to fulfill these two conditions:
>
> 1. It has to deliver the promised goods to its members; in other words, it needs to be truthful to its own tenets. This does not mean that the dwelling-place of the ancestors, or nirvana, for instance, has to be somewhere, or that the person who commits a mortal sin goes to a physical place called hell. It means, however, that those who follow the Commandments or the Dharma or observe the Four Noble Truths will reach the end or fulfillment of life that the particular religious tradition describes independently of the many possible cosmological and anthropological interpretations of the same tenets. A true religion must serve its purpose for those who believe in it; it must achieve existential truth, honest consistency.
>
> 2. It has to present a view of reality in which the basic experience is expressed in an intelligible corpus that can sustain intelligent criticism from the outside without falling into substantial contradictions. This does not mean that God must exist in the crude or literal way in which an outsider may think. It means, however, that world views which accept the reality of

gods, for example, can present themselves in the arena of human critique and meet the questions put from the outside so as to be able to present a picture which is consistent if not convincing for everybody. A true religion must achieve essential truth, authentic coherence.[3]

In summary, a religion must satisfy three requirements: it must give "ultimate meaning," "deliver the promised goods to its members," and "present a picture which is consistent." If we start with the last of the three requirements, it is easy to see that the scientific picture of the world, from the big bang to the structure of DNA, is consistent, convincing to many, and defensible. As for requirement two, it certainly delivers the goods, whether in the form of scientific medicine or thermonuclear weapons. But does it really give "ultimate meaning?" People with conventional religious sensibilities usually think that scientific materialism is entirely devoid of ultimate meaning. However, that view merely shows that science is not their religion. For the devotees of science, the scientific world may be indifferent to their personal desires, but it offers a clear understanding of ultimate questions. We come from the big bang, planetary formation, and Darwinian evolution. When we die our bodies return to the material from which we were made. Our ultimate purpose is procreation and the propagation of our DNA. A still more hard-nosed view would say that there is no ultimate purpose, that belief in such a purpose is a form of sentimental weakness, that social and moral constraints come from our need for survival, and so on. These "ultimate meanings" do not appeal to everybody. Nevertheless, they are accepted by many intelligent people who consider more conventional religious views mere wishful thinking, sops for the weak minded. The true devotees of scientific materialism see their embrace of the impersonal scientific worldview as an expression of heroic reason, the highest of human faculties.

However, within this heroic devotion to scientific reason there is room for a kind of faith, which, though different in content, shares many of the qualities of conventional religious faith. The religion of science often brings forth deep expressions of faith worthy of the most revered religions. For example, a scientific colleague and friend of mine developed a severe case of Parkinson's disease, complete with tremors and halting speech. I was discussing it with him and offering my sympathy when he smiled sweetly at me and said, "They will find a cure before long." Such professions of faith in scientific progress are hardly rare and are often held with as much conviction as any conventional religious belief. The compatibility of such faith in science with traditional religious tenets does not deny that science is a religion.

As a culture, we pay homage to science at every turn, in both thought and action. In the United States, the alphabet soup of NASA, NSF, DOE, DARPA, NIH, NIMH,[4] and so on proclaims the marriage between science and the state. The three great scientific and technological achievements of World War II—deciphering the Japanese code, deploying radar, and detonating a fission bomb—signed the covenant between science and the military in the blood of many nations. This relationship is largely duplicated throughout the industrialized world. It also parallels the marriage between the Roman Catholic Church and the Holy Roman Empire. Five hundred years ago, a poor boy in the West with some talent could enter the Church to advance spiritually, intellectually, and socially. Now that pathway to advancement lies through science. For example, the graduate fellowship for my Ph.D. came from NASA, while NSF funded my early research and today pays for the lab equipment I use in teaching. The power of science to shape everything from international policy to our view of ourselves is so pervasive we tend to ignore it and take it as a given in modern life.

Considering science as similar in character to a monotheistic religious view may seem extreme, because science is usually portrayed only as the best method for seeking truth, not as a mythological system with a creed and values to which we must bend our knee. However, the famous (or infamous, depending upon your commitments) philosopher of science, Paul Feyerabend, summarizes his brilliant technical analysis of this issue by claiming:

> Science is much closer to myth than a scientific philosophy is prepared to admit. It is one of the many forms of thought that have been developed by man, and not necessarily the best. It is conspicuous, noisy, and impudent, but it is inherently superior only for those who have already decided in favour of a certain ideology, or who have accepted it without ever having examined its advantages and its limits. And as the accepting and rejecting of ideologies should be left to the individual it follows that the separation of state and church must be complemented by the separation of state and science, that most recent, most aggressive, and most dogmatic religious institution. Such a separation may be our only chance to achieve a humanity we are capable of, but have never fully realized.[5]

Feyerabend calls for separating science, "that most recent, most aggressive, and most dogmatic religious institution," from the state.

His call seems radical for two reasons. First, we normally do not think of science as a religion, and second, most modern people unquestioningly believe in the truth and value of science and the appropriateness of its marriage to the state.

I found an illustration of science as religion and of the fusion between science and the state in an unexpected place: Westminster Abbey in London, which I happened to visit while thinking about these topics. So much of English culture is on display in that architectural masterpiece of a church, but I was especially interested in the thousands of people buried there, from kings, statesman, saints, and artists to scientists. The religious relics in the abbey were destroyed in 1540 on the orders of King Henry VIII, and the only major saint still buried there is St. Edward the Confessor. Nevertheless, a powerful religious presence is still palpable thanks to daily worship and the extraordinary liturgical music performed there.

One of the most arresting tombs prominently displayed in the nave is that of Sir Isaac Newton (fig. 30). He is in good company

Fig. 30. Newton's tomb, Westminster Abbey (photo by author)

there in the "scientists' corner" with Charles Darwin, Lord Kelvin, Ernest Rutherford, and Sir J. J. Thomson. On his tomb, Newton is attended by winged cherubs, and his image is as heroic and saintly as that on any tomb in the abbey. Besides the cherubs, the reference in the inscription to Newton's "strength of mind almost divine" contributes to the unmistakably religious air. Newton is treated like a great "saint" in the Religion of Science.

Because modern science, or more precisely scientific materialism, is the dominant religion in our culture, its marriage to the state is a serious concern. History shows that when a religion assumes dominance because of its alliance with the reigning political power, sectarianism and persecution of the other religions follow. For example, in the West, when Christianity was both the dominant religion and a major political power, it fell into its worst excesses. Over the last thousand years or so, during the Crusades and Inquisitions, Christians put Jews, Muslims, Albigensians, and other "heretics" to the sword in appalling numbers. When modern Hindu fundamentalists become intertwined with the Indian government, then Muslims suffer and die. In the Middle East today, when Islam weds political power, then human rights, women, and authors deemed offensive are all abused. Such persecution occurs not only between religions, but also between different interpretations or sects of the same religion, as the following example from Buddhist history shows.

In the seventeenth century, the fifth Dalai Lama, known as the Great Fifth, consolidated religious and political power in Tibet. (The Dalai Lamas head the Gelukpa sect of Tibetan Buddhism.) Through cultivation of relations with the military power of the Mongols, the Great Fifth became both the religious and temporal leader of central Tibet. Upon assuming this power, he forcibly closed the monasteries of other sects of Tibetan Buddhism, burned texts, and sealed libraries.[6] These abuses, which stem from a marriage of church and state, happened in a tradition whose two central principles are wisdom and universal compassion.

What comparable abuses and persecutions can we expect from the marriage between the state and the religion of scientific materialism? There are certainly doctrinal struggles between science and other religions. Today, the struggle between Christian fundamentalism and science takes the form of heated debates on creationism versus evolution. Although I am clearly on the side of science on this one, I think we must be vigilant to not repeat the lessons exemplified above. However, the real struggle is not simply about doctrine, but about the guiding principles of knowledge and the fundamental philosophical presuppositions about the nature of the universe. For example, laboratory-based parapsychology studies have generated mountains of carefully taken data showing the nonlocal nature of mind and its ability to interact through nonsensory channels with the material world (e.g., through telepathy, psychokinesis, or clairvoyance).[7] However, these studies are neglected or ridiculed by the scientific establishment. The reasons for this neglect are not entirely clear, but I suggest that the implications of these studies are such a profound challenge to the prevailing scientific worldview that they are perceived as a genuine threat.

Even more insidiously, the ascendancy of scientific materialism causes an enormous devaluation of the inner world and its productions. When you believe that consciousness is an epiphenomenon of the brain, that is, merely a by-product of neurochemistry, the objective study of matter necessarily takes precedence over the inward investigation of consciousness. Looking for the neural source of awareness becomes vastly more important than an inward turning into the source of our own deepest subjectivity. Soul is thrown into the scientific junkyard alongside such once-vaunted, now-debunked scientific theories as phlogiston, ether, and élan vital.

The paramount demand in science is for rational, objective knowledge, free from the taint of any subjectivity. This demand has great value in many areas, but the systematic exclusion of any human wishes, needs, and concerns often leads to inhumanity, whether in modern warfare or modern medicine. Because the most influential scientists are so successful in their realm, they boldly believe (and often convince others) that their method and values should be applied to all realms—that there is only one truth and one path to it. What is more, in trying to free the world of error, they often violate their own most precious principles. Feyerabend has criticized this and other inconsistencies in several of his books with great brilliance and verve.[8] Such inconsistencies are particularly well illustrated by two episodes in the long-running hostilities between science and astrology. In light of the foregoing discussion, these episodes—the publication of the manifesto *Objections to Astrology* and the infamous debate over the "Mars effect"— can be seen as clear examples of religious conflict.

SCIENTIFIC MONOTHEISM AND ASTROLOGY

In the mid-1970s, after my brief fling with experimental radio astronomy, I attended a meeting of the International Astronomical Union in Grenoble, France. I was glad to be going to such an important meeting and to have the opportunity to share my recent research with my colleagues in astronomy and astrophysics. Upon entering the main meeting hall, I was accosted by two astronomers, who asked me to sign a document known as *Objections to Astrology*. This document had already been signed by 192 leading scientists, including eighteen Noble Prize winners. By then, I had been struggling for over a decade to balance my love of theoretical astrophysics with my psychological and spiritual needs. Part of that balancing act involved an immersion in astrology. Of course, after a decade of studying astrology, I could not sign the document.

Objections to Astrology was published in *The Humanist*[9] in 1975 and later in a book[10] with two supporting essays. The full statement follows.

OBJECTIONS TO ASTROLOGY

Scientists in a variety of fields have become concerned about the increased acceptance of astrology in many parts of the world. We, the undersigned—astronomers, astrophysicists, and scientists in other fields—wish to caution the public against the unquestioning acceptance of the predictions and advice given privately and publicly by astrologers. Those who wish to believe in astrology should realize that there is no scientific foundation for its tenets.

In ancient times people believed in the prediction and advice of astrologers because astrology was part and parcel of their magical world view. They looked upon celestial objects as abodes or omens of the gods and thus intimately connected with events here on earth; they had no concept of the vast distances from the earth to the planets and stars. Now that these distances can and have been calculated, we can see how infinitesimally small are the gravitational and other effects produced by the distant planets and the far more distant stars. It is simply a mistake to imagine that the forces exerted by stars and planets at the moment of birth can in any way shape our futures.

Acceptance of astrology pervades modern society. This can only contribute to the growth of irrationalism and obscurantism. We believe that the time has come to challenge directly and forcefully the pretentious claims of astrological charlatans. It should be apparent that those individuals who continue to have faith in astrology do so in spite of the fact that there is no verified scientific basis for their beliefs and, indeed, that there is strong evidence to the contrary.

Both Feyerabend[11] and Carl Sagan,[12] an archenemy of astrology, have criticized this statement. Feyerabend points out that the language is nearly identical to the introduction to the *Malleus Maleficarum*, the 1484 textbook on witchcraft issued by the Roman Catholic Church.[13] Indeed, the religious tone of the *Objections* is striking. Like priests expressing anxiety for their flock, the authors are "concerned about the increased acceptance of astrology in many parts of the world." Why, in fact, should the scientists be "concerned?" Apparently, they have the one truth and want to guard the rest of us from falsehoods, since astrology has "no scientific foundation for its tenets." The document is pervaded by the assumption that if something has no scientific foundation, then it should not be believed. Following these scientists, we should then rule out religion, metaphysics, mystical philosophy, depth psychology, and astrology, since little or no scientific evidence can be advanced for belief in any of these systems of thought.

What a simple cosmology. Everything within the monotheism of scientific materialism is truth; everything outside is error. Fortunately, these scientists are not taking the injunction of Deuteronomy literally: "Thou shalt surely kill him [the unbeliever]; thine hand shall be first upon him to put him to death." Nevertheless, they are clearly taking a hostile stance toward the unbeliever.

Sagan, who repeatedly characterizes astrology as "bunk," criticizes the *Objections* as "authoritarian." He, like Feyerabend, points out that if one criticizes a view because it has its roots in a "magical worldview," one should also criticize many areas of science, which also grew from a magical tradition. Furthermore, the absence of a scientific explanation for a phenomena is not sufficient grounds for dismissing it. As Sagan writes: "That we can think of no mechanism for astrology is relevant but unconvincing. No mechanism was known, for example, for continental drift when it was proposed by [Alfred] Wegener [a German geologist]. Nevertheless, we see that Wegener was right, and those who objected on the grounds of unavailable mechanism were wrong."[14]

Feyerabend points out[15] that the scientists have not done their homework, because in fact there is a large literature discussing different kinds of interactions between the planets and Earth. For example, the solar wind (the plasma emitted by the Sun) is dependent upon planetary positions. Knowing planetary positions allows predictions about the activity of the solar wind, which in turn interacts in various ways with Earth. Although the authors of the *Objections* may not have known this work, Jung refers to it in his seminal essay on synchronicity.[16] In addition, various biological functions do depend upon tidal forces generated by the positions of the Sun and Moon.

The reference in the *Objections* to the weakness of gravitational effects shows that its authors were assuming a *causal* mechanism for astrology. However, as I discuss in detail in chapter 8, it is inappropriate to view these interactions between the Earth and the Sun, Moon, and planets as causes. It is incorrect to assume that solar system bodies influence us the way the Moon influences ocean tides. A much richer understanding emerges when we view astrology as a symbolic language whose meanings *acausally* relate our inner experience to the outer astrological positions.

The image that scientists like to project, one of cool impartiality and rationality, contrasts both with the religious tone of the *Objections* and its complete lack of any substantial arguments against astrology. When a scientist has strong experimental evidence or powerful mathematical arguments for a position, there is no need for colleagues unrelated to the work to sign his research papers. The framers of this document are attempting to make up for the absence of evidence or arguments by impressing us with the number of famous signatures. However, when the BBC wanted to interview the Noble Prize winners who signed it, they declined because they had never studied astrology and knew nothing of its details.[17]

This tendency of scientists to violate their self-proclaimed impartiality and argue against astrology when they know nothing about it is common and continues to occur. For example, consider the remarks of Sir Martin Rees, the Astronomer Royal of England, when he visited the United States to receive the Franklin Institute's $250,000 Bower Award for "achievement in science." The *New York Times* interviewed him on April 28, 1998. Here are the last few lines of the interview:

> Q. How does someone who theorizes about the cosmos feel about a phenomenon like astrology?
> A. I don't know any astronomer who takes it seriously. The question is, should one campaign against it? If I were an East Indian, where the leaders subscribe to astrology, I would campaign against it. Maybe if I was an American in Reagan's time, with Nancy, I might do so also. But in Britain, we have, I think, a more sophisticated attitude than in U.S. popular culture. Neither creationism nor astrology are serious issues. So I don't really feel that it's appropriate to take a very strong line. Indeed, if one did so, one would be perceived as unduly solemn.
> Q. So what's your sign?
> A. Cancer.
> Q. And what does it mean to be a Cancer?
> A. I wish I knew.

Why should such a capable astronomer violate the tenets of science and criticize something he knows nothing about? Apparently, he and the other Noble Prize winners have sufficient faith in the monotheism of scientific materialism that they need not bother with careful study but can merely rule astrology out on a priori grounds.

What then happens to scientists of such deep faith when confronted with scientific evidence in favor of astrology? There is one such
example that illustrates another twist in the tangled net of relationships between astrology and science. In 1955, the French statistician
and psychologist Michel Gauquelin published *L'influence des Astres*,[18]
which first proclaimed the "Mars effect." He looked at the position of
Mars in the natal horoscope (the map of the heavens at the time and
place of birth) of famous athletes. He found a statistically significant
pattern: Mars appeared more frequently just after sunrise and just after
culmination. In other words, famous athletes are more likely to have
been born when Mars was just above the eastern horizon or just after it
reached its highest point in the sky (culmination). Figure 31 shows
data representing 2,088 athletes.[19] In this graph, the plane of the eclip-
tic (the apparent path of Mars across the sky) is divided into twelve
sectors of thirty degrees each, labeled from one to twelve starting just
after sunrise. Segments one and four correspond to just after sunrise
and just after culmination, respectively. Note the peaks that appear in

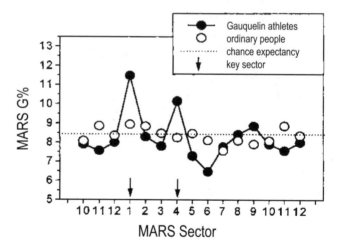

Fig. 31. The Mars effect

these two sectors. If the positions of Mars were distributed randomly,
then each sector would contain 8.33 percent of the athletes, as shown
by the dotted line. The strength of the effect increases with the
athlete's eminence, as gauged by their appearance in a selected group
of reference books. Failure to appreciate this point contributed to
the controversy.

The finding is not purely good news for traditional astrology, since the usual interpretations claim that a powerful Mars is more likely in sector twelve (called the first house in astrology) rather than sector one. In other words, although the data support astrology's central claim that the positions of planets correlate with personality structures, the details of the correlation are not consistent with the tradition.

However, this poor fit with traditional astrological theory is nothing compared to the difficulties that three different skeptical groups in Belgium, France, and the United States created for themselves. When these groups attempted to discredit the Mars effect, each became mired in scandalous behavior, when they shamelessly distorted the conclusions of the data. The details of the imbroglio are too convoluted to discuss here. It is sufficient to note that in the United States, prominent members of the Committee for the Scientific Investigations of Claims of the Paranormal (CSICOP, pronounced "psi cop") resigned over the scandal. The most balanced and careful investigation is given in *The Tenacious Mars Effect*,[20] written by Dr. Suitbert Ertel and Kenneth Irving, in conjunction with James Lippard, a confirmed skeptic of astrology. This book contains a detailed summary of the various scandals. The authors' careful reanalysis of the four separate data sets gathered by Gauquelin and the three skeptical groups shows that all four data sets support the Mars effect. The effect appears to be on solid scientific ground; however, some critics of astrology still claim it is not.[21] A foreword to *The Tenacious Mars Effect*, written by the skeptic Lippard, summarizes the situation:

> I was first exposed to the "Mars Effect" controversy while a university undergraduate in the mid-1980s, about the time I founded the *Phoenix Skeptics*. . . . Until then, I had supposed the skeptics to be the dispassionate voices of objectivity and reason, cleanly and completely debunking every alleged paranormal claim to come along. I had been a naive disbeliever, but was now confronted with an apparently paranormal claim, which appeared to offer some difficulty to the skeptics.
>
> After much communication with and observation of fellow skeptics, I concluded that skeptical groups can suffer from the same irrationality, dogmatism, and "group-think" as other groups. (Indeed, this seems to me now to be an essential characteristic of human social behavior). Evidence that resists refutation and threatens foundational beliefs of a group may cause the group to reject, suppress, or ignore that evidence.

Given the details of how badly the skeptics acted, this rebuke is mild. Let me caricature these events to make my point about the dark side of monotheistic scientific materialism: the scientists tried to "smite the unbeliever" with the *Objections*, reinforced with 192 of their best troops, and then they attempted to destroy the "goods" of the astrologers, that is, the data supporting astrology, through a series of unscrupulous actions.

In this particular controversy, the astrological side comes out looking good. However, astrologers, with their various excesses, undisciplined speculations, and lack of internal standards and consistency, are their own worst enemies. I also believe that if some combination of depth psychology and astrology were in the ascendancy, that is, the reigning monotheism, then its practitioners would act just as badly to repress competitors to its views. The impulse to destroy the infidel, the unbeliever, the one with the inferior view, seems built into every monotheism.

Both the *Objections to Astrology* and the controversy surrounding the Mars effect express the dark side of the monotheism of science. The example of the Mars effect especially shows how defending scientific monotheism often leads to scandalous inconsistencies within the practice of science—a significant conflict of ideals and actions. Perhaps the main reason the Mars effect generates so much controversy is that it explicitly attempts to bring astrology within scientific monotheism by showing that an astrological correlation is statistically significant. Rather than bring astrology under the scientific umbrella, an unlikely occurrence, it would be more valuable to generate a genuine dialogue between science and astrology, as between any two religions. The greatest obstacle to a fruitful dialogue is the tendency of most religions—whether Christianity, scientific materialism, or astrology—to believe that they alone possess the one all-encompassing truth. From this belief follows the companion belief that all other views are in error and must be contained, if not eliminated. Then instead of a dialogue teaching us about each system and how they interrelate, we have the injunctions of Deuteronomy and all its modern variants. Understanding and breadth of vision give way to conflict, intolerance, and impoverishment of world culture.

Chapter Seven

INDIVIDUATION AND SYNCHRONICITY

I have published many scholarly articles in physics and several interdisciplinary fields, but in early December 1993 I finish my first book, *Synchronicity, Science, and Soul-Making*. I take a colleague's advice and talk it over with his literary agent, whose name, promisingly enough, is Faith. After sending my manuscript to a variety of publishers, she and the publishers conclude that my book is too ambitious for the trade press, yet too far off the beaten path for an academic publisher. She says she cannot help and bids me merry Christmas.

I have worked too hard to quit that easily, so I send it off to more than a half a dozen publishers. By early February 1994, a small blizzard of rejection notices has begun burying my literary ambitions. It doesn't help that my colleagues warned me to expect this. A large publisher shows interest in my book, but that exciting prospect dies as my manuscript works its way up the editorial ladder. By April, a small publisher known for its philosophy and science titles is the only one that has not yet rejected me. I am depressed, as any author would be in similar circumstances, but the rejection is intensified because so much of my personality and case material are woven into the book. As could be expected under these stressful conditions, my dreams roar to life. I pile the form letters of rejection on my meditation altar as an offering. I have largely lost faith in the entire project. Early one morning I have the following strange dream:

> I was in the Dewitt Building in downtown Ithaca, New York, at an award ceremony in my honor. For my new book, I was being presented the James Hillman award for the most significant contribution to depth psychology for the year. Dr. Jenny Yates, a Jungian analyst in town, was presenting the award, which included a cash prize and an office in the Dewitt Building for one year. I was deeply honored.

After thinking about this dream for a few minutes, I am dismayed. "How could I be having such grandiose fantasies when I can't even get my book published?" I ask. Swinging between the opposites is not new to me, but my embarrassment prevents me from writing down the dream as I always do. Around seven in the evening I tell my wife about the dream (we often work on our dreams together). After telling her, I am in the process of writing it down when the telephone rings. My wife hands it to me and announces, "It's Jenny Yates!" I have not had any communication with Jenny in at least six months, although in the acknowledgments section of my book I thank her for helpful comments on an earlier draft.

"Hi, Jenny. I had an interesting dream with you in it last night. Who should go first?"

Being a true Jungian analyst, she wants to hear the dream before telling me her reason for calling. We do not interpret the dream, but it is obvious that something interesting is going on. She has just finished a telephone call with an editor who was reviewing my book. The editor, another Jungian analyst, is a friend of Jenny's from her training days in Zurich. Having found Jenny's name in the acknowledgments, the editor called her to find out more about the book and me. The editor is waiting for one more external review before formally offering to publish my book.

I was delighted by the news and simultaneously stunned by the realization that my dream was not just an ordinary one but part of a synchronicity, an event that violated the normal constraints of space and time. How could I, as a finite consciousness, bound by space and time, know that Jenny Yates would be the bearer of such good news? Stranger still, I was telling the dream to my wife at the very moment Jenny was on the telephone with the editor.

It is possible to dismiss such experiences as mere chance coincidences. The argument goes that innumerable things occur during a lifetime and, sometimes, weird coincidences just happen. However, many of us feel that these kinds of events are simply too improbable and too charged with psychological meaning to be dismissed in this way. Jung found that they frequently occurred during periods of great stress or in the course of deep psychological work. Toward the end of his life, after much experience with the phenomenon, he articulated the concept of *synchronicity* in 1955 in a famous essay, "Synchronicity: An Acausal Connecting Principle."[1]

Before discussing details, let me outline my purpose for reviewing synchronicity. In the last chapter, we saw how the scientific establishment not only dismissed the claims of astrology but also, in the process, subverted many of the principles by which science operates. In addition, one of the chief misunderstandings in that debate concerned the supposed causal claims of astrology. I pointed out that, contrary to the view of many of its critics, astrology should be understood as *acausal* correlations between our inner states and outer astrological positions.

Many people, along with Jung, believe that synchronicity provides a proper acausal framework for understanding astrology. However, as I have pointed out elsewhere,[2] there are serious difficulties with all previous attempts at understanding astrology as a class of synchronicity. In this chapter and the next, I will take a fresh approach to synchronicity and its relationship to astrology.

To understand Jung's concept of synchronicity, we must first understand the process of individuation. I touched on this process in the discussion of soul in chapter 4, but because individuation is so closely connected to synchronicity, we need to review it in a bit more detail.

INDIVIDUATION

Fig. 32. Digital image 1

An apt analogy for individuation comes from an unlikely source: digital imaging technology. The image in figure 32 looks like a few randomly placed pixels. If you could view this image under magnification, you would find that each pixel actually has 256 possible shades of gray, ranging from snow white to coal black. Even with an active imagination, it is impossible to see any pattern or meaning in figure 32.

Next, look at figure 33. Here you might be able to see some sort of shape, but at this stage, it is still mostly projection—attributing shapes that are in the mind of the viewer and not in the actual image.

Fig. 33. Digital image 2

In figure 34, you might actually start recognizing something. Yet, you may still wonder how much of what is seen resides in the image and how much is a projection. By figure 35, it is clear that you are seeing pixels from a photograph of a person's face. With a few hints, you might even guess who the person is. All becomes clear in figure 36, which shows all pixels of the photograph of the Dalai Lama.

Let me try to connect these images to Jung's idea of the process of individuation. Instead of each pixel being one of 256 possible shades of gray, imagine that each pixel shade is unique. In other words, imagine that there are an infinite number of possible shades and that no shade is repeated. Imagine further that each unique pixel represents a particular psychological experience: all your traumas and triumphs, your earliest and latest experiences—each represented in a pixel. Each of your dreams, whether you understood them or not, has a representation as a unique pixel, and so forth.

Early in our process of reflection, or sometimes even after years of effort, the set of pixels seems jumbled and senseless. We can see neither meaning, nor structure, nor intelligence in the scatter of pixels or psychological experiences—just as in figure 32. With more experience and psychological work, a vague and shifting pattern of meaning may appear. We persist in trying to understand our emotional reactions to events in the inner and outer worlds. We learn to remove our psychological projections on others, to reflect

Fig. 34. Digital image 3

Fig. 35. Digital image 4

deeply upon our dreams, to ferret out the intention or purpose of our experiences. In other words, we are trying, through psychological reflection, symbolic interpretation of dreams and fantasies, and the attempt at removing projections, to understand the heights and depths of our personality.

Along the way, various archetypally structured components of the personality emerge from the unconscious. For example, we learn about the shadow, that part of our personality that we repress for the sake of some ideal vision we hold of ourselves. Aspects of our personality that are incompatible with that vision are denied, repressed, or neglected. Nevertheless, they live on in the unconscious and influence our behavior, whether through a slip of the tongue, an emotional outburst, or some unexplained action. Unfortunately, those who know us well can often see the shadow much more easily than we can. The more unconscious we are of these components, the more freedom they have to express themselves without our control.

With more attention, we can become aware of the autonomous elements in our psyches that represent the opposite sex. Jung used the term *anima* for the female principle within the male psyche and *animus* for the male principle within the female psyche. These components of the psyche play a big role in our relationships both to the unconscious and to the opposite sex. Getting to know these and other archetypal figures and attempting to integrate them into our personality is analogous to catching glimpses of the various shapes in the photograph and trying to make a coherent image of the scattered pixels.

In the sequence of images shown, we note that there is always a latent image of the complete face that is unfolding in successive photographs. In some sense, the complete photograph is always there, but more of it becomes manifest as we proceed through the series. In a similar manner, the archetype of the self, the guiding intelligence expressing itself in the process of individuation, is a timeless principle that is always present as the orderly unfolding of personality. Of course, early in the process we have no clear knowledge of the image, just a splatter of confusing pixels (or experiences) that don't seem to fit together, that don't have any shape, sense, or coherence. The famous primatologist Jane Goodall, who, judging from her autobiography, has no significant knowledge of Jung's ideas, describes this process quite vividly:

> Through the years I have encountered people and been involved in events that have had huge impact, knocked off rough corners, lifted me to the heights of joy, plunged me into the depth of sorrow and anguish, taught me to laugh, especially at myself—in other words, my life experiences and the people with whom I shared them have been my teachers. At times I have felt like a helpless bit of flotsam, at one moment stranded in a placid backwater that knew not, cared not, that I was there, then swept out to be hurled about in an unfeeling sea. At other times, I felt I was being sucked under by strong, unknowing currents toward annihilation. Yet somehow, looking back through my life, with its downs and its ups, its despairs and its joys, I believe that I was following some overall plan—though to be sure there were many times when I strayed from the course. Yet, I was never truly lost. It seems to me now that the flotsam speck was being gently nudged or fiercely blown along a very specific route by an unseen, intangible Wind. The flotsam speck that was—that is—me.[3]

Fig. 36. Digital image 5, revealed as a photo of His Holiness, the Fourteenth Dalai Lama (photo by anthor)

When she writes, ". . . my life experiences and the people with whom I shared them have been my teachers . . . I was following some overall plan . . . being gently nudged or fiercely blown along a very specific route by an unseen, intangible Wind," Goodall gives a vivid description of the process of individuation.

However, the analogy I've built on these five images is misleading on several counts. First, we don't want to end up with an image of the Dalai Lama, as in this photo, but an image of ourselves as we truly are. The point of individuation is to become who we are meant to be, an expression of our authentic self, not some clone of another person or the expression of collective values. As James Hillman, former director of the C.G. Jung Institute in Zurich, is fond of saying, "Jung was the last good Jungian."

This uniqueness of each individuation is beautifully illustrated by the thirteenth-century tale *Queste del Saint Graal*, which the scholar of comparative mythology Joseph Campbell calls one of the most important myths at the foundation of the Western tradition. When the knights set out to find the Holy Grail, "They thought it would be a disgrace to go forth in a group. So each entered the forest at a separate point of his choice."[4] If a knight came upon another searching for the Grail and followed that knight's path, rather than his own, he immediately became lost. As Campbell goes on to say:

> This, I believe, is the great Western truth: that each of us is a completely unique creature and that, if we are ever to give any gift to the world, it will have to come out of our own experience and fulfillment of our own potentialities, not someone else's. In the traditional Orient, on the other hand, and generally in all traditionally grounded societies, the individual is cookie-molded. His duties are put upon him in exact and precise terms, and there's no way of breaking out from them. When you go to a guru to be guided on the spiritual way, he knows just where you are on the traditional path, just where you have to go next, just what you must do to get there. He'll give you his picture to wear, so you can be like him. That wouldn't be a proper Western pedagogical way of guidance. We have to give our students guidance in developing their own pictures of themselves. What each must seek in his life never was, on land or sea. It is to be something out of his own unique potentiality for experience, something that never has been and never could have been experienced by anyone else.

I believe Campbell overstates his case here. After all, the knights had their Merlin, their guru, upon whom they relied. Nevertheless, there is a genuine Western emphasis on the uniqueness and autonomy of the individual, and Jung's notion of individuation is grounded firmly in that tradition.

Parts of the self-portrait revealed in individuation will not be pretty, especially those expressing the shadow. Other aspects of our wholeness will reveal new talents and potentials that are essential to becoming who we authentically are. Deeper and more comprehensive knowledge of oneself, according to Jung, leads to the realization that there is great wisdom in the natural unfolding of personality. The ego, the center of the conscious personality, is not the source of the meaning, the intentionality, the purpose of life. Rather, the ego must learn how to communicate, largely through the symbolic interpretation of experience, with that wisdom expressing itself as the individuation process. We strive to set up a dialogue between the ego and the self, this archetype of meaning (or, in the language of chapter 4, the divisible aspect of soul). The communication is rarely easy, but it reveals an intelligence much wider and deeper than that of the ego. Consciously developing a connection with the self and attempting to embody this higher authority in our lives is the process of individuation, of coming to be who we are truly meant to be.

Another misleading aspect of the sequence of images above is that they quickly converge to a fully articulated image. Since the contents of the unconscious are inexhaustible and there will always be vast areas of unconsciousness in any human, according to Jung, the process is never completed. Another way of expressing this idea in terms of the series of images is to say that the process of individuation does not result in a final, fixed image. Instead, with more detail, a whole new aspect of the process reveals itself, or the current image transforms itself into something new and unexpected. When our development seems to have reached a plateau or played out its course, whole new dimensions unfold. Rabindranath Tagore, known simply as "the Poet" in modern India, expresses this very beautifully:

> I thought that my voyage had come to its end at the last limit of my power, —that the path before me was closed, that provisions were exhausted and the time had come to take shelter in a silent obscurity.
>
> But I find that thy will knows no end in me. And when old words die out on the tongue, new melodies break forth from the heart; and where the old tracks are lost, new country is revealed with its wonders.[5]

SYNCHRONICITY:
ACAUSAL CONNECTION THROUGH MEANING

According to Jung, synchronicity is an acausal connection, through meaning, of inner psychological states (such as dreams, fantasies, or feelings) with events in the outer or material world.[6] The keys to understanding this definition are the notions of acausality and meaning.

CAUSALITY/ACAUSALITY. For Jung, causality involves energy exchanges and our conventional notions of space and time. For example, in discussing synchronicity he writes, "We must give up at the outset all explanations in terms of energy, which amounts to saying that events of this kind cannot be considered from the point of view of causality, for causality presupposes the existence of space and time insofar as all observations are ultimately based upon bodies in motion."[7] Alternatively, as Jung's student and collaborator Marie-Louise von Franz writes, "Jung just presumed the same thing that nearly all physicists do today: that causality implies a provable interaction within the space-time continuum. All other formulations represent for Jung an overstretching of the concept of causality."[8]

In classical physics, any interaction can serve as an example for causality. For instance, gravity caused the apple to fall on Newton's head. Or, psychologically, anxiety caused me to forget a person's name. In synchronicity, there are no causal connections between the inner psychological states and the outer material events. The inner state neither causes the outer event nor vice versa. I call this *horizontal acausality*, since here the inner states and outer events are on the same epistemic level—both are consciously known.

There is also what I call *vertical acausality*, where the purported agent is transcendent and unknowable in itself. Of this type of relationship von Franz writes:

> According to the Jungian view, the collective unconscious is not at all an expression of personal wishes and goals, but is a neutral entity, psychic in nature, that exists in an absolutely transpersonal way. Ascribing the arrangement of synchronistic events to the observer's unconscious would thus be nothing other than a regression to primitive-magical thinking, in accordance with which it was earlier supposed that, for example, an eclipse could be "caused" by the malevolence of a sorcerer. Jung even explicitly warned against taking the archetypes (of the collective unconscious) or psi-powers to be the *causal agency* of synchronistic events.[9]

Thus Jung also eliminates any transcendent principle, whether archetypes or angels, as the cause for synchronicity.[10] We cannot attribute what happens "down here" in the empirical realm to what goes on "up there" in the transcendent realm. Despite the thoroughgoing horizontal and vertical acausality of synchronicity, Jung did not seek to abolish causality, but to supplement it with synchronicity.[11]

MEANING. Although the inner and outer elements of a synchronicity experience are acausally related, they connect through meaning. "Meaning" is a deceptively simple term, whose familiarity may mask its critical role in both Jung's thought in general and his ideas on synchronicity in particular.

Let's start with Jung's most exalted view of meaning. Section 3 of his synchronicity essay, entitled "Forerunners of the Idea of Synchronicity," begins with a discussion of Taoism, by far the most extensive treatment of any of the "forerunners." To prepare us for the discussion, Jung writes, "Although meaning is an anthropomorphic interpretation it nevertheless forms the indispensable criterion of synchronicity. What that factor which appears to us as 'meaning' may be in itself we have no possibility of knowing. As an hypothesis, however, it is not quite so impossible as may appear at first sight."[12] After this warning about the difficulty of grasping meaning in itself, he then goes on to tell us that there are many translations of *Tao*, but, he says, "Richard Wilhelm brilliantly interprets it as 'meaning.'"[13] Jung extensively quotes Lao-tzu's *Tao Te Ching* from Arthur Waley's *The Tao and its Power*, "with occasional slight changes to fit Wilhelm's reading," as Jung's translator, R.F.C. Hull, tells us.[14] For example,

> There is something formless yet complete
> That existed before heaven and earth.
> How still! How empty!
> Dependent on nothing, unchanging,
> All pervading, unfailing
> One may think of it as the mother of all things under heaven.
> I do not know its name,
> But I call it "Meaning."
> If I had to give it a name, I should call it "The Great."[15]

My point is not to argue the merits of Jung's equation between Tao and meaning, but to indicate how Jung understands meaning. This exalted and transcendent level of meaning, "formless yet complete, that existed before heaven and earth," is indistinguishable from what is normally referred to as the absolute. Given Jung's view, I regret that he did not select a more technical term, such as "transcendent meaning." It might have prevented many of the later misconceptions about synchronicity and its dependence upon meaning.

Lao-tzu characterizes the Tao as "Nothing" and Jung writes, "'Nothing' is evidently 'meaning' or 'purpose,' and it is only called Nothing because it does not appear in the world of the senses, but is only its organizer."[16] Meaning, or synonymously, purpose, is somehow an "organizer" of the world but "Tao never does; Yet through it all things are done."[17] Meaning organizes, but it does so acausally and in that sense "never does."

How does this lofty meaning or purpose enter the realm of opposites, of mundane life? Jung does not address this issue in the synchronicity essay; however, it is clear from his other writings that meaning or purpose primarily enters our life through what he calls unconscious compensation.

As we saw in chapter 4, for Jung, unconscious compensation is the chief form of interaction between the unconscious and consciousness. It is the psyche's way of correcting the ego's blindness or inappropriate views and guiding us in the process of individuation. This dynamic principle expresses the purposiveness or guidance of the unconscious. Rather than stressing the immediate causes of psychological phenomena, Jung was more concerned with their final purpose in our individuation. The question shifts from "What past experiences brought me here?" to "Where is this experience leading me? What does it demand of me? What purpose or meaning does it have for my evolution?" This shift de-emphasizes reduction—tracing present symptoms to past events—although that strategy is also employed in Jungian analysis.[18] As Jung said, "By finality I mean merely the immanent psychological striving for a goal. Instead of striving for a goal, one could also say sense of purpose. All psychological phenomena have some such sense of purpose inherent in them. . . ."[19]

Let me illustrate the notion of unconscious compensation by recounting a dream I had just a month before writing this sentence. At the time I was struggling with trying to formulate the last part of this book. I was badly bogged down in a whole series of dense philosophical issues. Even if I did get the ideas sorted out, I thought it was going to be nearly impossible to write about them in an engaging manner. It was not a major life crisis but certainly an anguished phase of the creative process.

I need to provide some background information first. My teacher, Anthony Damiani, had six sons. The second oldest, Paul, had great talent and the most interest in his father's work. He had a penetrating understanding of the various philosophies and religions that we studied, as well as a powerful emotional life. Paul's philosophical and psychological opinions were greatly valued. Despite Paul's introverted personality, he and I were good friends. Besides our intellectual and spiritual connections through Anthony, we worked together constructing the buildings at Wisdom's Goldenrod, often sailed on Seneca Lake together, and spent a little time socializing. Paul was deeply depressed after Anthony died. Within a year, Paul was dead too, from a freak accident; he was only in his thirties. His funeral was held one year to the day after his father died. It was a heavy blow to everyone.

Recently, after struggling for several days with trying to formulate the last section of this book, I had the following short dream:

> In the distance off to my right, I see somebody who looks like Paul. I strain to see more clearly and think, "It cannot be Paul, since he is dead." As the person comes closer, I notice he is walking with great self-confidence and yet naturalness. "I don't care what people say. It is Paul! There is no doubt." He now appears smiling, strong, trim, and older than I last saw him. He looks middle-aged, with fine lines on his face, but full of vitality and purpose. He comes up to me and I stand to greet him. I notice he is very tall, maybe seven feet. We embrace with great warmth.

I awoke and immediately felt lifted out of the fog of doubt that had been plaguing me. I interpreted the dream subjectively, not as having anything to do with the real Paul, but as symbolizing a part of me. This part was not dead, but in fact vibrant, full of purpose, mature, and much larger than I had thought. None of the tragic, moody, or introverted side of Paul was evident in the dream.

Here we see the unconscious offering encouragement through the warm embrace of Paul. It presented a compensation for my dim view of my abilities and marked the breaking of an intellectual logjam. However, the unconscious is certainly not always encouraging. It can also present us with some very unpleasant realizations about ourselves. For example, during a time when I held far too high an opinion of myself, I had a dream in which a pompous pig, dressed up in a three-piece suit and standing in my boots, was holding forth on what a grand fellow he was![20] There are yet other times when the unconscious compensation seeks to draw out a new view of a psychological problem or to encourage new developments. I stress, along with Jung, that such compensation is not a product of the ego. Rather, the ego is transformed by the accumulation of these compensations during the process of individuation.

In summary, the meaning or purpose in a synchronicity experience incarnates through an unconscious compensation, which expresses itself simultaneously in the inner and outer worlds. Synchronicity is thus a dramatic episode in the process of individuation. However, as in a dream, this meaning is not a creation of the ego. Instead, the meaning carries the transformative power of the self, actualizing through both the person and events in the world. Although the meaning has a personal aspect, since it is finely tuned to the needs of our individuation, it also has an archetypal and therefore universal aspect. As von Franz writes:

> For Jung, individuation and realization of the meaning of life are identical—since individuation means to find one's own meaning, which is nothing other than one's own connection with the universal Meaning. This is clearly something other than what is referred to today by terms such as information, superintelligence, cosmic or universal mind—because feeling, emotion, the Whole of the person, is included. This sudden and illuminating connection that strikes us in the encounter with a synchronistic event represents, as Jung well described, a momentary unification of two psychic states: the normal state of our consciousness, which moves in a flow of discursive thought and in a process of continuous perception that creates our idea of the world called "material" and "external"; and of a profound level where the "meaning" of the Whole resides in the sphere of "absolute knowledge."[21]

For Jung, "absolute knowledge" is not mediated by the senses, not the empirical ego's knowledge, and thus is not limited by the usual categories of spacetime. More important for my purpose is to emphasize, as von Franz does, the intimate connection between individuation, meaning, and synchronicity. Making this connection between meaning and individuation necessarily involves us in purpose, teleology, or final cause, and this must be so, otherwise we might falsely believe that each unconscious compensation is merely an attempt to restore some local balance. Instead, the final purpose or teleology of a life reveals an orderly process or intelligence actualizing itself through these separate unconscious compensations, these particular incarnations of meaning. As Jung says, instances of unconscious compensation "seem to hang together and in the deepest sense to be subordinated to a common goal, so that a long dream-series no longer appears as a senseless string of incoherent and isolated happenings, but resembles the successive steps in a planned and orderly process of development . . . the individuation process."[22]

When we understand synchronicity as an expression of the guidance of the self, as a presentation of meaning through the mechanism of unconscious compensation, we glimpse dramatic episodes of "the successive steps in a planned and orderly process of development." Thus, we are inevitably involved in a consideration of ultimate purpose or final cause. This purpose inherent in all psychological phenomena implies foreknowledge. In his synchronicity essay Jung writes:

> Whether we like it or not, we find ourselves in this embarrassing position as soon as we begin seriously to reflect on the teleological processes in biology or to investigate the compensatory function of the unconscious, not to speak of trying to explain the phenomenon of synchronicity. Final causes, twist them how we will, postulate a foreknowledge of some kind. It is certainly not a knowledge that could be connected with the ego, and hence not a conscious knowledge as we know it, but rather a self-subsistent "unconscious" knowledge which I would prefer to call "absolute knowledge."[23]

The emphasis is on final causes, life's purpose, and how the psyche guides our unfolding of that foreknowledge of what we are meant to be through unconscious compensation. The meaning embedded in experience draws us onward along our particular path, our individuation. In a sense, the future is pulling us in a particular direction. Such "drawing" or "pulling" is not causal. Rather, the numinous meaning embedded in a synchronicity has the power to lead us toward a fuller expression of that unique wholeness, the self.

Here enters a difficulty for modern persons, especially those of us heavily influenced by science. It is not merely that teleology or final purpose is out of fashion in modern science. More fundamentally, the scientific view firmly holds that the past determines the present. For example, a central task of theoretical physics is, given the initial conditions, to predict the outcome of future experiments. This is as true in quantum mechanics, so replete with acausality, as it is in classical physics. The most comprehensive expression of this approach is found in modern cosmology, in which the present state of the universe is traced to its very earliest conditions. In the traditional scientific view, events that may occur in the future have no effect on the present. This view contrasts sharply with the idea that a foreknowledge of what we are meant to be is playing itself out in our experience, eliciting a fuller expression of our unique wholeness.

FINDING THE MEANING IN SYNCHRONICITY

Within this framework of unconscious compensation, meaning, and teleology or final purpose, we can begin seeking the lessons hidden in my synchronicity experience with my earlier book. In this example, it is unreasonable to say that the editor's interest in my book caused my dream or that my dream caused the editor to be interested in my book. We also cannot say that Jenny Yates' telephone conversation caused the dream, because the dream occurred before that conversation. Nor, if we follow Jung, can we say that any transcendent principle, whether the unconscious or a particular archetype, caused the synchronicity. Nevertheless, the dream and the ensuing events are meaningfully related.

Because the dream seems to have given me information before I could have received it through normal channels, such as the telephone, this experience gives evidence for a knowledge transcending space and time, Jung's "absolute knowledge." Usually, synchronicity experiences are preceded by a significant activation of the unconscious. In my case, the unconscious was activated by my dire fears about laboring for years on a manuscript, only to have it rejected by publishers.

It is possible to view the synchronicity experience as a forceful unconscious compensation, as the Tao incarnating in both the inner and outer worlds with the intent or purpose of transforming me. I had lost faith in myself and the entire project. The dream and associated synchronicity experience sought to compensate for that lopsided conscious view. Since my conscious view was so negative, the dream compensated with the opposite extreme—the idea of a literary award and cash prize for the book. This response is typical of the kinds of unconscious compensations that occur when our views are badly unbalanced. As Jung says:

> As a rule, the unconscious content contrasts strikingly with the conscious material, particularly when the conscious attitude tends too exclusively in a direction that would threaten the vital needs of the individual. The more one-sided his conscious attitude is, and the further it deviates from the optimum, the greater becomes the possibility that vivid dreams with a strongly contrasting but purposive content will appear as an expression of the self-regulation of the psyche.[24]

As we've seen, Jung holds that such unconscious compensations imply some foreknowledge, some abstract vision of what we are meant to be, some future state of completion or wholeness, which draws us onward. Otherwise, how could the psyche "know" that my conscious view was unbalanced or inappropriate? My conscious assessment of the value of the book was so unbalanced and so damaging that the unconscious had to compensate with an image of receiving an award for my work.

However, the compensation is more specific than simply pumping up a deflated ego. To show this I need to say more about what the Dewitt Building, Yates, and Hillman mean to me.[†] First, the Dewitt Building. In the late 1960s, I was deeply involved in the anti–Vietnam War activities and related social actions that were so visible in the universities during that era. One project I particularly liked occurred in the Dewitt Building, which was formerly the junior high school for Ithaca. After the city built a new school, the building fell into disuse. Then a dedicated and able political activist and graduate student in French literature, Jack Goldman, launched the Ithaca Neighborhood College in the Dewitt Building. This expression of idealism offered free courses to anybody who cared to take them on everything from auto mechanics to Maoist thought. After paying a five-dollar registration fee, you could take as many courses as you liked. Because I appreciated Jack and the ideals embodied in the project, I put in a fair amount of time and effort on it. After a few years, the city sold the building to a developer, who converted the upper floors into apartments and offices and the ground floor into shops and restaurants. Although the Ithaca Neighborhood College did not last long, I still appreciate its idealism, community service, and revolutionary approach to education.

In the dream, because the award ceremony and the awarded office are both in the Dewitt Building, it seems that the "Dewitt state of consciousness" is an important part of the book project. The unconscious appears to be delivering a symbolic reminder that the book, whatever its limitations, is rooted in idealism, connecting to the larger community, and is a fresh approach to education in the broad sense of the term.

The dream may also have offered a little window into the book's future. After it was published, my first bookstore reading occurred in a store owned and operated by the same Jack Goldman of Ithaca Neighborhood College. Interestingly, that bookstore now occupies a significant fraction of the ground floor of the Dewitt Building.

[†] A psychological disclaimer: I remind Hillman, Yates, and their friends that I am taking a subjective view of the dream, where each symbol expresses an aspect of my psyche. What counts for the present interpretation is my psychological associations to those people, not their literal truth as individuals.

Let me turn now to Jenny Yates, who is a woman in midlife; a much-loved professor of religion and psychology at Wells College, in Aurora, New York; and Ithaca's only Jungian analyst. What little contact I have had with Jenny has always been pleasant. She came to dinner at our home once, and I have seen her at a few activities at the Jung Club in Ithaca, which she organized. Once we went to lunch, on which occasion she made a few brief comments about an early version of the book. She is a deeply intuitive person, even mediumistic, with a strong scholarly bent.

In the dream, Jenny seems to symbolize the intuitive or medium, one of the roles played by the feminine principle within a man, what Jung calls the anima. Especially because the book was about synchronicity, one of its central concerns is the intuitive side of life. The anima, as the wellspring of intuition, was engaged throughout the conception and writing of the book. In the dream, Jenny is presenting the award, delivering the "message" of the dream, an action that seems to symbolize directly the role of anima as a bridge to the unconscious. More particularly, Jenny seems to symbolize the intuition that "sees in the dark" or has insights into the workings of the unconscious.

James Hillman is a brilliant and original writer in Jungian psychology. To differentiate himself from Jung and emphasize his own approach to the psyche, Hillman calls himself an archetypal psychologist. I have always appreciated Hillman's writings. Even if I don't always agree with him, they are some of the most insightful and stimulating writings I have read in psychology. I greatly admire his stylistic elegance, breadth of vision, the depth and originality of his scholarship, and especially his independence of thought. However, his approach is sometimes excessively Apollonic and dry. He then becomes unnecessarily obscure and removed from the realities of everyday living and its problems. Nevertheless, he has generated a great body of work. The dream occurred before I had ever met Hillman, but I knew his reputation for being cold and aloof. Since the dream, I have developed a modest personal relationship with him through conversations at various meetings where we were both presenting papers. This acquaintance has deepened my appreciation for both his strengths and limitations.

For me, getting the "Hillman award" would symbolize recognition for clear, original scholarship that advances our understanding of the depths of the soul and its interaction with the world. Receiving it from Jenny Yates emphasizes the intuitive, nonrational aspect of the work. Its association with the Dewitt Building makes a connection to the background of idealism and nonconformist spirit from which the book grew. I repeat, this dream seems compensatory for the extremely negative conscious view I then held of both the book and myself as a writer. The dream is not saying that I truly embodied all these wonderful attributes, but that these attributes are the compensatory forces, the attempt of the unconscious to present the other side of the total picture.

I speculate that if this dream had occurred without an accompanying synchronicity experience, it would not have been able to effect the necessary compensation. I was simply "too far gone" for a dream to accomplish any transformation. It seems that an arresting synchronicity experience was required to bring adequate attention to the dream.

Besides these personal meanings, every synchronicity experience is an empirical expression of the ultimate unity of the inner and outer world. For example, von Franz says:

> The most essential and certainly the most impressive thing about synchronicity occurrences . . . is the fact that in them the duality of soul and matter seems to be eliminated. They are therefore an *empirical indication* of an ultimate unity of all existence, which Jung, using the terminology of medieval natural philosophy, called the *Unus Mundus*.[25]

Thus, acausal synchronicity simultaneously incarnates transformative meaning in the subject and in his or her world. As a far-reaching and relatively frequent phenomenon, it has great significance for our philosophical and scientific worldview.

For a final perspective on synchronicity, we can turn to Aristotle's four types of cause. As an example, suppose we go with Aristotle on an imaginary trip to Florence, Italy, where we view Michelangelo's exquisite sculpture of David. We ask Aristotle what caused this statue to be. First, he identifies the *efficient cause*, Michelangelo's chiseling and working of the stone. In this cause, we have one well-defined thing (a tool) producing an effect on another well-defined thing (the marble). This is Jung's use of cause. Second, Aristotle explains that the marble is the *material cause* of the statute, the actual stuff of it. Third, we see in its extraordinary grace the archetype of the hero, the giant-slayer, the *formal cause* of the statue. Fourth, we seek the *final cause*, the ultimate purpose of the statute. Here we understand the statue as an expression of Michelangelo's individuation, his soul's expression of itself through tools, stone, and archetypal form.

The hallmark of synchronicity is its acausality, its lack of efficient cause, both vertically and horizontally. However, there must be some event in consensual reality (such as a telephone call from an acquaintance bearing good news) that meaningfully corresponds to a psychological state. That outer event is the material cause or "stuff" of synchronicity. The archetype as formal cause characterizes the meaning that connects the inner and outer worlds. Finally, the ultimate cause or final purpose of the synchronicity is the protagonist's individuation. As long as we remember that synchronicity is acausal at the level of efficient cause, we can more fully appreciate it through its material, formal, and final causes.

SYNCHRONICITY AS AN EXPRESSION OF TRANSFORMATIVE SELF-KNOWLEDGE

Does the synchronicity experience just discussed represent a form of transformative self-knowledge? I will argue that it does by applying the seven characteristics of such knowledge discussed in chapter 3— *intuitive, holistic, unique to the individual, transforming, unrepeatable, teleological,* and *sacred*—to synchronicity experiences.

1. Synchronicity experiences always involve an *interior intuition.* Certainly, there must be an objective event to correlate meaningfully with the subjective state. However, the intuition of meaning, the cornerstone of synchronicity, is an interior intuition, one issuing from our deepest subjectivity. It is true that the articulation of the meaning may take much reflection and time, but during the experience, there is a firm belief that the event is meaningful.

2. Synchronicity is *holistic knowledge* in two senses. First, the bridge between the inner and outer events is an incarnation of meaning central to our individuation and thus to our entire life, its purpose, direction, and significance. It therefore affects the whole of us in the fullest sense. Second, as von Franz pointed out above, synchronicity experiences gives us a personal expression of the unity underlying soul and matter.

3. Synchronicity experiences are always conditioned by a universal archetype; however, the meaning is always *unique* to the person and her individuation. Even if the same dream occurred to somebody else, the association to the dream symbols and the particular meaning that emerged from the synchronicity experience would,

of necessity, be different. Each synchronicity experience, despite archetypal conditioning, is a unique, unrepeatable event.

4. Since a synchronicity experience always marks a significant mile-stone in a person's individuation, it therefore has a *transforming effect* on the protagonist. Of course, as in any experience, this trans-forming effect is greatest when we have ferreted out the meaning embedded in a synchronicity. Otherwise, it is largely a case of "Wow! That was strange!" Then the experience may be arresting, but in the absence of consciously assimilated meaning, its transformative effect is limited. The same is true of all psychological experience. For example, consider a person who has an overpowering dream, but can make no sense of it. She feels the meaning carried in the numinous symbols but cannot articulate it. Such a dream can still transform a person, both consciously and unconsciously. However, deep reflection on the symbolic significance of the dream and a sincere effort at assimilating its meaning will significantly enhance its transformative power. The work of extracting meaning from synchronicity is another illustration of the well-known fact that individuation must be a conscious effort at cooperating with the intentions of the self.

5. It is obvious that such an experience is *unrepeatable*. I certainly have been filled with self-doubt more than once since the "Hillman Award" dream and have again been encouraged by the unconscious, as in the recent dream about meeting Paul. But each compensa-tion, each psychological experience, is unique and meaningful only within a context that is forever changing.

6. By the very nature of an unconscious compensation, we are in-volved with *teleology*. As Jung stated in one of the passages already quoted, we are involved in final causes or teleology whenever we "investigate the compensatory function of the unconscious, not to speak of trying to explain the phenomenon of synchronicity." What within me knew that, contrary to my conscious position, I had too low an opinion of my book project? Besides my inappropriate atti-tude toward the book, the synchronicity experience showed a foreknowledge within the unconscious of how things would turn out. Some transcendent knowledge is being unfolded, a bit like the way the latent image of Jung unfolds as more pixels are added. When the individuation process displays a long string of such ex-

pressions of the unconscious, we are naturally led to the idea that there is a timeless "vision" of what the self demands of us. Then each experience can be understood as the self drawing us toward that vision, eliciting our authentic being from each life experience.

7. A genuine synchronicity experience is always an arresting and numinous experience, and therefore it is *sacred* knowledge. For example, von Franz says, "Synchronistic events constitute moments in which a 'cosmic' or 'greater' meaning becomes gradually conscious in an individual; generally it is a shaking experience."[26] Recipients of synchronicity experiences often feel they are being given a gift, or the experience fills them with religious devotion. As Jean Shinoda Bolen says in her book on synchronicity, "Every time I have become aware of a synchronistic experience, I have had an accompanying feeling that some grace came along with it."[27]

Synchronicity, and to a significant extent, other expressions of transformative self-knowledge, are much more likely to occur in periods of deep difficulty and stress. This is when the grace is most likely to come. In other words, when you are feeling fine, your ego is strong, and life is going well, the chances of a major synchronicity are small. Jung stresses that it is only when the unconscious is activated, either through some crisis or deep therapeutic work, that synchronicities occur. This assertion does not deny that good things, both spiritually and psychologically, can happen when we are feeling strong and adapted. Nevertheless, with sufficient experience, it becomes clear that only when we are broken open, only when the ego is at least a little crushed, can the most powerful transforming experiences occur. In religious literature, there is a long tradition of suffering and woundedness being the gateways to spiritual experience. A fragment of a Rumi poem expresses this directly.

> Trust your wound to a teacher's surgery.
> Flies collect on a wound. They cover it,
> those flies of your self-protecting feelings,
> your love for what you think is yours.
>
> Let a teacher wave away the flies
> and put a plaster on the wound.
>
> Don't turn your head. Keep looking
> at the bandaged place. That's where
> the light enters you.

And don't believe for a moment
that you're healing yourself.[28]

Our wounds, failures, sufferings, deep disappointments, and distresses are the matrix out of which transformation occurs, the place "where the light enters you." I do not deny the value of positive and affirming experiences for our transformation. Nor do I glorify suffering. Nevertheless, whether it is individuation of the personality or the more ambitious transcendence of all pairs of opposites in what the East calls liberation, there is no swifter horse than that of suffering. As the Buddha tells us in the first Noble Truth, all experience is pervaded by suffering, so we need not look for it. Life delivers it freely and there is no need to take unnecessary rides on that swift horse.

Chapter Eight

Toward an Understanding
of Astrology

March 12, 1999: I am standing in a motel room in Phoenix, Arizona, lecturing to the walls. It feels tedious and unnatural, but this act of desperation seems to have helped polish the talk. I now think it's going to work. I've given the lecture before but never been happy with it; I haven't been able to hit the right level of technical detail or set the right feeling tone. Having just used these ideas about the double nature of soul a few days ago in writing a chapter for my new book, I am particularly eager to do them justice tonight. Since I will be speaking to the Phoenix Friends of C. G. Jung, it seems especially fitting that these ideas deepen and extend Jung's notion of soul.

Giving the practice talk has put me in a lovely feeling state. I am grateful for the privilege of being able to discuss such noble ideas, and my teacher Anthony's presence seems almost palpable. He used to get so inspired when speaking on this topic. I wish he could hear the talk tonight.

It's after 5:30 P.M. and my hosts are going to meet me in the motel lobby and give me a ride to the lecture at 6:45. I have a little over an hour to grab a quick bite and shower. I have to get going!

"There's a nice restaurant across the street and down a little ways," the motel clerk tells me.

I walk briskly in the brilliant sunshine alongside a six-lane highway full of zooming cars. It feels good to get out and move. But where is that restaurant? After walking for five minutes or so, I see the restaurant, but it must be another five minutes away. Maybe this is "down a little ways" by car, but it is a full ten-minute walk. Now I am really squeezed for time.

"Damn it! Why did Elaine take that rented car and leave me

stranded like this? How the hell am I going to make it on time?" But then I catch myself.

"Inspiration killed by my negativity? No. I won't let it happen."

Finally, I reach an intersection. The restaurant beckons from directly across the street. There are stopped cars in the nearest two lanes, but the third lane, farthest from me, is empty. Despite the flashing red hand telling me not to cross, I think I can make it to the median divider. I run out into the crosswalk, in front of the two lanes of stopped cars to my left. Just into the third lane: thud!

I am lying on the ground and hear a car skidding to a halt ahead of me. I drag myself up from the pavement. I am way outside the crosswalk now and cars are flying by on all sides of me. There is a deep pain in my left shoulder and I am sore all over as I stumble toward the little black sports car that just hit me. My heart is racing.

"I am really sorry," I tell the driver.

"You scared the hell out of me! Are you all right?"

"Can you call an ambulance? My shoulder is busted and I am pretty banged up."

I feel an extraordinary combination of extreme gratitude and pure terror. He pulls the car off to the intersecting road and calls the police with his cell phone. Two beautiful young women come running up to me.

"Are you all right? Wow! I never saw anything like that! You just flew through the air. Can we help?"

With the low sun streaming through their hair to give them halos, they look like angels. I ask them if they can get the book I was carrying. I point it out to them. It must be fifty feet from the site of impact. Shortly after they retrieve the book, the police arrive and ask them to fill out an accident report. They tell me I'll have to fill one out when I am in the hospital.

Although the pain is severe, I still want to give that talk. From past experience, I know that the chances for giving an inspired talk increase when my ego is off center stage, as it is now. I ask the police, "Do you think I can make a 7:30 lecture?" They stare at me as though I am from Mars. In fact, maybe I am. Who else would run out in front of cars to save time?

While they are taking Polaroid pictures of the sports car (fig. 37), I sit on the grass beside it and look it over. The right headlight is smashed; a bit of my blood is on the hood, along with scuff marks; and the right side of the windshield is badly cracked.

"The patient is ambulatory and we are taking him to the emergency room now," says the paramedic on his cell phone. I get on a gurney and appreciate lying down. On my back, I notice the vast cobalt blue sky. It seems to lift me up and out of myself.

"You have a beautiful sky here," I remark.

"Oh, you'll really like the ceiling of the ambulance," one paramedic retorts.

They put an intravenous line into my hand, put an oxygen mask on me, and test for internal injuries, nerve damage, and so on. They are so kind. I feel such genuine concern for them. I don't want them to worry about me. I know I am OK. I want to reassure them, to put their minds at ease. I thank them repeatedly and inwardly give sincere thanks to all the higher powers.

"You were amazingly lucky," a paramedic says. "You really damaged that car and you seem pretty good."

Fig. 37. Vic's teacher (courtesy of Scottsdale, Arizona, Police Department)

At the hospital emergency room, the kind and capable hospital staff takes care of me. More questions, more probing, blood pressure measurements, and more amazement. They clean the wounds on my left knee and put ice packs on my right leg and left shoulder. The nurses point out to each other the book I was carrying and keep remarking on the title. It is *Crossing to Safety* by Wallace Stegner. The coincidence never occurred to me before they mentioned it.

After being there for about twenty minutes, I hear a great roar from a helicopter. It sounds like it is coming through the roof. There is much bustling about and people leave me for more pressing matters. They wheel in a burly man in his thirties, his head in a restraining cage to prevent spinal injury. His plaid shirt is soaked in blood. For a second our eyes meet and I fall into deep pools of terror. I feel such compassion for him and realize that it could easily have been me.

I am extremely thirsty, but they will not give me water for fear I will vomit. After an hour and a half, the police come and make me fill out an accident report. I give them all the detail possible and fully admit my guilt and stupidity. Another helicopter delivery interrupts us. They give me a ticket for ninety-eight dollars for crossing against the light. After three hours in the emergency room, x-rays, and various tests, all they can find is that I have a badly separated left shoulder, banged-up legs, and a nice selection of bruises, aches, and pains. I have no broken bones and not even scrapes from where I hit the pavement. They put my arm in a sling and discharge me. In my shaken state, I take a cab back to my motel.

I have a prescription for some powerful painkillers. Although I am in a good bit of pain, it seems manageable. Despite the doctor's warning that I won't be able to sleep without the painkillers, I decide to skip them tonight and not look for an open drugstore. I'll just take some aspirin. I think it is more important for me to face the significance of what happened with a clear head.

I call my wife in Tucson. No answer. I leave a message saying it is not an emergency, but please call me back. I keep putting ice on my various bruises and reading *Crossing to Safety*. I am looking for some clues to the meaning of it all. Because of the difference in time zones, I only got a few hours of sleep the night before. However, I am so full of pain, adrenaline, and joy that I cannot consider sleeping now.

Instead, I try a method I have developed over the years for dealing with nightmares and dreams with troubling imagery. I get out of bed, sit in a meditation posture, close my eyes, and hold the troubling images as vividly as possible in my mind. I set aside any intellectual formulations and interpretations and just concentrate on the images. I become one with them, soak myself in them, no matter how horrendous they are. In this way, these feeling-laden messages from the feminine unconscious are granted autonomy, allowed to speak. This attention eventually drains the fear and loathing from them and I can get back to sleep. It allows the images to do their work, to perform the unconscious compensations even when I don't understand them analytically. Several times, I try this technique on my accident. I let the thud, blackness, pain, and terror wash over me in all their ferocity. I directly confront my horror at what easily could have been. Still, the adrenaline pours through me. It is difficult getting comfortable in bed, but I eventually get to sleep around 3:30 A.M. I awake a few hours later and feel like the voltage in my nervous system is set way too high. Despite the pain and exhaustion, I am in a state of extreme joy and gratitude.

I have been to the edge of the abyss. In my thanksgiving, I rededicate myself to realizing the nature of soul in all its complexity.

Searching for an Explanation, Part 1:
In Honor of Sir Isaac Newton

While in the emergency room, I tried to reconstruct what happened in the accident. I never did see the car, nor did the driver see me. When I ran in front of the car, its right headlight hit the left side of my left knee. There must have been little or no weight on that leg, otherwise my knee would have been shattered. Instead, judging from the huge bruise on the inside of my right calf, my left foot slammed into my right calf and knocked me off my feet. Then, as the marks and blood on the car hood showed, I flipped up onto the hood with my feet toward the driver's side. The windshield then slammed into my left shoulder, throwing me up and outward, and the car drove underneath me as it screeched to a halt. I could not remember either how I went through the air or how I landed.

The only experience I had for comparison was something that happened more than thirty years earlier, when I was motorcycle road-racing. While going around a sweeping turn at over a hundred miles per hour, I hit an oil slick and instantly lost control of the bike. I can still vividly recall how the horizon changed direction as I tumbled down the track, the other bikes roaring past me, and how I skidded to a halt on the track. It all seemed to happen in slow motion. However, in this car accident I had none of those details. The impact must have knocked me unconscious, and I flew through the air like a rag doll and hit the ground in that state. That must have prevented me from trying to catch myself, and my being unable to resist, it reduced my injuries from the fall.

Around 6:00 A.M. the next morning, I returned to the accident site. I went there as part of my exercise of facing the terror of the accident as directly as possible. I had also realized that two simple measurements and some easy calculations could yield a rough estimate of how fast the car was going. I needed to measure the distance between the site of impact and where the headlight glass landed and to get the height of the headlight. Assuming the headlight pieces had the same horizontal velocity as the car, it would only be a high school physics problem to estimate out how fast the car was going.

The glass was still there. I paced off the distance—I learned many years ago how to pace off strides that are very close to three feet each.

The first fragments were fully thirteen paces from the impact site in the crosswalk and the farthest ones were eighteen paces. The headlight glass was thus from thirty-nine to fifty-four feet from the site of impact. I revisited the site at noon on the next day and remeasured the position of the glass fragments. I wanted to see if the traffic moved them. I could measure no noticeable change in the position of the glass. I even returned a little over a week later, just before flying home. I paced off the distance of the fragments again and found no noticeable change. Even before I did the calculations, I knew the car must have been going pretty fast to throw glass more than fifty feet.

So, one way I dealt with the experience of the accident was to immerse myself in the physical details—calculations, estimations, approximations. I went about the calculations in the following way: For an estimate of the car's velocity, there are two major uncertainties. It is a good approximation to say that the horizontal velocity of the headlight glass fragments was the same as the car's velocity. After all, the glass was moving with the same velocity as the car before impact. However, the impact made the headlight explode, both outwardly and against the car. This would give the fragments some velocity in the vertical direction. It would also give a spread of horizontal velocities around the car's velocity. Furthermore, the glass did not all start from the same height above the ground. However, all is not hopeless, because I have a measurement of the farthest distance that the fragments went, along with the shortest distance. The other uncertainty is how far the glass fragments slid on the pavement before coming to a halt. I consulted with my colleague, Professor Emeritus Jack Dodd of Colgate University, who has been an expert witness concerning several car crashes. He advised me to use ten feet as a generous estimate of the sliding distance. I used twelve feet for this calculation. With these uncertainties, I calculate, using Newtonian physics, that the car must have been traveling thirty-five miles per hour, with an uncertainty of about ten miles per hour in either direction. These estimates seem high, but the driver was passing the stopped cars on a highway with a speed limit of forty-five miles per hour. It wasn't even his car; he was test-driving it. It would not surprise me if he had been enjoying its acceleration and handling.

Being hit by a car going at that speed and ending up with only a badly separated shoulder and a few cuts and bruises is amazing—but not a miracle. The Catholic Church defines miracles as divine interventions that suspend the physical laws of nature. I agree with

David Hume, who long ago pointed out the incoherence of such an idea. Nevertheless, within the context of what could have happened in my accident, I am extremely fortunate. Appreciating, even roughly, how fast the car was going only deepens my gratitude.

Searching for an Explanation, Part 2:
In Honor of C. G. Jung

The day after the accident, I eased my battered body into the Jacuzzi at the hotel pool and let the water go right to my chin. The hotel was full of baseball players from the Oakland Athletics farm teams. I always appreciate the vitality and confidence that emanate from good athletes. Those guys were not only muscular and handsome gods; they were friendly and full of fun. Their exuberance contrasted so sharply with my broken state. In my decrepit and grateful condition, I had some surprisingly vivid sexual fantasies about several of the beautiful women around the pool. This prompted me to reflect on the old apple tree outside my office window back home. The closer it got to dying, the more apples it produced. The life force is a powerful urge, and I was thankful it was still expressing itself through me.

The Buddhist truths of impermanence, the preciousness of human life, that death is certain and only the time and conditions are uncertain, had become living realities for me. Although I had lectured and written about these things, they had become more real than the pain in my shoulder.

As the terror and adrenaline rush subsided, the gratitude and devotional feelings grew. I wanted only to live each moment as though it were my last and devote myself to finding my true nature. Before, I had gotten so passionate about all sorts of inconsequential things, but all that ballast of normal consciousness had been thrown overboard as I sailed on sacred seas. From that time on, I would have no time for trivial concerns or activities.

Despite the reality and sincerity of my realizations and planned reforms, I was a boring saint, full of pious platitudes and worn nostrums. There was a tincture of sadness in me because I knew Elaine would not have to suffer my sainthood for too long. The shadow would erupt soon enough and send all my philosophizing out the window. The old Vic would surely return, but for the time being, all was light and gratitude. I wanted to make the most of it.

We had planned to do some touring around the Southwest on our way to Santa Fe, where I was to give another talk. However, I needed to recuperate, so we found an extraordinary hacienda in the desert just outside Tucson and stayed for several days. I was in a state of unmitigated bliss. Every detail of the desert was radiant, fresh, and clear. The lodge owner loaned me a little CD player, and I listened to the music intended for my canceled workshop in Phoenix. Each note of the second movement of Samuel Barber's violin concerto was a blessing. I wrote some e-mail to friends back home telling them what happened and expressing the depth of affection for them that in normal circumstances would go unsaid. The flood of loving and supportive e-mail that came back surprised me and moved me to tears.

Looking back, it is clear that the week following my accident was the most beautiful spiritual experience of my life. I certainly would not have chosen that way to get such an experience, but it was still priceless.

There are some obvious and important lessons from the accident. I have been blessed with a lot of energy, but I often squeeze in too many experiences and rush like a madman to execute them all. I can abuse my blessing. While that is a critical lesson, I sense there is more to it. Beside my own subjective conclusions, however, consider the uncanny aptness of the title of the book I was carrying: *Crossing to Safety*. The subject of the book isn't relevant, but under the circumstances the title is striking. It is taken from this poem by Robert Frost.

I COULD GIVE ALL TO TIME

To time it never seems that he is brave
To set himself against peaks of snow
To lay them level with the running wave
Nor is he overjoyed when they lie low
But only grave, contemplative and grave.

What now is inland shall be ocean isle
Then eddies playing around a sunken reef
Like curl at the corner of a smile;
And I could share Time's lack of joy or grief
At such a planetary change of style.

I would give all to Time except—except
What I myself have held. But why declare
The things forbidden that while the Customs slept
I have crossed to Safety with? For I am There
And what I would not part with I have kept.[†]

[†] *Complete Poems of Robert Frost* (New York: Holt, 1964), p. 447.

The poem's reference to time is striking in light of my abuse of it. Let me venture an interpretation. Time (capitalized) is a Saturnine presence, "grave, contemplative and grave." The main point in the first two stanzas is the inevitability and impersonality of the change associated with Time. For example, in the second stanza, "What now is inland shall be ocean isle, then eddies playing around a sunken reef." The geologic transformation from continent, to island, and then to sunken reef is inevitable and impersonal.

The third stanza, from which the book's title is drawn, is more profound. He would give all to Time, except for "What I myself have held." Is he only holding the memories of a rich life? Whatever they are, he does not want to be too explicit about them ("why declare the things forbidden"). He has to slip these forbidden things past the sleeping "Customs" and thereby cross to "Safety." Here we have some mysteries: three common words made strange with capital letters— Customs, Safety, and There. Frost cannot be just hanging on to old memories, especially in light of the pervasive impermanence emphasized in the first two stanzas. He is willing to give all to the devouring jaws of Time, except what he has held to be most sacred, most essential, and most truly Robert Frost—that which Time cannot destroy. That to which he clings must be slipped by the Customs, a word that connotes far more than uniformed people searching suitcases. I suggest that the Customs are our personal and cultural beliefs, that we are entirely finite and limited creatures—fit food for the tiger of Time. Occasionally, in moments of spiritual uplift or severe crisis, those Customs sleep and we break free of the limiting belief in our finitude. Then we "cross to Safety." But what safety can there be in anything or any place subject to the inevitable decay of time? We find the capitalized Safety whenever we reach capitalized There—a state of consciousness beyond the grasp of Time's destruction. In short, we can only cross to Safety by making contact with a consciousness or aspect of soul beyond the reach of Time. Frost claims to have some experience of this state for he says, "I am There and what I would not part with I have kept."

This interpretation of Frost's poem accords with my state of mind just before the accident, when I was completely saturated with the idea of the double nature of soul. As I discussed in detail in chapter 4, the classical philosopher Plotinus holds that the very essence of soul is that it is simultaneously finite, and thus subject to the destruction of time, yet also infinite, undivided, and immortal. In each experience, at every level, no matter how mundane or exalted, we are both limited, finite creatures who are subject to decay and simultaneously immortal, transcendent beings. Any intimation of the immortal aspect of soul is a profound spiritual experience and therein lies our true "crossing to safety."

In my accident, I crossed to safety physically and was profoundly grateful for it. However, I also crossed briefly to the side of immortal soul and that safety is of a deeper order, as Frost intimates. I am not saying that had I suffered more physical harm, I would have been equally grateful. Nor could I hold on for very long to that light from beyond my ego. Although I could not sustain it, I will always cherish it. The experience taught me the great value of appreciating the world simultaneously from the viewpoints of both Newton and Jung—from the head and the heart. Through the stark conclusions of physics, I appreciated the transforming grace more fully, while the grace helped me appreciate the lawfulness of the Newtonian cosmos and even showed me its limitations.

In this light, I can interpret my accident as an initiation into the indivisible and immortal aspects of soul, into that realm beyond the reach of time, the realm of true safety. It came about through near-destruction of the body, the expression of the finite aspect of soul. In a sense, I had a mild form of near-death experience, one of those life-transforming events that come to some people when they are very close to death and are resuscitated. I did not have the usual visionary component, but I did experience a transpersonal reality and its transformative effects.

The experience also taught me that no matter how much psychological work I do in cultivating a fuller expression of the divisible aspect of soul, that aspect of soul offers no safety. A deep realization of the magisterial grandeur of soul requires cultivating both its aspects. If I am ever to get over the fear of death that so paralyzed me during my airplane ride to Arecibo, I won't get There by psychological work alone.

ASTROLOGY AND EXPLANATION

In my response to the accident, I sought two very different kinds of explanation, what I'll call here type 1 and type 2 explanations. These two views of my experience illustrate a distinction that will help us understand the difficulties that arise in seeking explanations for astrology. In a type 1 explanation, the emphasis is on *causality*, that is, one well-defined thing affecting another through the exchange of forces, energy, or information. For example, the right headlight hits the left side of my left knee, which has little weight on it; my left foot slams into the left side of my right calf; and I am flipped up on the hood without having my knees shattered. This is a completely *impersonal* and universal process, governed by Newtonian physics. Although the timing had to be just right, nothing about the event was special or unique to me. You could replace me with a crash dummy and study the phenomena with a high-speed camera. Since the phenomena are all entirely *objective* in this explanation, not dependent upon our likes or dislikes or whatever local customs apply, we could repeat the experiment with the crash dummy as many times as necessary and expect *repeatable* outcomes. The meaning that emerges from such explanation is restricted entirely to the impersonal, material, *factual* level of the event. In other words, it is *devoid of higher meaning or purpose*. The emphasis is entirely on the literal significance of events.

In contrast, type 2 explanations are *acausal*; that is, not governed by forces and physical energy exchange. Instead, they are *symbolic* expressions of *transformative meaning*, of significant episodes in a person's individuation. Because of this, they are *unique* to the individual and his or her development. If it had been somebody else in front of that little sports car, the accident would have had a different significance, one unique to that person. Of course, such experiences are *unrepeatable*. Yes, I could run in front of a speeding car more than once, but each time it would be a different experience, since I am transformed and therefore different after each event. Finally, rather than being objective in the scientific sense, these experiences are deeply *subjective* intuitions of meaning. Table 3 summarizes the differences between these two modes.

When we ask how a particular astrological configuration correlates with a psychological experience, our demands for explanation are

Table 3. Two Kinds of Explanation

Type 1 Explanations	Type 2 Explanations
Causal	Acausal
Impersonal and universal	Unique to the individual
Repeatable	Unrepeatable
Devoid of higher meaning or purpose	An expression of transformative meaning
Objective	Subjective
Factual and literal	Symbolic

usually of type 1. For example, the scientist in me asks, "How can the motion of the planet Pluto, with about one two-hundredth of the Earth's volume at an average distance of some six billion kilometers, correlate with my dark excursions into the unconscious?" The phrasing of the question, with its reference to size and distance, shows that I am seeking a type 1 explanation in terms of causal physical laws. Those seeking a scientific explanation for astrological influence always seek a causal mechanism. I am using the term *causal* as Jung did, to mean one well-defined thing influencing another by an exchange of energy, force, or information.

Such attempts to model astrology along causal lines express a deep commitment to a Cartesian-Newtonian worldview. Such a view, often unconsciously held, posits a world of independent objects that causally influence each other. This view may be appropriate for understanding classical physics and many everyday occurrences, such as the dynamics of a collision, but it is wrong for astrology. Like depth psychology, astrology is best understood as being rooted in type 2 explanations. In fact, when discussing synchronicity, astrology, and related phenomena, Jung preferred to think in terms of the unitary ground underlying both psyche and matter, what the old alchemists called the *Unus Mundus*.

The quantum mechanical view, which supplants the Cartesian-Newtonian view, has, as Jung noted,[1] properties similar to those of the Unus Mundus. Quantum mechanics denies the existence of properties of objects independent of measurement and is replete with nonlocal connections and noncausal interactions. Although I know of no quantum mechanical explanation for astrology, this theory can still inspire us to seek some noncausal or acausal framework for astrology. If we do this, we are following in Jung's footsteps. Inspired in part by quantum mechanics through his association with the great physicist Wolfgang Pauli, Jung developed an acausal understanding of synchronicity in terms of a type 2 explanation. Since Jung believed that astrology was a form of synchronicity, he therefore believed in such an acausal explanation for astrology. However, although astrology and synchronicity certainly have similarities, I believe there are pitfalls in seeing an explanatory relationship between them.

ASTROLOGY AND SYNCHRONICITY: FIT OR MISFIT?

Like science, astrology has its own specialized terminology, which we must review briefly before we can consider the relation of astrology to synchronicity. In astrology, the positions in the sky of the planets, Sun, and Moon at the time and place a person was born constitutes his or her *horoscope*. For example, when I was born, Mars was very near the eastern horizon and in the constellation of Capricorn. But Mars takes about two and a half years to move, or transit, through all the constellations in the zodiac, thereby making one complete orbit. During that time, it makes various angles with its original position and with the other planets in my horoscope. These angular relationships between the present position of a planet and the position of the planets in the horoscope are called *transits*. For example, as I write this, the planet Saturn is making a ninety-degree angle (called a *square* in astrology) with the position of my *natal* Sun (the Sun's position at my birth).

According to the traditional interpretation, this configuration (referred to as transiting Saturn squaring natal Sun) is a challenging time when we are confronted with our limitations both inwardly and outwardly. It can be a time of low vitality, conflicts with authorities, increased seriousness of purpose, and taking on responsibility. It may be a time when our deeper nature and purpose is drawn out of us. However, the interpretation of any transit must also reflect the other transits occurring at the same time and the many details of my horoscope. For example, as I write this, transiting Pluto is also squaring my natal Sun. The astrologer's challenge is to synthesize these two major transits with the other transiting planets within the context of my horoscope. Such synthesis forms the core of the complex art of astrological interpretation. Anyone with astrological experience can testify that this process can deliver detailed and uncanny insights into our experience.

To see how astrology fits into a synchronicity framework, consider transiting Saturn squaring natal Sun. We can say that the objective event (Saturn square Sun) meaningfully correlates with the subjective experience of Saturnine forces opposing our will and sense of self. The same meaning incarnates both objectively, in the positions of the planets, and subjectively, as we reflect on our experience through the traditional astrological interpretations. Transiting Saturn does not *cause* our limitations, but the position of the planet and our struggles both express the same archetypal meaning symbolized in the traditional astrological interpretations. What could be a better expression of synchronicity? This conclusion suffers from two related problems: one with meaning, and the other with the frequency of such occurrences.

Jung stresses that meaning is "the indispensable criterion of synchronicity." His position is that without our recognition of the meaning, there is no synchronicity. Yet astrology claims to be effective all the time, whether we are aware of any meaning in our experience or not. It works even for people who are unaware of it. When the South Sea Islander in her tropical paradise falls into an inexplicable depression as transiting Saturn squares her natal Sun, it does not matter, according to the astrologers, whether she knows anything about astrology nor even reflects on her depression. Famous athletes need not know about Mars in their horoscope for their performance to give evidence of the Mars effect.

Regarding frequency, Jung stresses that synchronicity is a creative and sporadic eruption of the unity underlying psyche and matter: "It is only the ingrained belief in the sovereign power of causality that creates intellectual difficulties and makes it appear unthinkable that causeless events exist or could ever occur. But if they do, then we must regard them as *creative acts*, as the continuous creation of a pattern that exists from all eternity, repeats itself sporadically, and is not derivable from any known antecedent."[2] Outside of some serious psychological or spiritual crisis, synchronicity experiences like those discussed in this chapter and in the previous one are infrequent. In contrast, astrology claims to be effective twenty-four hours a day, 365.25 days a year. With or without meaning, it is as continuously effective for an archenemy of astrology, such as Sagan, as it is for you and me.

The possible lack of meaning and the constancy of astrological correlations illustrate the difficulty of fitting astrology into a synchronicity framework. These difficulties can be resolved by clarifying a notion that Jung calls *acausal orderedness*.

ACAUSAL ORDEREDNESS

One of the most opaque and yet significant parts of Jung's synchronicity essay attempts to place synchronicity in a larger framework. After working hard on this and related material for several years, I am convinced that Jung does not have an adequate model for astrology or parapsychological phenomena as distinct from synchronicity. Nevertheless, his attempt at building a larger framework is a good place to start:

> The meaningful coincidence or equivalence of a psychic and a physical state that have no causal relationship to one another means, in general terms, that it is a modality without a cause, an "acausal orderedness." The question now arises whether our definition of synchronicity with reference to the equivalence of

psychic and physical processes is capable of expansion, or rather, requires expansion. This requirement seems to force itself on us when we consider the above, wider conception of synchronicity as "acausal orderedness." Into this category come all "acts of creation," *a priori* factors such as the properties of natural numbers, the discontinuities of modern physics, etc. Consequently, we would have to include constant and experimentally reproducible phenomena within the scope of our expanded concept, though this does not seem to accord with the nature of the phenomena included in synchronicity narrowly understood. The latter are mostly individual cases, which cannot be repeated experimentally. This is not of course altogether true, as Rhine's experiments show and numerous other experiences with clairvoyant individuals. . . . I incline in fact to the view that synchronicity in the narrow sense is only a particular instance of general acausal orderedness—that, namely, of the equivalence of psychic and physical processes where the observer is in the fortunate position of being able to recognize the *tertium comparationis*. But as soon as he perceives the archetypal background he is tempted to trace the mutual assimilation of independent psychic and physical processes back to a (causal) effect of the archetype, and thus to overlook the fact that they are merely contingent. This danger is avoided if one regards synchronicity as a special instance of general acausal orderedness. . . . This form of orderedness [synchronicity narrowly defined] differs from that of the properties of natural numbers or the discontinuities of physics in that the later have existed from eternity and occur regularly, whereas these forms of psychic orderedness are *acts of creation in time*.[3]

It is possible to interpret this critical passage on the basis of Jung's writings alone. Nonetheless, it is reassuring to find corroboration of my interpretation from the writings of his close associate, Marie-Louise von Franz. She is the only writer known to me who discusses the ideas in this important passage. However, both she and Jung have fallen into some difficulties and inconsistencies.

Jung would understand my "Hillman Award" dream as "synchronicity narrowly defined." This is a special case of the broader category he calls *general acausal orderedness*. All acausal "acts of creation in time" (synchronicity in the narrow sense) are distinguished from acausal orderedness through our recognition of the *tertium comparationis*, the third comparison term—meaning. In other words, it is possible to discriminate between synchronicity and acausal order because "the observer is in the fortunate position of being able to recognize" the archetypal meaning expressing itself both inwardly and outwardly. Later in the quotation, Jung warns that once we recognize the archetypes expressing themselves in the meaning, we must avoid thinking of the archetypes as causing the synchronicity. (That is, synchronicity has no vertical or horizontal causality.) Although meaning is a critical tool for discriminating between synchronicity and acausal orderedness, both phenomena are acausal and may therefore involve aspects that transcend space and time.

A complication arises with the possibility of unconscious synchronicities, where the meaning escapes us, just as when we do not understand a numinous dream. These psychological experiences can still transform us, however. That is, the meaning may still be effective, thus weakening the distinction between the two phenomena. Because of this blurred boundary, an experience can migrate between classifications, from acausal orderedness to synchronicity, once we understand the embedded meaning. In principle, the reverse migration is also possible. The dividing line between the two phenomena cannot be as sharp as we might like.

For clarity, I will henceforth use the term *synchronicity* only for sporadic, acausal connections of meaning (synchronicity in the narrow sense). I use the term *acausal orderedness* for the constant and reproducible connections without meaning for individuation—acausal quantum phenomena, for example. General acausal orderedness encompasses both synchronicity and acausal orderedness. Figure 38 summarizes Jung's classifications.

GENERAL ACAUSAL ORDEREDNESS

Constant, reproducible, acausal order	Inconstant, acausal connections through meaning
• Quantum phenomena • Properties of natural numbers	• Synchronicity

Fig. 38. General acausal orderdedness

Acausal orderedness includes "*a priori* factors such as the properties of natural numbers, the discontinuities of modern physics, etc." The phrase "discontinuities of modern physics" needs amplification. Other references in Jung's synchronicity essay[4] and von Franz's[5] writings reveal that it refers to various quantum phenomena, such as the half-life of radioactive atoms or the nonlocal correlations seen in the tests of Bell's Inequality.[†] These and all sorts of other well-studied acausal quantum phenomena have no causes for individual events and thus are fully acausal according to both Jung and the physics community.

Jung's understanding of natural numbers also needs amplification. Jung writes, "We define number psychologically as an *archetype of order* which has become conscious" (Jung's italics).[6] Because number is the archetype of order and archetypes act acausally,[7] Jung places the properties of natural numbers in the category of acausal orderedness. Jung and von Franz were also impressed that number plays such an extraordinarily important role in modern physics, where the old adage that "God is a mathematician" seems literally true. Thus, numbers are ordering structures for *both* the inner and outer world, hence their critical role in synchronicity and divination, as in astrology or the use of the *I Ching*. For Jung, the properties of natural numbers are as much given or objective as they are defined by mathematicians. His largely Platonic view of numbers as ideal forms means that no human constructs cause their properties. von Franz, who was personally given the assignment by Jung to research the archetypal nature of numbers,[8] writes:

> In the psychic sphere, an acausal orderedness can be found in the properties of the natural integers. The natural integers are a psychic content that just simply is the way it is. Five, for example, is a prime number. That is just the way it is. We cannot ask why five is a prime number. . . . we cannot account for this causally. The question "Why?" or "Where does that come from?" or "What makes it that way?" appears to be meaningless. . . . The properties of natural integers are thus a psychic orderedness, as half-lives are a physical orderedness. Both are phenomena that Jung characterized by the concept of "acausal orderedness," by which he meant an *a priori* "just so" order that we cannot account for in terms of cause and effect or probability.[9]

Here incoherence enters the definition of acausal orderedness. As I have stressed, Jung always uses *causality* in the sense of "efficient cause," or some form of energy, force, or information exchange, just as a physicist would. But what does the a priori nature of natural num-

---

[†] In the last two decades, hundreds of studies have shown that pairs of quantum mechanical particles can be correlated so that what happens to one particle instantaneously affects the other particle, regardless of the distance between the particles. Such nonlocal correlations exhibit a kind of acausal wholeness in which the relationship between the two particles is more fundamental than their separate identities.

bers have to do with this type of cause? Yes, prime numbers are "just so," "a priori," and not caused by anything, but that property differs greatly from the acausality of synchronicity, parapsychological phenomena, or various quantum phenomena.

The way Jung consistently uses the term *acausality* only makes sense when a causal explanation is conceivable for the phenomenon under consideration. For example, you could say that elves cause synchronicity, or, more reasonably (but incorrectly), that archetypes cause synchronicity. Similarly, you could postulate (wrongly) that electromagnetic interactions between the brain and the environment cause parapsychological phenomena. Finally, causal hidden-variable theories have been devised to account for quantum phenomena. Although recent experiments rule such quantum theories out, they were coherent theories. Although certain well-established parapsychological phenomena rule out electromagnetism-based explanations, those too were reasonable theories. Finally, there are several less direct arguments that rule out the archetypes as causal agents of synchronicity.

In contrast, would it make any sense to consider some causal explanation for the prime nature of the number five? Such a cause is inconceivable, simply because "efficient cause" is not applicable at this level: *causality* and *acausality*, the way Jung always uses the terms, make sense only for phenomena that express themselves in space and time. From this point of view, a causal explanation for the properties of natural numbers is unthinkable. This conclusion follows simply because these numbers exist on a different level than that of synchronicity, parapsychological phenomena, or quantum phenomena.

It therefore seems we have two choices. First, we can broaden the notion of acausality so that it encompasses the properties of natural numbers. That, however, would violate Jung's normal use of the term and make acausal orderedness so broad a category that it would lose its value. Second, we could remove the properties of natural numbers from acausal orderedness, since they appeal to a different notion of acausality than other members of the category. However, Jung clearly wanted them in this category. Yet, he writes, "we define number psychologically as an *archetype of order* which has become conscious." That might prompt us to ask, Why aren't other archetypes placed in acausal orderedness, since they are just as "a priori" and "just so" as the properties of natural numbers and they too order our experience?" If we demand coherence in our definitions of such fundamental categories, we must choose one of these uncomfortable alternatives. I suggest that removing the properties of natural numbers from acausal orderedness does less violence to the category.

Jung draws a sharp distinction between the sporadically occurring synchronicity and the constant and reproducible phenomena in acausal orderedness. He writes, "Consequently, we would have to include constant and experimentally reproducible phenomena within the scope of our expanded concept, though this does not seem to accord with the nature of the phenomena included in synchronicity narrowly understood." The acausal quantum phenomena are constant and reproducible, but synchronicity, strictly or narrowly defined, is sporadic and unpredictable. With this background, I return to astrology.

Astrology, Acausal Orderedness, and Synchronicity

Jung's test of astrology involved searching for particular correlations between the horoscopes of married couples. One of the indicators he used, for example, was whether the natal Sun for one partner was conjunct the natal Moon of the other partner (that is, at an angle up to plus or minus eight degrees). Jung used fifty such indicators. However, he could not find a statistically significant correlation confirming astrology. I believe there are several reasons for this failure. First, marriage has a vast range of complex and interdependent meanings, both conscious and unconscious, and thus is a difficult phenomenon to pinpoint astrologically. Second, Jung borrowed his indicators from the second-century astronomer Ptolemy. Whatever marriage meant in the twentieth century when Jung did his analysis, it surely had a different meaning in Ptolemy's time. Third, Jung's database was much too small to establish a statistically significant correlation.

More troubling than the lack of statistical evidence for astrology are the problems presented, again, by meaning and frequency. For example, imagine a married person totally ignorant of Western astrology—our South Sea Islander, for example. Such a person would not even consider correlations between her horoscope and that of her spouse. Would that couple be appropriate subjects for Jung's test? The astrologers would say yes, but such correlations would certainly hold no meaning for the couple. Since Jung believes that meaning is "the indispensable criterion of synchronicity," such correlations could not be synchronistic, as I have already argued. Furthermore, the constancy of the astrological correlations, as opposed to the sporadic and infrequent nature of synchronicity, also argues against considering astrology as synchronicity. Of course, the critics of astrology claim that there is little or no scientific support for astrology, so they would challenge the idea that astrology is always operating, with or without meaning.

If astrology is a type of synchronicity, attempting a statistical test of it also presents several subtle, if not insurmountable, problems. For example, Jung writes, "Synchronicity is not a phenomenon whose regularity it is at all easy to demonstrate."[10] von Franz goes further when she writes, "Precisely insofar as synchronistic events are 'acts of creation,' they are not predictable and thus not susceptible to scientific investigation—unless the scientific method is fundamentally changed."[11] Or as she writes later, "Since synchronistic events seem to be irregular, they cannot be grasped statistically; nevertheless, acausal orderedness can be investigated experimentally, because it is something general and regular."[12] Jung's attempt at a direct statistical test of astrology thus implies a contradiction. If we believe with von Franz that synchronicity is "not susceptible to scientific investigation," then by attempting a statistical test of astrology Jung is showing that astrology is not a type of synchronicity—the opposite of his intent.

For the sake of argument, imagine that Jung found a strong and repeatable correlation between horoscopes of married couples. He does not state in his essay whether the couples in his database were interested in astrology. It seems doubtful that all of them were. Let us assume they were not all avid astrologers. Then this successful statistical test would reveal a constant and reproducible connection not dependent on any associated meaning. This result would then be a fine example of acausal order but not of synchronicity, again the opposite of Jung's intent.

I have argued in a similar vein against considering parapsychological phenomena measured in the laboratory as synchronicity.[13] The experiments done by the pioneering American parapsychologist J. B. Rhine heavily influenced Jung. These experiments, along with their more recent and even more compelling successors, lack the critical elixir of transformative meaning so essential to both individuation and synchronicity. In addition, as the modern parapsychological research so effectively shows, the results are repeatable and constant. Largely because of their lack of meaning and their reproducibility, I have suggested classifying parapsychological phenomena as acausal orderedness, along with acausal quantum phenomena, rather than as synchronicity. I suggest the same reclassification of astrology for the same reasons. In astrology, however, there are interesting complications.

Perhaps more significant than Jung's failure to verify astrology statistically was the very experience of attempting verification. With a small sample of 180 couples (360 horoscopes), Jung found the promising result that ten percent of the couples had natal Sun-Moon conjunctions. However, as he collected more horoscopes, the statistical significance of his results vanished. He attributed his early success to "a secret, mutual connivance [that] existed between the material and the psychic state of the astrologer."[14] In other words, Jung believed that his emotional involvement in the experiment elicited a genuine synchronicity.[15]

To test the idea that the emotional state of the person selecting the horoscopes could elicit a synchronicity, he then asked three different women, whose psychological state Jung accurately knew, to pick twenty pairs of horoscopes at random. Jung understood that such a small sample could never yield statistically significant results. Nevertheless, these selected pairs of horoscopes were then tested for the appropriate correlations. To his delight, each woman picked out horoscopes that had a high number of correlations reflecting *her* psychological state. This confirmed his suspicion about a "secret mutual connivance" between the unconscious of the researcher and the horoscopes. Such experiences confirm the frequent observation that both astrologers and psychotherapists attract clients with problems related to the practitioner's own state. This tendency suggests that genuine synchronicities can occur in astrology.

Given the above discussion, I suggest the following categorization of astrology. When astrology is continuously functioning by correlating planetary positions with psychological states—but there is no meaning for the persons involved—then it is an expression of acausal orderedness. The Mars effect is a candidate for this category. Like various parapsychological phenomena, this type of astrology is acausal and yet "constant and experimentally reproducible," but it does not carry meaning critical for the experimental subject's individuation. It is this reproducibility that allows for the impressive modern experiments verifying parapsychological effects.[16] Because of the multileveled symbolic richness of astrology, statistical tests of it are much more difficult to design, but if astrology is truly an expression of acausal orderedness, its "constant and experimentally reproducible" effects should be statistically verifiable.

On the other hand, when a horoscope is read symbolically and reveals profoundly meaningful connections between the objective planetary positions and our subjective psychological state, then we experience a true synchronicity. Such individuation experiences are not always possible (like any true, sporadic synchronicity). However, when a skilled reader works with a horoscope, synchronicity experiences should be approximately as frequent as those found by a good Tarot or *I Ching* reader.

For these reasons, astrology can be *both* an expression of reproducible acausal orderedness and, when the meaning is present, a true, sporadic synchronicity. In other words, when astrology is working unconsciously for the South Sea Islander or the famous athlete, it is an expression of continuously functioning acausal orderedness—type 1 astrology. On the other hand, when studying our horoscope and its transits delivers a genuine insight into our psychological state, then the experience can become a genuine synchronicity—type 2 astrology. Because of the complexity of astrology, this dual status seems unavoidable. Figure 39 summarizes the results. The shaded area separating the two regions reflects the difficulty of distinguishing between the two types of general acausal orderedness.

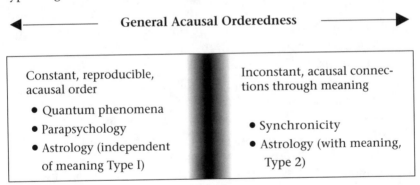

Fig. 39. General acausal orderedness, reclassified

Reproducible acausal orderedness (various quantum phenomena, parapsychological phenomena, and type 1 astrology, as in the Mars effect) falls within conventional science. Inconstant, nonreproducible synchronicity (including type 2 astrology), with its dependence on our unique individuation, falls outside of conventional science.

This discussion has presented some major revisions to one of Jung's important ideas. Namely, I have proposed that we should distinguish parapsychological phenomena from synchronicity, classify parapsychological phenomena as acausal orderedness, classify astrology as both acausal orderedness (type 1) and synchronicity (type 2), and remove the properties of natural numbers from acausal orderedness. The increased clarity and coherence of the revised scheme, the affirmation of the centrality of acausality and meaning, and the precision that the revisions bring to considerations of experimental studies make these changes seem more like refinements than a revolt. Like an early explorer, Jung opened new territory with his notion of synchronicity. Nearly half a century later, we are still attempting to map out the details of the original vistas.

Astrology and the Double Nature of Soul

Here it is useful to consider the relationship between astrology and the double nature of soul. Recall Plotinus's concept of the unique nature of soul: it is finite, divisible, and temporal, while simultaneously, at every level, infinite, indivisible, and eternal. If we follow Plotinus, we can never *separate* these two aspects, since they are what constitute its unique nature, any more than I could separate the front of my hand from the back. Of course, we can *distinguish* these two aspects of soul, just as I can distinguish the sides of my hand.

I suggest that the planetary positions at the time and place of an individual's birth, along with the subsequent transits, progressions, and other dynamic aspects of celestial motion considered in astrology, are all articulations of the divisible nature of soul. In other words, the subject of astrology is the divisible or finite aspect of soul. However, the indivisible or infinite aspect of soul is fully present as the meaningful correlation between our experience and the planetary positions. The unity that underlies astrology and accounts for its effectiveness (either type 1 or 2) is thus an expression of the indivisible nature of soul. Directly experiencing the indivisible aspect of soul is difficult, since it requires a completely still mind and thus a temporary lapsing of divisible soul, what we instinctively take to be our fundamental identity. Despite this, every time we observe strong correlations between our experience and the planetary positions, we are obtaining empirical evidence of the indivisible nature of soul. Of course, as an item of empirical evidence, this experience is only a partial and divided content of soul and thus not a direct experience of our indivisible nature. Nevertheless, it can be a moment of great spiritual uplift to have any experience of the indivisible and infinite aspect of soul within which we continuously live. To experience how, for example, a sense of limitation correlates with a Saturn transit, is to glimpse at evidence of our indivisible nature, to get a little peek beyond our finite and limited selves.

Chapter Nine

CAN SYNCHRONICITY
BE SCIENTIFICALLY TESTED?

I am teaching our department's introductory course for physics majors. The laboratory program for this course begins with an elegant experiment that measures the average velocity of gas particles using the kinetic theory of gases. Lab sections typically have fourteen to sixteen students, which means seven or eight pairs, each working with their own apparatus (fig. 40). One of the interesting aspects of this lab is its use of liquid nitrogen, a gas so cold it has become liquefied. The temperature of liquid nitrogen is −320 Fahrenheit, −196 Celsius, or 77 Celsius degrees above absolute zero. This temperature is so far from anything we normally experience that it is difficult for students to appreciate what it implies. I therefore begin the lab period by stressing to the students how this extreme cold makes the nitrogen dangerous to handle. I explain how they must work with it and wear safety goggles to avoid splattering it in their eyes.

I get the students going by filling their dewars (just fancy thermos bottles) with liquid nitrogen and start them taking measurements. It is not possible to attend quickly to every team with a problem, so I have a lab assistant, Monica, a capable senior physics major. After about an hour and a half, by which time everybody has solved their initial problems with the

Fig. 40. Students in introductory physics lab (photo by author)

apparatus and begun taking measurements, I leave for the men's room. I return in five minutes and notice the class is working diligently, but it is eerily quiet. Parents know that if you enter a room with children and it is unusually quiet, then something strange went on just before your arrival.

I motion to Monica to come to the back of the lab, where I ask her, "Why is it so quiet in here?"

"Oh, there was a little accident while you were gone. Tim was refilling his dewar and spilled liquid nitrogen on the front of his pants. He instantly pulled off his pants and his underwear. At first, the rest of the students were stunned. When they realized he was OK, they roared with laughter. He got his pants on just before you entered the room!"

This lab story illustrates one of the fundamental presuppositions in science: the difference between experience and experiment—something Tim learned directly. Ravi Ravindra[1] has very effectively made this distinction and inspired my thinking about this and other fundamental presuppositions in science. A clear understanding of these presuppositions is a prerequisite for the task of thinking about synchronicity and astrology in a scientific context.

One group that has undertaken this task is the Synchronicity Committee, an international group of scientists and Jungians currently led by Drs. James Hall and Jan Marlan. They are seeking a deeper understanding of synchronicity through their combined effort, part of which is to consider scientific synchronicity experiments. This chapter explores whether such experiments are in fact feasible. First, however, we must review the critical presuppositions that characterized the scientific worldview.

THE FUNDAMENTAL ASSUMPTIONS IN SCIENCE

EXPERIENCE, EXPERIMENT, AND THE PERSONAL EQUATION. Every year our department recognizes and encourages the best physics and astronomy students with a gift of a specially boxed copy of Richard Feynman's three-volume set *The Feynman Lectures in Physics*. Each staff member signs the books, and they are presented in a formal ceremony. On the first page of this masterpiece, Feynman says, "The principle of science, the definition, almost, is the following: The test of all knowledge is experiment. Experiment is the sole judge of scientific 'truth.'"[2] This view expresses itself in the enormous effort we make in both teaching and research to understand and become proficient in experimental work. Here I distinguish between experience and experiment, reserving for the latter term only the meaning it has in science.

In an experiment, we ask a precisely defined question under carefully controlled settings. The prevailing scientific theory strongly conditions the question asked and even tells us what we can measure. For example, before the current understanding of electromagnetism emerged, there were several attempts to weigh electrical charge. With our current theory, we understand just how exceedingly difficult this approach would be, and we devise other methods, based on electromagnetic theory, for quantifying electrical charge.

Since we never make a measurement without having some expectations that are guided by theory, control is essential. Without adequate control over the experiment and its environment, we cannot be sure we are testing the theoretical predictions. For example, in the lab experiment just discussed, we have a theoretical model for the behavior of gases. If we assume the gas molecules act like point masses with no internal structure and collide like billiard balls guided by Newtonian physics, then we can develop what are called the ideal gas laws. These laws relate such fundamental variables as pressure, temperature, density, and average particle velocity. With some care, we can control the experiment so that we know the conditions appropriate for when the ideal gas laws apply. Then we can predict how measured variables relate to the average velocity of the particles in the gas. This relationship allows students to measure gas pressure in the apparatus as a function of time and, using the ideal gas laws, infer the average gas particle velocity. Although clear theoretical structure and controlled experiments are the hallmark of modern physics (the paradigm for all the sciences), my discussion also applies to all the quantitative and laboratory-based natural and biological sciences.

Although experiments always involve a clear theoretical structure within which they are planned and executed with great control, serendipitous discoveries do occur. For example, in 1965 Arno Penzias and Robert Wilson were working on a sensitive horn antenna designed for a communication satellite system. They found a strange signal coming from all parts of the sky. They tried to eliminate it by doing everything from checking and fine-tuning all parts of the antenna to cleaning out a pigeon nest and its associated droppings. The signal persisted and they published their strange result.[3] In the same issue of the *Astrophysical Journal,* other astronomers showed that this result was the first detection of the radiation left over from the earliest moments of the cosmological big bang, something theoretically predicted nearly twenty years earlier.[4] Although the experimental result was initially mysterious, the control and precision involved in making the measurements allowed them to be taken seriously. With the theoretical interpretation and subsequent confirmations, these results gave the astronomical community great confidence in the standard big bang model for the universe and resulted in a Noble Prize for Penzias and Wilson in 1978. It is important to notice that, despite the serendipitous nature of the finding, it only took on significance within a well-established theoretical structure—the standard model for the big bang.

Whether in observational astronomy or particle physics, we teach students to leave their personal equation—their feelings, philosophical and psychological presuppositions, and personal peculiarities—out of the experiment. The ideal is to become completely objective and detached observers.

Our second-year curriculum for aspiring physicists includes a course in which students learn to build electronic components that allow experiments to be automated. With automation, the experimenter need not even be present when the data are taken. Here, through a combination of modern electronics and computing, we come close to the ideal of the detached observer. Of course, humans must interpret the data within a theoretical structure. Therefore, you cannot completely eliminate the observer in science.

Contrast all this with our student who spilled liquid nitrogen. The cardinal principle of control was certainly missing. Thanks to my introductory discussion, Tim did have some prior expectations based upon theoretical knowledge of liquid nitrogen. However, he certainly did not leave out his personal equation nor was he detached. In fact, the inclusion of his personal equation, his fears of bodily harm, and all the rest of his subjectivity, transformed the experiment into an experience. In other words, the involvement of soul in events transforms them into experience, whether the events are scientific experiments or bodily hormonal responses. In contrast, the removal of subjectivity, whether through electronics and computing or controlled laboratory procedures, allows experiences to become scientific experiments.

SCIENTIFIC OBJECTIVITY AND PRIMARY AND SECONDARY QUALITIES. Scientific objectivity rests upon a particular set of expectations and assumptions about nature. For example, Galileo Galilei developed the idea of primary and secondary qualities of objects. Primary qualities are those such as position, length, mass, energy, and velocity—quantities studied in the physics laboratory. Secondary qualities are those such as sweet, sour, hot, cold, color, and smoothness—due largely to our sensory experience of the world. Both Galileo and John Locke, an English philosopher who further developed Galileo's idea, argued that only the primary qualities of objects were appropriate for scientific study. Of course, secondary qualities are the raw material for much sensitive art. However, since science is seen as *the* way to truth and our experience is largely of secondary qualities, the implication is that the truth about the world cannot be obtained through normal experience. In other words, human experience, unaided by science, cannot attain a truthful view of the universe. Of course, this view seriously estranges us from nature.

Yet, there is good reason to have suspicions about appearances. For example, the Sun, Moon, planets, and stars all seem to rotate around the Earth, but scientific observation and reasoning show that this is only an Earth-centered view. My desk feels smooth and solid, but modern physics tells me it is mostly empty space. As these examples show, important insights in the physical world do come from the scientific focus on primary qualities. However, since we know only secondary qualities directly, this focus excludes normal human experience from the view of nature offered by science. If we hold that science offers the only true view, then normal human experience cannot accurately know the natural world—at least as science defines it. In this way, modern science estranges us from nature.

For example, imagine you are in an inspiring place in nature and watching an extraordinarily beautiful sunset. The sky is incandescent with warm colors, clouds and sunlight are forming majestic patterns, and you are fully absorbed in its beauty. The mood deepens to a life-changing experience of timeless beauty, both inwardly and outwardly. In contrast to an experiment, this experience is neither controlled, nor detached, nor based upon primary qualities. A scientist might study the same sunset by monitoring changes in the spectrum of the sunlight with time to obtain information about the Earth's atmosphere. For you the sunset is an occasion for experiencing timeless beauty, while the scientist learns about greenhouse gases and global warming. Are you and the scientist really encountering the same sunset? Is one view more valid than the other?

The objectivity so prized in scientific analysis rests upon shared commitments that go way beyond the focus on primary qualities. For example, in the sunset study, the measurements made, along with the analysis and interpretation, rest on a shared understanding of how the interaction of light with atoms is governed by quantum mechanics. Another such commitment is that the data and the analysis must all be publicly available for replication by any trained scientist.

Yet another essential commitment in science, rarely acknowledged, is what Erwin Schrödinger, a leading physicist of the early twentieth century, called the principle of objectification. According to this principle, the mind objectifies its world and necessarily leaves itself out of the picture, as it must, since by its very nature it cannot be turned into an object like other items in the world. He says, "Mind has erected the objective outside world of the natural philosopher out of its own stuff. Mind could not cope with this gigantic task otherwise than by the simplifying device of excluding itself—withdrawing from its conceptual creations. Hence the latter does not contain its creator." Since our interest is so focused on the world of objects, the true subject, which Schrödinger calls the subject of cognizance, then falls to the background. This subject, by its very nature, cannot exist in the world of objectively existent objects, the domain of science.

Jung makes a very similar statement when he writes:

> Every science is a function of the psyche, and all knowledge is rooted in it. The psyche is the greatest of cosmic wonders and the *sine qua non* of the world as an object. It is the highest degree odd that Western man, with but very few—and ever fewer—exceptions, apparently pays so little regard to this fact. Swamped by the knowledge of external objects, the subject of all knowledge has been temporarily eclipsed to the point of seeming nonexistence.[5]

Both Schrödinger and Jung are asking us to pay more attention to the "subject of all knowledge." Here I am primarily interested in noting that the removal of this subject is a pivotal assumption characterizing science. With our focus on the objects of science, whether in the classroom or the lab, we disregard the truth that "Every science is a function of the psyche, and all knowledge is rooted in it." Instead, the subject becomes a ghostly entity we seek to avoid, while it haunts our every step.

It is only within this detailed and far-ranging set of shared commitments that the scientist has made an objective analysis. In fact, only those with adequate training in and adherence to those shared commitments are eligible for membership in the scientific community. In other words, objectivity in science is actually an intersubjective agreement based upon a large network of shared theoretical and observational commitments.

Let's contrast this intersubjective agreement with the aesthetic and spiritual experience of the sunset. Such an experience cannot be controlled like a scientific experiment. Someone can sit in the same spot and watch one glorious sunset after another, and there is no guarantee that they will have a life-changing experience of timeless beauty—or of anything else. Of course, the focus is on secondary qualities. The personal connection and involvement in experience is in stark contrast to the function of a detached observation, which can be done by a computer-driven measuring device. The aesthetic or spiritual experience is not publicly available for replication. You can neither replicate nor automate such experience. Instead, you can only prepare the right conditions and then be fully present in the experience with all your unique psychological attributes.

In a spiritual or psychological experience, our state of consciousness is of paramount significance. Some experiences are not available for an unrefined or insensitive state of consciousness. In contrast, anybody with the requisite scientific training, which does not demand any inward transformation or refinement, can do the experiment.

Finally, for many artists and essentially all mystics, the subject/object split lapses in many important classes of experience. This fusion between the subject and object strongly contrasts with Schrödinger's principle of objectification, which demands that science always keep a sharp separation between the objects in the world and the excluded subject of cognizance.

UNIVERSAL LAWS AND ABSTRACTIONS. One of the greatest achievements of the sciences is the ability to generate universal mathematical laws, which apply for all time and space to an enormous number of special cases. For example, the theory of general relativity culminates in one elegant equation: $R_{\mu\nu} - .5g_{\mu\nu} = -8\pi GT_{\mu\nu}$. This equation governs the relationship between the curvature of four-dimensional spacetime (represented on the left side of the equation) and the distribution of matter in spacetime (the right side of the equation). This one equation is actually a compact form for specifying sixteen distinct equations. Unfortunately, finding general solutions for this equation is mathematically difficult. Nevertheless, this single equation governs a range of phenomena from cosmology and black holes to the collisions of billiard balls and the flowing of water down sink drains. Although the laws of hydrodynamics were known well before general relativity, they are, nevertheless, contained within general relativity's one master equation. This extraordinary power to explain a large body of diverse phenomena with a few compact equations is one of the greatest triumphs of modern science. This quest for more general and profound universal laws is a major motivation in science. For example, in contemporary physics, there is a major effort to unify all the four forces in nature (gravity, electromagnetism, strong nuclear force, and weak nuclear force) in one grand unified theory or theory of everything.

Part of the price paid for this universalizing power is the high level of abstraction inherent in modern science in general and physics in particular. Whether doing research or teaching students, we always struggle to understand just how the abstract mathematical laws connect to the observed phenomena. In addition, today's scientific phenomena usually cannot be apprehended with unaided senses. Galileo could do an experiment by visually examining objects falling from the leaning tower of Pisa; today such observation no longer suffices. Instead, the phenomena we study usually give only a tiny and indirect glimpse of themselves in an oscilloscope trace or a digital readout. Based on these glimpses and a great deal of theory, we construct our models of the physical world.

Even in the introductory laboratory exercise mentioned above, the phenomena studied are abstract. Yes, the students work with liquid nitrogen, dewars, thermometers, pressure gauges, and other physical objects. They take data at specific times. However, they certainly do not have any sensory contact with the phenomena studied. Instead, using the ideal gas laws, they construct in the imagination a model or picture of what they believe is going on in nature. This approach implies that the deep reality of the world is a model built with mathematical physics. All the rest is an appearance of this underlying reality. According to this logic, only those sufficiently trained to appreciate this mathematical structure have contact with reality. As Galileo said:

> Philosophy is written in this grand book the universe, which stands continually open to our gaze. But the book cannot be understood unless one first learns to comprehend the language and to read the alphabet in which it is composed. It is written in

the language of mathematics, and its characters are triangles, circles, and other geometric figures, without which it is humanly impossible to understand a single word of it; without these, one wanders about in a dark labyrinth.[6]

Of course, since Galileo's day mathematics has become much more abstract and powerful. Today we must work much harder to understand the mathematics necessary to keep us from wandering "in a dark labyrinth." Furthermore, the very power and generality of the mathematical laws imply a reduction in the importance of the individual event, the unique example, whether a particular genetic mutation, a photon emission, or a synchronicity event.

The Nobel Prize–winning immunologist Sir Peter Medawar states all this very powerfully. He tells us, "As science advances, particular facts are comprehended within, and therefore in a sense annihilated by, general statements of steadily increasing explanatory power and compass—whereupon the facts need no longer be known explicitly, i.e., spelled out and kept in mind. In all sciences we are being progressively relieved of the burden of singular instances, the tyranny of the particular."[7] Certainly, a particular person's individuation, never seen before and never to be repeated again, has no place in this view.

The productivity of the abstract and universal laws in modern science is unquestionable. Unfortunately, great achievement with these laws often leads to equally great blindness about their shortcomings. For example, Stephen Weinberg, a Nobel Prize winner and one of the people making important contributions to a unified theory of the four forces in nature, writes:

> When the Spanish settlers in Mexico began in the sixteenth century to push northward into the country known as Texas, they were led on by rumors of cities of gold, the seven cities of Cibola. At the time that was not so unreasonable. Few Europeans had been to Texas, and for all anyone knew, it might contain any number of wonders. But suppose that someone today reported evidence that there are seven golden cities somewhere in modern Texas. Would you open-mindedly recommend mounting an expedition to search every corner of the state between the Red River and the Rio Grande to look for these cities? I think you would make the judgment that we already know so much about Texas, so much of it has been explored and settled, that it is simply not worthwhile to look for mysterious golden cities. In the same way, our discovery of the connected and convergent pattern of scientific explanations has done the very great service

of teaching us that there is no room in nature for astrology or telekinesis or creationism or other superstitions.[8]

Weinberg is saying that the universal laws, what he calls "the connected and convergent pattern of scientific explanations," rule out "astrology or telekinesis or creationism or other superstitions." I object to placing astrology and telekinesis (the moving of matter by mental intent alone) in the same category as creationism. I can only assume that he does this because he views them all as challenging science at a fundamental level. (Incidentally, telekinesis, unlike astrology, is actually supported by mountains of carefully taken data.[9])

True, no laws exist that explain astrology or telekinesis in the way that the laws of general relativity explain the cosmological expansion. However, it is an enormous leap from that admission to saying that they can be ruled out in principle. Weinberg's assertion rests on two unfounded assumptions. First, he assumes that contemporary physics offers us a complete and exhaustive view of the universe, that the present laws of physics encompass all phenomena. We have no way of conclusively showing that the laws of physics are complete and can account for all possible phenomena. Second, he assumes that because he cannot imagine an explanation for these phenomena, then they cannot exist or be real. Our inability to imagine an explanation hardly proves the nonexistence of the phenomenon. Nature has repeatedly shown us that she is much more inventive than we are. Such poor arguments only show the dangers inherent in an uncritical love of the great success of abstract and universal laws in science.

FEELINGS AND OUR LEVEL OF BEING IN SCIENCE. All laboratory work, including computer simulation and analysis, whether in an introductory physics lab or at a national observatory like that at Arecibo, Puerto Rico, involves occasional frustrations and difficulties. Often students get emotionally upset at these inevitable difficulties and I remind them, "The equipment will not respond to threats or attempts at emotional manipulation. Getting your feelings aroused only makes it more difficult." They know this, of course, and my pious pronouncements probably don't help them embody the scientific ideal of a detached and feelingless observer.

The impersonality integral to science gives rise naturally to the goal of removing all feelings from the doing of science. It is true that our feelings can often lead us astray, whether in science or other areas of life. However, science does not recognize that feelings can be refined, developed, and with practice honed into a reliable source of knowledge. In contrast, mystical traditions around the world recognize that the refinement and purification of our personality and feelings are prerequisites for getting even a glimpse of higher reality. This follows because our level of psychological and spiritual development determines our perception and hence our ability to apprehend reality. For example, Plotinus tells us that to have a vision of Ultimate Beauty, the highest principle, the inner eye that knows it must be refined and made like that which it desires:

> If the eye that adventures the vision be dimmed by vice, impure, or weak, and unable in its cowardly blenching to see the uttermost brightness, then it sees nothing even though another point to what lies plain to sight before it. To any vision must be brought an eye adapted to what is to be seen, and having some likeness to it. Never did eye see the sun unless it had first becomes sun-like, and never can the Soul have vision of the First Beauty unless itself be beautiful.
>
> Therefore, first let each become godlike and each beautiful who cares to see God and Beauty.[10]

The need to become godlike before we can see God is in striking contrast to the preparation needed to become a good scientist. Although the process of getting a Ph.D. in science is a rigorous initiation, the feelings need not be refined nor the personality of the scientist transformed in any way. The demand for replicable, publicly available data and analysis overrides any consideration of the level of psychological and spiritual development of the scientist.

MATERIALISM AND MEANINGLESSNESS. Modern physics, being the study of matter and energy and the relationship between the two, is materialistic by definition. For physics, the universe is a dance of inert and insentient matter and energy choreographed by mathematical laws. None of the dancers—the elementary particles or their larger groupings from molecules to stars—has any interiority, will, purpose, or consciousness. They are just passive amid forces external to them. In a fully materialistic view, those entities who exhibit consciousness, such as humans, do so because of a sufficiently complex arrangement of matter and energy in their brains. Then the brain is really a sophisticated computer made of meat.

Oddly, in the West it was the reforms of the Christian church fathers, initiated during their long war against paganism and polytheism, that laid the groundwork for this materialism. James Hillman brilliantly sketches this history and concludes:

Soul was confined to the persons of Christ and those baptized in his name, all else burnt out of Being or moving
mechanically around a clockwork orbit. Animals were bereft of
psyche, and children, even when baptized, did not have the full
reality of souls. Both modern science as it was then being formed
and modern Christianity as it was then being reformed required
that subjectivities be purged from everywhere and everything
except the authorized place of persons: the rational Christian
adult. To experience otherwise was heresy and witchcraft.[11]

The pagan view of a world animated with intelligences called gods had
to be defeated so that the "one true God" would be sovereign. Here we
have echoes of the injunction in Deuteronomy to slay the nonbeliever.
Removal of subjectivity from all but persons and God allowed
Newtonian physics to build a model of the world as a giant clock, with
God, the architect-engineer, relegated to the role of disconnected spec-
tator. Soon the increasing tide of secularism, aided by physics, removed
the need for God altogether. Christianity defeated paganism, only to
be defeated in turn, at least among most modern intellectuals, by materialism.

By reducing all phenomena in the universe to insentient matter
passively responding to forces that are themselves devoid of subjectivity and purpose, materialism reduces the world to a meaningless display
for those with a sufficiently complex form of matter to reflect on it. As
Weinberg says, "The [materialist] reductionist worldview *is* chilling and
impersonal. It has to be accepted as it is, not because we like it, but
because that is the way the world works."[12] I admire Weinberg for his
brilliance in physics and his heroic tough-mindedness in the face of its
implications. With his voice still ringing in our ears, let us turn to the
issue of scientific testing of astrology and synchronicity.

SCIENTIFICALLY TESTING SYNCHRONICITY

As I explained in chapter 8, there are two types of astrology. Type 1
expresses acausal laws of nature, while type 2 expresses synchronicity.
Type 1 studies, such as those on the Mars effect, present scientific data
that confirm the central hypothesis in astrology—that our experiences
correlate with planetary motions. As I have stressed, this confirming
scientific evidence is scanty. Nevertheless, difficult as such tests are, it
is possible in principle to make meaningful scientific studies of this
type 1 astrology. However, type 2 astrology, an expression of
synchronicity, presents more difficulties when we seek to test it scien-

tifically. Let's turn to some of those difficulties by examining each of the above characteristics of the scientific worldview as they relate to testing synchronicity scientifically.

Experience, experiment, and the personal equation. When we turn from experiments to experiences, as we must in discussing synchronicity, control of nature is essentially impossible and generally undesirable. The value of synchronicity lies in its being a spontaneous response of nature, an expression of our individuation. It embodies a critical unconscious compensation. Here the self is educating the ego, and therefore the ego cannot control the course and the curriculum. For this reason, control is antithetical to synchronicity. For example, in a divinatory technique, such as the *I Ching* or Tarot, we try to provide nature with maximum freedom for its response. We throw coins randomly to use the *I Ching* or thoroughly shuffle the Tarot deck before laying out the cards.

Theoretical expectations may be present but, more often than not, they get in the way of the experience presented. Certainly, our individual presence in the experience is required to transform mere events into experience. Our subjective involvement in the events is what turns them into experience. In short, a synchronicity experience, when we are fully present with all our individual preferences and peculiarities, is very different from a controlled experiment by a detached observer who bases her actions and interpretations upon clear theoretical structures.

Scientific objectivity and primary and secondary qualities. If we dig a little beneath all the talk about the role of the observer in modern physics, we see that it involves only a notion of "bare subjectivity." By bare subjectivity, I mean the ability to record factual knowledge, which most believe a computer can do. (Nobody doubts that the choice of experiment and its interpretation require a human.) Whether or not a computer is an adequate expression of bare subjectivity is not essential. The critical point is that such bare subjectivity has no internal structure, nothing that differentiates one bare subject from another. In other words, there is no individuality in this subjectivity.

This critical point deserves amplification. Consider the electron. We know its charge, mass, and spin with great precision. However, we also know that all electrons are identical. Yes, an electron can occupy different states. One travels freely at nearly the velocity of light in a jet from the vicinity of a black hole or in a particle accelerator, while another binds to a proton to form a hydrogen atom in a distant galaxy or in my glass of water. However, aside from such extrinsic conditions as their state of motion or their inclusion in an atom, these electrons are intrinsically indistinguishable. If there are ten electrons moving freely in a box, we have no way to distinguish one electron from another. In other words, electrons do not have little serial numbers stamped on them that would allow us to treat them as individuals. All this is at the very foundation of modern physics. In a completely analogous way, one bare subject in physics can replace another without any change in the experiment. There is simply nothing to distinguish one bare subject from another.

Despite the widely varying philosophical interpretations of quantum mechanics, there is full agreement that the kind of subjectivity talked about is bare, in this sense. This agreement in no way diminishes the importance to science, with all its centuries of a purely objective orientation, of having to address the importance of our involvement in measuring quantum events. Nevertheless, the kind of subjectivity involved in quantum measurement is of a different order than the wholeness and uniqueness of a person involved in a synchronicity experience.

In synchronicity, an acausal bridge of meaning connects the subjective inner event with the objective outer event. Since this unfolding meaning is intimately connected with our individuation, our coming to a fuller expression of who we are meant to be, the whole of a unique person and his or her subjectivity are involved. As von Franz says, "The realization of 'meaning' is therefore not a simple acquisition of information or of knowledge, but rather a living experience that touches the heart just as much as the mind."[13] The subjective pole of a synchronicity experience thus involves the full person, with all their lusts, secrets, limitations, fears, and all the excellences of the soul and its spiritual aspirations. This "fully dressed subjectivity" makes each individual unique. This uniqueness is our most fundamental sense of identity. We certainly could not exchange one person for another in a synchronicity experience, since the experience is really an expression of a particular person's individuality. To complicate matters, synchronicity is replete with sensuous secondary qualities, thereby making more difficulties for a scientific test that must rely on primary qualities.

UNIVERSAL LAWS AND ABSTRACTIONS. The emphasis on universal laws and on freedom from what Medawar calls the "tyranny of the particular" presents special difficulties for scientifically testing synchronicity. As Jung and von Franz stress, synchronicity is a unique event, exquisitely tuned to the needs of the particular person's individuation at that moment. Individuation is indeed the "tyranny [or joy] of the particular."

Even so, general laws and structures do govern our psychological and spiritual development and allow the rational cultivation of a higher level of being. For example, Jung elaborated archetypal structures that play a dominant role in psychological development. Various spiritual traditions have developed disciplines based upon universal psychosomatic structures—chakras, for one example. Despite these general or universal structures, the emphasis at all levels is on the uniqueness and the particularity of the individual aspirant. As we well know, each individuation is unique, never seen before in the history of the universe and never to be seen again. Almost every spiritual tradition stresses the need for a spiritual mentor, because, despite any universal structures or scriptures, the spiritual journey must address the particular strengths, weakness, accomplishments, and peculiarities of the individual.

FEELINGS AND OUR LEVEL OF BEING IN SCIENCE. A major synchronicity, like a big dream, often seems to be given for free, without effort and preparation. Such is the spontaneous nature of synchronicity. However, without refinement of feeling and an appreciation of symbolic consciousness, the recipient has no hope of grasping the meaning and thereby benefiting from the experience. Since few of us are born with these talents, developing them often requires years of patient work and the help of an analyst or close friend with more experience in the inner realms.

MATERIALISM AND MEANINGLESSNESS. As I've discussed elsewhere, I believe it is easier to comprehend synchronicity within the philosophical framework of idealism.[14] However, the issue here is not materialism versus idealism, but rather that the cosmos known to science is populated only by entities devoid of interiority, will, and intelligent purpose. In scientific materialism, there is no room for the incarnation of meaning in outer objects. In contrast, the whole thrust of synchronicity is to appreciate a cosmos in which the same intelligence, the same archetype, is structuring both our inner world and the correlated outer events. This view necessarily implies that there are autonomous principles in the cosmos other than man, such as archetypes, that do embody interiority, will, and intelligent purpose. Individuation must imply some teleology, that events have a purpose—an idea banished in science since Darwin. Astrology is even more pagan in believing that the planets are expressions of archetypal intelligence—that Apollo, Mercury, Venus, Mars, Jupiter, Saturn, Uranus, Neptune, and Pluto and their friends are continuously (but acausally) displaying intelligence, autonomy, purpose, and intent.

IS JUNG'S TEST OF SYNCHRONICITY SCIENTIFICALLY ACCEPTABLE?

At the end of his life, according to a 1983 essay by von Franz,[15] Jung suggested that once it was clear that an archetype had been constellated (or activated), because of some serious psychological stress, for example—then several divinatory procedures, whose functioning depends upon synchronicity, could be employed. The results of all these procedures, from the *I Ching* to the Tarot, should converge to the same archetypal meaning. According to von Franz:

> Jung suggested investigating cases where it could be supposed that the archetypal layer of the unconscious is constellated—following a serious accident, for instance, or in the midst of a conflict or divorce situation—by having people engage in a divinatory procedure: throwing the *I Ching*, laying the Tarot cards, consulting the Mexican divination calendar, have a transit horoscope or a geomantic reading done. If Jung's hypothesis is accurate, the results of all these procedures should converge. However, unfortunately, up till now no results of any such experiments have been published. An Institute under the leadership of a professional in Jungian psychology should, in my opinion, undertake this matter.[16]

Jung attempts to address the fullness of the individual in part by keeping the subject the same while changing the divinatory procedures. The usual scientific practice is to keep the method the same and test the results with a large number of identical systems, whether electrons, persons, or giant elliptical galaxies. After all, the scientist does not want to be subject to the "tyranny of the particular." Is Jung's proposed experiment, which allows room for the unique individual, actually a scientific experiment?

Let me put on the hat of a conventional and conservative scientist and discuss his proposal, relying on points made above about the nature of science. I assume that Jung does not want to just "preach to the choir" but do this experiment in a sufficiently rigorous way that it is convincing to scientific skeptics. In other words, the test aims to show statistically that synchronicity is a genuine phenomenon. Although this point is not explicitly mentioned, it is a natural interpretation, especially in light of Jung's failed attempt to statistically test synchronicity through the astrology experiment reported in his original synchronicity essay. A statistical test implies that the results will be quantifiable. Herein lie many knotty problems.

The first difficulty comes from the inadequate theoretical structure within which to do this experiment. Despite many efforts,[17-19] the theory of synchronicity is far too formless and unconstrained. Talk of acausality is acceptable, since quantum physics has taught us how to live with that. However, the reliance on meaning (an extremely suspect idea within science) and its relationship to individuation makes the theory far too vague and too accommodating of an inordinately large class of experiences. This dependence upon the subjective sense of meaning is troubling in two ways. First, it forces us to rely on a subjective evaluation of what is meaningful. In the final analysis, it is one individual, the subject in a synchronicity experience, who must decide what is meaningful. Set aside the problem of the subject mistaking or twisting the meaning for his or her own purposes. In any case, right or wrong, the subject is the final arbiter of meaning. Second, even when an event is judged as meaningful, the structure and connection of this meaning to individuation are open to innumerable interpretations, all of which involve relying upon the feelings and subjective judgments of the protagonist. Where physicists use mathematics to guide them to understanding, depth psychologists and those interested in synchronicity must use feelings as a guide to the meaning and significance of these events. Given this, how could we possibly judge whether the results converge? What objective and quantitative measure of convergence could we develop?

The related problem of controls is especially difficult. First, we need objective criteria for judging when "the archetypal layer of the unconscious is constellated." What precise criteria could we use to decide when the deeper levels of the unconscious are constellated or activated? Different people have different thresholds for an activation of the unconscious. Second, divination is extremely slippery. For example, a hexagram from the *I Ching* has multiple layers of meaning, each of which bears several interpretations. In addition, judging how these meanings apply to a given question is certainly difficult and subject to many different interpretations.

These difficulties do not prevent us from doing an experiment. However, they make it extremely challenging to do the experiment in a scientifically convincing manner. Let's imagine that through some extraordinarily heroic effort, the experimental protocols are worked out in a sufficiently rigorous manner. Then, given the number of possible variables and the complexity of the experiment, it would have to be done by independent groups on thousands of people to get a statistically significant result. Judging from the reception that measurements of such parapsychological phenomena as psychokinesis and clairvoyance get from the skeptical scientific community, there would be many complaints about the experimental protocol that would require tightening of controls and various improvements. Then the experiments would have to be repeated. In the parapsychological case, history shows[20] that even with a mountain of carefully taken data, the skeptical scientific community has a tremendous resistance to accepting the data, let alone its implications. I believe that the resistance comes in large part because the parapsychological data profoundly challenge many aspects of the scientific worldview. The resistance would be even greater in the case of synchronicity.

In view of all the difficulties with Jung's proposal for a test of synchronicity, I strongly doubt that it is worth doing as a *scientific test* of synchronicity. However, for those already committed to depth psychology, it might be a way of obtaining significant insights into synchronicity. Is any scientific test of synchronicity doomed? I am cautious about making such pronouncements, since history teaches us that what one generation considers impossible a later one turns into everyday reality. Nevertheless, synchronicity's lack of an adequate theoretical structure; its uncontrollability; and its reliance on subjectivity, feelings, and scientifically suspect terms such as meaning make it exceedingly difficult, if not impossible, to test scientifically.

Although von Franz did not consider the issue of synchronicity experiments in detail, she believed that it was impossible to verify synchronicity scientifically. She says, "Precisely insofar as synchronistic events are 'acts of creation,' they are not predictable and thus not susceptible to scientific investigation—unless the scientific method is fundamentally changed."[21] I agree with her conclusion, but not her focus on the unpredictable nature of synchronicity. Many unpredictable events, whether the decays of a radioactive atom or the occurrence of an earthquake, are routinely studied scientifically. Later von Franz says, "I do not think it is possible to introduce synchronicity into the body of the sciences as they exist today."[22]

Despite the virtual impossibility of testing synchronicity scientifically, it is worth thinking carefully about such experiments and especially our motivation for wanting to do them. Part of that motivation is that the sheer dominance of the scientific worldview creates a kind of intellectual pressure to find a place within that worldview for aspects of our inner experience. Added impetus for seeking some form of harmony also comes from both Jung and Pauli, who often championed closer ties between depth psychology and modern science. However, given the structure of science just reviewed, it is unreasonable to expect it to be an adequate approach to reality in all its fullness. A concern for meaning and an interest in deep subjectivity are not medieval superstitions to be banished with the scientific sword. That so many believe science in its present form is the royal road to reality, the yardstick for *all knowledge*, shows the poverty of our present situation, despite our being surrounded by so many scientific triumphs.

Having distinguished scientific knowledge from what I call transformative self-knowledge in Part I and reviewed some of the interactions and tensions between these two kinds of knowledge in Part II, we are ready for the final leg of our journey in Part III. There I will attempt to bring some harmony between these two kinds of knowledge without reducing one to the other or putting them into a hierarchy. We begin the journey by returning to India for both inspiration and some useful ideas that will light our way.

Part III

TOWARD THE HARMONY OF SCIENCE AND THE SACRED

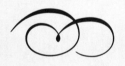

Chapter Ten

A THREEFOLD VIEW OF THE ABSOLUTE

About a half an hour before dawn, we are walking down the dusty main street of the small town of Kanchi Puram, India. The sound of bullocks plodding along mixes with the creak and rumble of the huge wooden wheels of their carts. The gray, pre-dawn light reveals silhouettes of sleepy drivers huddled under blankets against the chill. The still, moist air is heavy with smells—some of which come from people squatting at the edges of the street and relieving themselves. Besides a few muffled voices, there is the occasional crack of a whip over the heads of the bullocks. In the distance, a truck growls along the highway.

We are exhausted from long delays, even longer flights, and crossing too many time zones. Yet, excitement and anticipation at being in the presence of a person that the philosophic mystic Paul Brunton called "the greatest living sage" overcomes our fatigue. For years, I have read about him, seen photographs of him, and heard first-hand accounts of the great spiritual power emanating from this frail little man in his mid-nineties. Some mysterious power combined with my spiritual ambition pulls me to him. Soon we are led into the mutt—a combination temple and lodging for His Holiness Sri Sankaracharya, the sixty-eighth holder of a title that goes back nearly twelve centuries to the great Adi Sankara. This first Sankara was India's most revered re-former of Hinduism and exponent of the nondualistic philosophy of Advaita Vedānta—believed by many to be one of the greatest philo-sophical systems in the East or West. Advaita stresses the nondual nature of the absolute.

In the mutt, we join several dozen Indian devotees who are sit-ting on a concrete platform a few feet above what looks like a stage with a dirty brown canvas curtain. I try to meditate, but despite my excitement, fatigue descends on me and turns the meditation into a struggle against drowsiness. I open my eyes to see a cow and her young calf being led in for their morning blessing. One of the many honorific titles for Sankaracharya is "Protector of the Cows." Just after I am settled, the cow sends a jet of urine as big as the stream from a garden hose onto the concrete platform. A beautiful Indian woman in a flowing silk sari reaches into the stream with her hand and blesses herself with the urine, just as a Roman Catholic would use holy water.

The curtain is suddenly pulled aside to reveal a tiny baldheaded man with a close-cropped white beard. Heavy black glasses sit on his delicate, light-brown face. He is squatting on his haunches, naked except for a dhoti folded into a small loincloth. One cataract-dimmed eye wanders off, while the other one sweeps the crowd before him. Wooden prayer beads are looped about his neck and three streaks of white paste cover each side of his forehead. The devotees surge forward, their fervent chanting and praises filling the air. Some make full-body prostrations. Many engage in a unique gesture of obeisance: they put right palm to left cheek and left palm to right check, then quickly and lightly pat their cheeks. Several women light little oil fires in brass dishes and blow the smoke toward him while chanting praises in high tremolo voices. His Holiness surveys it all calmly and turns his palm outward in a tender blessing of the straining throng (fig. 41).

He is nearly deaf, so his attendants receive requests for blessings from individuals in the crowd and then shout them into his one good ear. They have to shout so loudly that they risk spitting on him, so

Fig. 41. Sri Sankaracharya (courtesy of Sankaracharya Mutt, Kanchi Puram, India)

they hold a hand in front of their mouths, palm inward, as they bellow at him. He strains to hear them and often asks them to repeat the message. Meanwhile, he touches fruit and flowers that have been eagerly passed up to him by the crowd. His touch transforms the fruit and flowers into blessed offerings or *prasad*. Soon there are great mounds of prasad piled all about him. I don't understand Tamil, but many messages are sprinkled with English words, so I can guess that they range from requests for blessings on marriages and students going off to school, to simple expressions of devotion. He rarely speaks, only occasionally whispering something to his attendants, who pass on the words to the devotees. He places some of the offerings on his head as a way of offering them in turn to the feet of his guru, which are always symbolically on his head. The attendants pass the blessed objects back to the crowd, which strains to see and be seen by the holy man.

A few minutes after I am settled, a powerful trumpeting sound blasts through the cacophony. The crowd makes room for an elephant, which is waving its trunk above its head like an enormous cobra. The attendants pass blessed bananas and coconuts back to the elephant. No eyes but mine leave Sankaracharya to watch the elephant enjoy her prasad of blessed offerings.

Before coming to India, I tried to prepare myself by reading several essays by the late Krishnachandra Bhattacharyya,[1] the great twentieth-century Indian philosopher. Although his work is some of the densest and most difficult philosophical writing I have ever read, nobody penetrates more deeply into the heart of philosophical Hinduism. I believed such essays as "Studies in Vedāntism," "Sankara's doctrine of Māyā," and "The Advaita and Its Spiritual Significance," would prepare me for my spiritual pilgrimage. Now, in the face of the pandemonium of both the crowd and, worse, my own reactions, those efforts seem completely irrelevant, even a joke. What does my struggle to understand philosophical Hinduism have to do with this madness?

Fig. 42. A beloved temple elephant receiving her daily decorations or sacred makeup (photo by author)

Only after several days of acclimating to South Indian religious culture and meditating during and between audiences with Sankaracharya did I begin to see beneath the forms of religious devotion and discover the relevance of my preparatory studies. Eventually, my three journeys to India to visit His Holiness gave me some understanding of how, in the midst of all that frantic devotion, elaborate ritual, and giving and receiving of prasad, he taught the core of Advaita Vedānta, the nondual interpretation of the ancient texts known as the Vedas. The principle of nonduality distinguishes Advaita from monotheism, which holds that there is a highest principle, some high level of being, and then all the rest, such as matter and evil. For example, in Christianity the one true God, exalted in Deuteronomy, opposes the absence of good, known as Satan. The highest principle in monotheism usually has some structure and a relationship to all else. In contrast, in a nondual view, there is nothing else but the absolute. All views of its structure and relationships place illusory limitations on that which is unlimited.

The core of Advaita is tightly summarized by the first paragraph in Bhattacharyya's essay, "The Advaita and Its Spiritual Significance," which reads (with my inserts in square brackets):

> The illusoriness of the individual self is apparently the central notion of Advaita Vedānta. Every vital tenet of the philosophy— Brahman [the nondual absolute] as the sole reality, the object as false, Māyā [illusion] as neither real nor unreal, Īśvara [creation principle] as Brahman in reference to Māyā, moksa [liberation from all opposites] through knowledge of Brahman and as identity with Brahman—may be regarded as an elaboration of this single notion.[2]

Let me approach the "illusoriness of the individual self" through a more positive description of Advaitic realization. Consider the symbolization of the swan or *hamsa*, which has a special significance for the Advaita and my experience of Sankaracharya. The word *hamsa* is a variation of *so'ham*, "I am That" (Brahman), the highest realization, wherein the seeker experiences the essential unity of his innermost nature with Brahman, the nondual absolute. The great exemplars of the tradition, such as Sankaracharya, are called *paramahamsas*—great swans. Although the swan spends most of its time in the water, its feathers remain dry, just as the advaitin lives in the world, yet remains unaffected by its pleasures and pains. The swan travels on land, water, and air, just as the adept traverses all the realms from the earthly to the most sublime. In Indian myth, the swan separates milk from water, just as the advaitin discriminates the eternal *Atman* (the supreme Self) from the noneternal world, the true self from the illusory ego. The Atman, which is in essence identical with Brahman, is just as immanent in the world as milk is seemingly inseparably mixed with water. The swan also symbolizes the *jivanmukta*, one liberated from the play of the opposites and in continuous contact with the absolute while still alive in this world. The swan has freed itself from bondage to the illusory ego and its realm of opposites.

The Advaita teachings and Bhattacharyya's writings are not only inspirations for inner life; as we will see, they can also provide a framework for discussing the relationship between science and spirituality. For that, I turn to Bhattacharyya's essay, "The Concept of the Absolute and Its Alternative Forms," which deals with the relationship between our everyday consciousness and the absolute.

The Concept of the Absolute and Its Alternative Forms

Finite reflective consciousness, our normal state of consciousness, always involves a subject, an object, and relationship between them. For example, I see a tree outside my office swaying gracefully in the wind. The conventional Vic is the subject, the tree is the object, and the relationship is one of enjoyment and appreciation. Such reflective consciousness is appropriate for revealing any finite object, from quarks to giant elliptical galaxies. However, it cannot grasp the limitless consciousness that illuminates and reveals all experience, nor the infinite, nondual absolute. So how, within finite reflective consciousness where philosophy is done, can we formulate coherent views of the infinite absolute? Bhattacharyya answers that consciousness takes three forms—knowing, willing, and feeling—and as a result, there are, *within reflective consciousness*, three alternative forms of the absolute.

Knowing. Knowing seeks to reveal the object as independent of the knowing consciousness. For a simple example, consider my Social Security number. It is independent of my knowing and in no way constituted by my knowing. If I forget the number or even when I die, the number has a well-defined existence independent of my knowing. According to Bhattacharyya, "The content of the knowing act is unconstituted by the act. The particular act of knowing discovers and does not construct the object known. . . . Knowledge would appear to mean that the object known is in some sense independent of it. . . ."[3]

Knowing is the principle approach in science. As I discussed in chapters 5 and 9, science seeks a view of the universe as objective, independent, and free from the peculiarities of the observer and her consciousness. Every effort is made to remove the personality of the scientist from the science. Although there is much discussion of the role of the observer and measurement in relativity and quantum mechanics, the overall goal of science is clearly to establish a view of the universe that is unconstituted by the human act of knowing. In chapter 2, I stressed that we could never fully achieve this level of objectivity, a point I illustrated by a little lesson about instrument response functions in radio astronomy, but here we need to consider the issue of objectivity more carefully.

Einstein eloquently articulates the independence of the scientific cosmos from the knowing of the scientists in a passage that gives his motives for pursing science:

> It is quite clear to me that the religious paradise of youth, which was thus lost, was a first attempt to free myself from the chains of the "merely personal," from an existence which is dominated by wishes, hopes, and primitive feelings. Out yonder there was this huge world, which exists independently of us human beings and which stands before us like a great, eternal riddle, at least partly accessible to our inspection and thinking. The contemplation of this world beckoned like a liberation, and I soon noticed that many a man whom I had learned to esteem and to admire had found inner freedom and security in devoted occupation with it. The mental grasp of this extrapersonal world within the frame of the given possibilities swam as the highest aim half consciously and half unconsciously before my mind's eye. [4]

For Einstein the world "exists independently of us human beings" as an "extrapersonal world." Nevertheless, it is "accessible to our inspection and thinking."

Despite Einstein's view, other prominent voices within physics emphasize that the world in fact does not exist independently of the scientist and her knowing. Danish physicist Neils Bohr differed on this point for decades with Einstein. For example, Bohr says, "The limit, which nature herself has thus imposed upon us, of the possibility of speaking about phenomena as existing objectively finds its expression, as far as we can judge, just in the formulation of quantum mechanics."[5]

The development of both relativity and quantum mechanics has focused attention on the role of measurement in physics. I have treated this in detail elsewhere.[6] Here I'll briefly summarize the salient issues. In relativity, we learn that a physical quantity only has a well-defined value in a particular reference frame or from a particular point of view. For example, let's say a redwood tree is measured to be 350 feet tall in a reference frame at rest with respect to the tree. For an astronaut moving with respect to the tree (along its vertical axis) at 98 percent of the speed of light, the same tree measures 70 feet tall. Relativity teaches us that this length is just as real, just as physically significant and true, as the 350-foot measurement. Length, time, mass, and several other fundamental quantities are deeply dependent upon the reference frame from which the measurements are made. Although this dependence upon the reference frame is a pillar of relativity, it does not imply that the object measured is in any way constituted or constructed by the knowing consciousness. For example, we can easily automate data taking through modern electronics and computing. Now our robot will make the appropriate reference-frame-dependent observations whether the scientists knows it or not—or is even in the same country when the observations are made.

In quantum mechanics, we also learn that whether an electron displays wavelike or particlelike behavior depends upon the experimentalist's detailed choices about what to measure. Prior to or independent of measurement, the electron does not have well-defined properties of either type. Physicist John Wheeler has summarized this by saying, "Useful as it is under everyday circumstances to say that the world exists 'out there' independent of us, that view can no longer be upheld. There is a strange sense in which this is a 'participatory universe.'"[7]

As is well known to those in daily contact with the doing of physics, "participatory" does not mean that something depends *directly* upon the consciousness of the observer. In fact, as I mentioned above, the physicist or astronomer need not even be present when the measurements are made. Computer-driven equipment can do all this work. Yet, measurements must be interpreted and understood by a person and therefore become elements of our knowing. Our interpretations are deeply influenced by everything from the physical theory under consideration to the sociology of physics research. For example, it is well understood that a theory, a mathematical construction of consciousness, tells us what we can measure and what our measurements mean. In this limited, but important, sense, the object is constructed by the knowing consciousness.

Therefore, modern developments do show that there is a limited, but important, dependence of the scientific object on the consciousness of the scientists. Despite this, the whole thrust of physics is to eliminate the preferences, proclivities, emotional and intellectual commitments, and personality of the observer—to strip away the contribution of our personal consciousness. Consequently, in science we can only give a limited affirmation to Bhattacharyya's view that "[t]he content of the knowing act is unconstituted by the act. The *particular* act of knowing discovers and does not construct the object known."

For knowing, the absolute is formulated as *truth*, that which can never be denied with any increase in knowledge. That is, to apprehend the absolute we are to know so deeply and fully that our contribution to the knowledge is eliminated and truth becomes self-revealing and self-evident. Thus, for the Advaita tradition, the entire cosmos, including all the beings within it, is known as Brahman, the absolute nondual truth, which shines forth self-evidently. Such knowing is not personal and contains none of the limitations of reflective knowing.

WILLING. In contrast to knowing, the content of willing is actually constituted by the willing consciousness. Consider the following unlikely example: I decide to undertake a total fast, neither eating nor drinking. The fast is a direct result or outflow of my willing. The fast is constituted by my willing and, though distinct from the willing, it is unthinkable without it. The act, end, or empirical embodiment of the end "is constituted by willing in the sense that apart from willing it is nothing at all."[8] The content and the willing consciousness are distinct, but the content is unthinkable without the willing.

More dramatic examples are found in the lives of the shapers of history, from military generals to peace activists. For example, consider Nelson Mandela, the center of the revolution in South Africa and the first president of a post-apartheid nation. When he was on trial for sabotage in 1963, he admitted the charges against him and ended his statement in court with the following words:

> During my lifetime, I have dedicated myself to this struggle of the African people. I have fought against white domination, and I have fought against black domination. I have cherished the ideal of a democratic and free society in which all persons live together in harmony and with equal opportunities. It is an ideal, which I hope to live for and to achieve. But if needs be, it is an ideal for which I am prepared to die.[9]

A little knowledge of Mandela's life clearly illustrates how his heroic willing expressed itself directly in the transformation of himself and South Africa. Without Mandela, apartheid probably would have died a bloody and fiery death under the weight of its inherent evil. However, its actual peaceful demise, the revolution that took place, and the details of the transformation are unthinkable without considering Mandela's willing. His emphasis on freedom also dovetails beautifully with Bhattacharyya's notion that the formulation of the absolute for willing is *freedom*, limitless expression of the absolute.

At a spiritual level, the attempt at breaking free of the play of the opposites, understood as liberation in Buddhism and Hinduism, is often approached through intense meditation disciplines. Here we can see the liberation thus attained as a direct expression of the willing consciousness. In the Advaitic tradition, to see the absolute through willing is to appreciate that the entire universe is the sport or play of Brahman, the dance of *līlā*, in which Brahman is completely free to manifest or not to manifest.

FEELING. In feeling, consciousness is indistinct from the content felt. However, we cannot say that there is a true unity between the feeling consciousness and the felt content. Such unity is not possible within reflective consciousness, which always involves the trio of empirical subject, object, and relationship between them. We can say, though, that there is a lack of separateness or distinction between the consciousness and content—not just simple confusion of subject and object, but their unification at a higher level. For example, imagine that you are deeply absorbed in a favorite piece of music. The feeling experience of rapture and delight is a high state of consciousness wherein the empirical subject is barely distinguishable from the music itself. Here feeling and the content of feeling flow into each other to form this higher unity.

A beautiful example of feeling's nondistinction between consciousness and content in a spiritual context occurs in the following fragment of a Rumi poem entitled "The Sunrise Ruby":

> In the early morning hour,
> just before dawn, lover and beloved wake
> and take a drink of water.
>
> She asks, "Do you love me or yourself more?
> Really, tell the absolute truth."

He says, "There's nothing left of *me*.
I'm like a ruby held up to the sunrise.
Is it still a stone, or a world
made of redness? It has no resistance
to sunlight."

This is how Hallaj said *I am God,*
and told the truth!

The ruby and the sunrise are one.[10]

Here is the feeling approach to the absolute, where the subjective and objective sides become indistinguishable in a higher unity. "I'm like a ruby held up to the sunrise. Is it still a stone, or a world made of redness? . . . The ruby and the sunrise are one. . . . This is how Hallaj said *I am God,* and told the truth!" According to Bhattacharyya, the absolute for feeling is *value.*

Much of the traditional religious literature of India associates a "knowing" approach to the absolute as *jñāna-yoga* and a "feeling" or devotional approach as *bhakti-yoga.* A "willing" approach to the absolute can be split into two possibilities: *karma-yoga,* the path of inspired action and selfless service, and *raja-yoga,* the path of deep meditation. These different paths are usually put in a hierarchy, with jñāna-yoga as the most exalted path. However, Bhattacharyya's conceptual formulation has none of this hierarchy. In fact, the threefold nature of the formulation is more an expression of the limitations of reflective consciousness rather than anything intrinsic to the absolute.

In everyday practice, as with Sankaracharya, the three approaches intertwine and reinforce each other. For example, he was in the lineage of the most famous and revered of jñāna-yogis (knowing), Adi Sankara, and he taught and wrote about that approach early in his life. Throughout his life, however, and especially toward the end, he was the center of largely bhakti-yoga (feeling) daily activities. As a karma-yogi (willing), he also spent a considerable amount of time in daily ritual ceremonies and, through his organization, supporting large-scale public service projects, such as feeding the poor and education.

The greatest spiritual figures usually combine two or three modes of apprehending the absolute. A particularly good example of combining bhakti-yoga with jñāna-yoga comes from Adi Sankara. Here are three bhakti stanzas of his "Eight Stanzas to Bhavāni," the Great Mother:[11]

I

No father have I, no mother, no comrade,
No son, no daughter, no wife, and no grandchild,
No servant nor master, no wisdom, no calling:
In Thee is my only haven of refuge,
In Thee, my help and my strength, O Bhavāni!

V

Addicted to sinning and worthless companions,
A slave to ill thoughts and to doers of evil,
Degraded am I, unrighteous, abandoned,
Attached to ill objects, adept in ill-speaking:
In Thee is my only haven of refuge,
In Thee, my help and my strength, O Bhavāni!

VIII

Defenseless am I—ill, aging, and helpless,
Enfeebled, exhausted, and dumbly despairing,
Afflicted with sorrow, and utterly ruined:
In Thee is my only haven of refuge,
In Thee, my help and my strength, O Bhavāni!

ELABORATIONS AND CLARIFICATIONS

Our experience of the world comes to us through our physical senses. Only in reflection do we understand how our limited mind-body complex plays such a dominant role in our apprehension of the world. Analogously, Bhattacharyya explains that our finite consciousness formulates the infinite absolute through knowing, willing, and feeling. Given this triple formulation, it is then natural to ask, "Are there actually three absolutes, or one?" Bhattacharyya answers this question toward the end of his essay:

> It is impossible to avoid this triple formulation of the absolute, though the notion that there are three absolutes would be just as illegitimate as the notion of there being only one absolute. The absolute is not a *known content*, about which the question of "one or many" has meaning. . . . It is meaningless, therefore, to cognitively assert that there are three absolutes or one absolute. The absolute has, however, to be formulated in this triple way. Each is absolute, but what are here understood as *three* are only their verbal symbols, they themselves being understood together, but not *as together*.[12]

The threefold nature of the above conceptual formulation of the absolute stems from the limited nature of human consciousness. The absolute, by its very nature, transcends quantification. However, the last sentence in the above quotation is obscure. I believe the following geometrical analogy helps make sense of it. But, if you have no taste for coordinate geometry, then just skip this explanation.

A Vector Analogy for Representing the Absolute

The representation of vectors in a particular coordinate system offers a helpful analogy for understanding how we finite beings formulate the absolute. However, before speaking about any coordinate representation of vectors, we need to understand them as purely geometrical objects independent of any coordinate system. Consider a vector, **V**, in three-dimensional Euclidean space. The most fundamental view of a vector is as a *geometric entity* consisting of a directed line segment. Because a vector has only a length and a direction in which it points, it makes no reference to a location or a particular coordinate frame. Any vector may thus be translated about (that is, we can move it to another location), but if we change either its direction or length, we create a new vector. For example, consider the vector shown in figure 43.

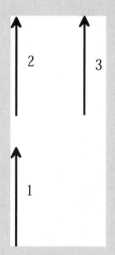

Fig. 43. Three instances of the same vector

Start from position 1, at the lower left. Since a vector is a geometric entity consisting only of a directed line segment, you can translate the vector parallel to itself vertically upward to position 2 and still have the same vector. You can also translate the vector to the right to position 3, being careful not to change its direction, and still have the same vector. However, if you rotate the vector just slightly in any direction you thereby change the direction in which it points and generate a new vector of the same length. Of course, if you keep the direction the same and shorten the vector, you again have a new vector.

For calculations, we often want to *represent* a vector in a particular coordinate system. For some applications, it is most convenient to use the rectangular Cartesian coordinates consisting of mutually perpendicular axes in the x, y, and z directions, as shown in figure 44.

The standard representation of vector **V** begins with an image of it projected in the x-y plane. To do this, imagine going out an infinite distance along the positive z-axis (vertically up- ward in the diagram) and shining a light back down toward the x-y plane. The shadow of **V**

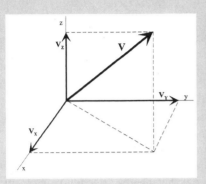

Fig. 44. Cartesian vector representation

in the x-y plane, shown as a dotted line, is then the projection of interest. That line in the x-y plane is then projected (by shining a light back on it from infinitely far in the positive y-axis) onto the x-axis, giving the *component* of **V** along the x-axis, V_x. In a similar way, the shadow of **V** in the x-y plane is projected onto the y-axis to give the vector components V_y. The component V_z can be found by simply projecting the original vector **V** onto the z-axis directly. Now the original vector, **V**, can be represented by the *vector addition* of the components V_x, V_y, and V_z. Vector addition is a special kind of addition that we need not consider in detail.

Note, however, that there is nothing special about the particular orientation of the x, y, and z axes. We can orient them according to our convenience. For example, in figure 45, the coordinate system has been reoriented (while keeping the origin point fixed) so that the y-axis is in the same direction as the vector, **V**. The x, y, and z axes

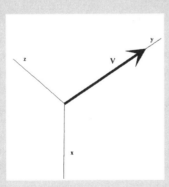

Fig. 45. Alternative vector representation

are still mutually perpendicular and have the same relationship to each other as in the previous figure. However, in this orientation, **V** has no components in the x or z directions. Instead, $V = V_y$. The axes could be oriented in an infinity of other ways. For example, they could be rotated so that **V** lies entirely in the x-z plane with components only along the x and z axes.

In the analogy, consider **V** as a purely geometric quantity, to be the absolute. Being purely geometric, it is complete and self-contained and needs no reference to any axes. We could say that all possible rep-resentations are contained integrally within it. Now consider the x, y, and z axes as corresponding to the human functions of knowing, willing, and feeling. Along with these functions comes the notion of number. If one function dominates your personality, you may view the absolute (**V**) solely through knowing, willing, or feeling (that is, as $V = V_x$, V_y, or V_z). Of course, there are an infinite number of combinations of these three views of the absolute, depending upon your orientation—your particular individuality. This fact is reflected in the combination of these approaches in daily practice.

Now, within this analogy we can ask whether there is one or many "representations" or formulations of the absolute. As purely the absolute, analogous to a geometric view of **V**, it has no representation and therefore no reference to either human consciousness or number. However, as represented, we see that it is equally legitimate, and equally misleading, to say that it has some number of representations or that there are some number of conceptions of the absolute.

Note how the last Bhattacharyya quotation ended: "Each is absolute, but what are here understood as *three* are only their verbal symbols, they themselves being understood together, but not *as together*." I will take this sentence one phrase at a time and interpolate explanatory words in square brackets. "Each [representation] is [a concept of the] absolute, but what are here understood as *three* [representations] are only their verbal symbols" [since within reflective consciousness we can only get symbols of the absolute]. The sentence is completed with "they [the representations] themselves being understood together [as different conceptual views of the absolute], but not *as together* [as constituting a triune absolute]." Unlike in the coordinate representation of vectors, you cannot simply sum the representations of the absolute, which would be analogous to vector addition, to give you the true absolute. Such summation of conceptual representations will never add up to the absolute, since getting even a glimpse of the absolute requires that we depart from *conceptual* consciousness, that is, experience a shift in both consciousness and level of being.

As the geometric analogy attempts to show, both the three-fold nature of the absolute and our various representations of it in knowing, willing, and feeling are limited symbolic expressions of that which is unlimited. So far, I have been stressing the conceptual formulation of the absolute; that is, the product of our attempt to grasp what transcends us. A complementary view sees the absolute as expressing itself through us. The first approach is from the bottom up (limited consciousness representing unlimited absolute), while the second is top down. Let's expand upon the top-down view.

Since each person has a unique psychological and philosophical orientation, the absolute expresses itself in a distinct way through each individual. For some orientations, the absolute expresses itself primarily through knowing, as in the case of the great formulator of jñāna-yoga, Adi Sankara. However, he clearly had what we might call (in the language of my geometric analogy) "a large component of the absolute along his feeling axis," as the Hymn to Bhavāni shows. Whether these components combine to produce someone like Adi Sankara or the great Tibetan reformer and philosopher, Tsong Khapa, or someone like Hitler, each individual life expresses the nondual absolute.

Yet, "the illusoriness of the individual self" is apparently the central notion of the Advaita Vedānta." In that the Advaita consistently formulates its position from the Himalayan heights of the nondual absolute, individuality is illusory. Nevertheless, from the point of view of the manifest world, each individual is a unique expression of the absolute. Even the jivanmuktis, those who have realized the absolute while living, are still unique individuals. An absorption in the nondual, undifferentiated absolute does not destroy the uniqueness of the individual. My experience with a few such persons shows me that they are more individual, more unique, than anybody else I have ever met. The expression of the absolute through a jivanmukta is necessarily conditioned by that person's historicity and individuality—after all, the expression comes through his or her space- and time-bound personality. If such self-realization involves continuous communion with the absolute, then nonduality demands that the historical individual be integral to the absolute.

Yes, from the point of view of absorption in the nondual, undifferentiated absolute, individuality is illusory, but here in the world, where the hamsa swims, individuality is an expression of divinity. As Tagore says, "Oh grant me my prayer, that I may never lose the bliss of the touch of the one in the play of the many."[13]

The Triple Absolute and Transformative Self-Knowledge

According to the Advaita, consciousness is rooted in our highest self or Atman, which is, in its essential nature, identical to the absolute. This is the import of the famous saying, "Thou art That." Since the absolute is self-luminous and self-knowing, our self-knowing is ultimately rooted in the absolute. Therefore, individual self-knowledge is the absolute knowing itself through us. In other words, each time we get a deeper understanding of ourselves through any of the three modes of consciousness, we experience a limited expression of the absolute self-knowing.

From the foregoing discussion of the functions of consciousness, we see that self-knowledge can come through a transformation of our knowing, willing, or feeling. In any one experience, the functions of consciousness can be present to varying degrees. For example, one experience may be primarily an expression of knowing, while another is mostly feeling with some limited component of willing. There are endless possibilities for each individual. Many of the personal experiences discussed in this book are primarily transformations of my feeling. Those are the most difficult and the most rewarding for me. I'll close this chapter by recounting a small instance of such a transformation of feeling that occurred on my first visit to Sankaracharya.

Meditation has never been easy for me. It always requires, at least in the beginning of a session, a willful approach. Despite that and the pandemonium surrounding Sankaracharya, I am able to meditate for about eight hours a day while in his presence. Since we spend about twelve hours a day at the mutt, I can spend several of those hours just gazing at him and all the activity that swirls around him, along with reading devotional poetry by Tagore. Not understanding Tamil also helps me concentrate. Most of what the attendants shout in Sankaracharya's one functioning ear is just loud noise and therefore easier to ignore. Sometimes I hear English words such as "tax audit" and "labor dispute" mixed in with the Tamil requests from devotees. Everybody is begging for his or her special little favor. It all seems so petty.

"Here is a jivanmukta and you people are acting like street beggars. India's great philosophical treasures are lost on you."

I cherish the times when the big dirty canvas curtain is drawn, removing Sankaracharya and his humble sleeping area from view. Although he is just on the other side of the canvas, everybody leaves and the place falls silent. I hear only an occasional few words between Sankaracharya and his attendants, the birds in some nearby trees, and the more distant roar of buses, trucks, and air horns. These are the best times for really pushing inward.

From the sheer number of hours meditating and from being in his presence, my mind is getting quiet. In the first days of this journey, I kept a journal. I wanted to be able to recall all the vivid details and deepen my reflections on events. After several long days of meditating, gazing at the sage, and reading devotional poetry, words and ideas come noticeably more slowly and often seem useless and vain. After a full day with Sankaracharya, I have to make an effort just to speak. I feel that I am close to some breakthrough. I want a big explosion, something to "kick the bottom of the bucket out," as they say in Zen. I want to leave the old Vic behind like a worn-out shoe. My spiritual ambition is showing.

Most people only stay a short while to see Sankaracharya and receive his blessing. Since we are there every possible hour of the day, the attendants soon give us a special area for sitting. We now sit closer to the sage on a low step in front of the railing that keeps the throng from falling in on top of Sankaracharya. Today the crowds are particularly frenzied to get close to make their plea or catch a glimpse of him. In their frenzy, somebody kicks me in the small of the back and breaks my concentration.

"Why don't they just be still and feel his presence instead of begging for trinkets." I protest silently. Since my meditation has been rudely interrupted, I read some Tagore to try to recreate my mood. I find the following prose poem:

> Where dost thou stand behind them all, my lover, hiding thyself in the shadows? They push thee and pass thee by on the dusty road, taking thee for naught. I wait here weary hours spreading my offerings for thee, while passers-by come and take my flowers, one by one, and my basket is nearly empty.
>
> The morning time is past, and the noon. In the shade of evening my eyes are drowsy with sleep. Men going home glance at me and smile and fill me with shame. I sit like a beggar maid, drawing my skirt over my face, and when they ask me, what it is I want, I drop my eyes and answer them not.
>
> Oh, how, indeed, could I tell them that for thee I wait, and that thou hast promised to come. How could I utter for shame that I keep for my dowry this poverty. Ah, I hug this pride in the secret of my heart.
>
> I sit on the grass and gaze upon the sky and dream of the sudden splendour of thy coming—all the lights ablaze, golden pennons flying over thy car, and they at the roadside standing agape, when they see thee come down from thy seat to raise me from the dust, and set at thy side this ragged beggar girl a-tremble with shame and pride, like a creeper in a summer breeze.
>
> But time glides on and still no sound of the wheels of thy chariot. Many a procession passes by with noise and shouts and

glamour of glory. Is it only thou who wouldst stand in the shadow silent and behind them all? And only I who would wait and weep and wear out my heart in vain longing?[14]

The aspiration and yearning in Tagore, the sense of "wear[ing] out my heart in vain longing" so accurately describes my state. I also clearly recognize as my own the "dream of the sudden splendour of thy coming." I want to dazzle them all with the light emanating from every pore in my body.

It suddenly strikes me that I am just as much a beggar as any leper in India.

I whine, "Oh, Sankaracharya, please help me get a little glimpse of the higher self. I came all this way, and I am meditating so hard."

How is my whining fundamentally different from asking for help with a tax audit or a labor dispute? I watch His Holiness. This frail little man, despite obvious exhaustion, gives the same tender blessing to everybody there, from the "diamond people," with exquisite saris and heavy jewelry, to a rickshaw driver in rags with cracked and gnarled feet. He seems to be fully aware of "the illusoriness of the individual self" and blesses us all as unique expressions of Brahman, from the most arrogant beggar to the humblest supplicant. In my shame, I recall another piece of Tagore's writing:

> I came out alone on my way to my tryst. But who is this that follows me in the silent dark?
>
> I move aside to avoid his presence but I escape him not. He makes the dust rise from the earth with his swagger; he adds his loud voice to every word that I utter.
>
> He is my own little self, my lord, he knows no shame; but I am ashamed to come to thy door in his company.[15]

Chapter Eleven

SCIENCE AND CONSCIOUSNESS

I have finally thrown it over, all of it. Even as late as high school, I had loved being a Catholic and appreciated how important it was in developing my inner life. Now I can no longer tolerate all that senseless dogma. After long sessions of theological questioning with the priests running the Newman Club at Dartmouth College, I always leave unsatisfied. Their explanations seem so contrived, so unreasonable, so far from the style of explanation I have learned to appreciate in science. On top of all that, my body leads me into one mortal sin after another. My gaze lingers just long enough on a beautiful woman to generate a delicious sexual fantasy and the consequent mortal sin and eternal damnation in the fires of hell. Absurd! Better to throw the whole mess overboard. Now I will concentrate on science and on trying to leave this planet a little better than I found it. Nevertheless, I still miss Catholicism a little, and the old voices occasionally echo in my head.

Tonight I am working late again. The classroom I am using for my office this summer gets so quiet after dark. Then I can get some serious work done. It is a warm August night, the windows are all open, and all I can hear is crickets. Next month my first-year graduate courses toward my master of science degree at Dartmouth will start, and I'll have to divide my time between research and coursework. I have never been so intent, so concentrated, in my life as in the last few months. I am very close to cracking this research problem wide open and excitement keeps bubbling up to the point of distraction.

I am calculating the complete radiation spectrum for a charged particle of arbitrary velocity moving in a plasma (an ionized gas) with an embedded magnetic field. The magnetic field causes any charged particle to spiral or corkscrew down the field lines. The spiraling causes the particle to radiate electromagnetic energy in a complex pattern. Because this phenomenon occurs often, my research problem is of real interest for physics and astrophysics. The Noble Prize–winning physicist Julian Schwinger solved the problem of a particle of arbitrary velocity spiraling down a magnetic field in a vacuum decades earlier. However, the presence of the plasma is a significant complication. Unlike the vacuum, the properties of the plasma itself depend on both the angle of propagation of the particle's radiation with respect to the magnetic field and the frequency of the radiation. This is a serious piece of theoretical physics, and the mathematics is straining me. Earlier in the summer, I had to take a little detour to learn some sophisticated mathematical techniques. It is all exquisitely beautiful stuff, and now it is clear I can make the calculation without any significant approximations. A couple of days ago, I started over from the very beginning to calculate it all again, without looking at my previous efforts, to see whether I could duplicate my earlier results.

My excitement is causing me to make the silliest mathematical mistakes, so I have to back up a couple of steps and do the latest piece again. The crickets seem to be mocking me. One more monster manipulation and I'll be done. I am sweating and my hands are shaking as I get my earlier calculations to see if they match tonight's results. Yes! There is no doubt I have done it! Weeks ago I showed I could simplify my results and get Schwinger's formulas for the vacuum case. I also showed that I could keep the plasma in the problem but restrict the particle to moving in a straight line and get the Cherenkov formulas developed a decade earlier. All these checks give me confidence in my results. What a great relief!

I move to the window to bathe myself in the cool breeze and listen to the crickets. They seem much friendlier now. I am a bit giddy. What a lovely piece of physics! I have moved into completely unoccupied territory. None of those guys who wrote those painfully difficult papers in plasma physics knows this result. Nobody in the world but me knows this result! I can't wait to tell my graduate advisor. He is a lovely guy, but he gave me almost no help. That made it tougher, but now that I am here, it is all the sweeter.

Suddenly, my giddiness is tempered as I realize how laborious it will be to evaluate these results using a computer. Yes, these formulas are all exact, but to calculate the actual power output for radiation at a given frequency in a given direction, I will have to write a program to evaluate these hairy formulas for particular values of particle velocity, plasma density, and magnetic field strength. "But hey, I just did the hard part," I tell myself. "The computer part won't be so bad."

I am full of gratitude. I want to give thanks to something above me because I could see a little farther than those guys in the journal articles. But I am confused. I cannot thank the god of arbitrary rules, the enemy of the body and its desires. I am completely burned out but too excited to sleep. I decide to walk around on this loveliest of nights.

At 4:30 A.M., the campus is deserted. I walk downtown, although I know nothing is open. It's lonely out here. That little warm spot inside me where I carry my secret scientific knowledge makes me even lonelier. I have been working so hard that I have no social life at all. I have turned into a real physics geek. Soon it will be light. I had better get to bed.

I get up after only a few hours of sleep and decide to celebrate by taking the day off. I don't know what to do with myself. There aren't many people on campus during the summer. What few friends I have are busy, so I go for a long walk along the wooded shores of the Connecticut River. I lie down on a dense bed of pine needles and gaze up through the trees. I start thinking about how I will write up my results for a physics journal. It will be great to see my name "in lights." Should I put my middle initial in my name in the journal article?

In the middle of these pleasant musings, I start to feel a little hollow, confused, and maybe even a bit depressed. I can't figure out why, or what is going on. I guess after any big effort some depression or letdown is natural. When women give birth, they often get depressed, despite the joyous nature of the event. Maybe I'm having my own form of that reaction. Whatever it is, I can't identify it or shake it for the rest of the week. I guess my burnout is worse than I thought.

Over the next couple of days, I do a little mathematical mopping up and then take off for a hiking trip of several days in the Mount Washington area of the White Mountains. The weather is ideal, and I am pleasantly surprised to find that I am not as badly out of shape as I feared. Things become clearer in the cold winds above timberline. There is no doubt that I still love science and will continue working in it, but I realize that my little discovery really has nothing to do with me, with or without my middle initial. Yes, my writing style will be noticeable in the article in the *Astrophysical Journal*, but so what? You start with well-known laws of physics, manipulate them in a certain way, and after a bunch of mathematical effort, out comes the result. It is totally impersonal, even mechanical. Any decent theoretical physicist, once pointed in the right direction, could persist and work it out. It has nothing to do with me and who I am. Sure, not everybody can do such work. Yes, some steps required creativity or at least cleverness. There were moments of real beauty and satisfaction when I saw how all the complex pieces fit together in one lovely final result. Despite these real fulfillments, the very impersonality of the work proves that it has nothing to do with who I really am.

My conclusion on Mount Washington is as true for the big guys like Einstein, Schrödinger, Bohr, and all their friends as it is for me. Yes, their work was truly magnificent, orders of magnitude more profound and beautiful than my little work. Nevertheless, somebody else would have eventually worked it out. Einstein was a genius lone wolf, but somebody else would have eventually worked out relativity.

One of the great strengths of science is its impersonality. Science does not depend upon who does the work, on their philosophical, religious, or psychological beliefs. It is truly universal. This impersonality makes science a much more potent force for changing, even destroying, of cultures than the old colonialist beliefs in manifest destiny and all its misguided ideas. I am not saying that there are no philosophical presuppositions in science. There certainly are, but they are not personal.

But where does the individual, the unique person, fit into this scientific picture? As discussed in chapter 5, Einstein found that contemplating this impersonality of science liberated him from "an existence dominated by wishes, hopes, and personal feelings." However, the impersonality of science leaves no room for the divisible or finite aspects of soul. I did not understand this limitation while doing my first significant piece of scientific research. Now I understand that the confusion and melancholy I felt then had its roots in the incompleteness of the scientific picture. The Catholics told me I had a soul, but they only confused me when they tried to talk about it. Did I unconsciously expect science to replace Catholicism? Maybe reality is nothing more than impersonal laws of physics. You work hard, accomplish a few things that you like, suffer from one problem or another, and die. That is all there is to it. The universe just grinds blindly along. It is all just as impersonal as Fourier transforms, Maxwell's equations, infinite sums of Bessel functions, integrations in the complex plane, and the rest of the formalism in my calculation. But there must be more.

I recall that when I was a kid, I had this weird little belief that somewhere there was somebody exactly like me doing exactly the same thing I was doing at the time. This thought would pop into my mind frequently as I looked into the mirror brushing my hair. "Right now there is somebody exactly like me who is brushing his hair." Science has no principle that connects the guy who fell in love with physics with that kid brushing his hair, or with the crabby old man I might become, who bitches endlessly about his aches and pains. None of the cells in my body will persist from hair-brushing kid to crabby old man, yet some consciousness in me, some subjective light of awareness, has no doubt that those different piles of atoms and molecules house the same person.

Science has disinfected its temples of subjectivity in all its forms. That purging has made it powerful and vital. But the disinfected temples can now be occupied by computers; they no longer require flesh-and-blood people with hopes and fears, aspirations and disappointments, triumphs and defeats, and all those little details that define us as unique individuals. Yet, I believe we are more than just those piles of little details, just as we are more than piles of atoms.

My first joyous piece of original research occurred in that summer between my undergraduate and graduate years. That was also the first time I realized how lopsided and incomplete science is, how great a virtue and vice it was to remove subjectivity and consciousness from the scientific picture.

CONSCIOUSNESS AND A FINAL THEORY OF EVERYTHING

Some of the most fundamental physics research occurring today is the attempt to unify the theory of the four forces of nature into one compact set of equations. The goal is a fundamental theory that unifies at a deep level gravity, electromagnetism, the weak nuclear force, and the strong nuclear force. Such a theory would admit of no explanations in terms of deeper principles. For example, Newton understood why the apocryphal apple fell at 9.8 meters per second squared, but Einstein understood the same event through the more profound view that gravity is an expression of the curvature of four-dimensional spacetime due to the distribution of matter. In a final "theory of everything," as it is called, there would be no deeper theory; no latter-day Einstein would come along and explain a falling apple at a deeper or more fundamental level than that offered by the theory of everything. In addition, the theory of everything would contain explanatory principles for all physical phenomena, from the earliest particle formations in the big bang to the way a seed falls from a bird feeder.

It is neither my task nor expertise to explore the possibility and structure of such unification attempts. For that, we can turn to books such as Steven Weinberg's *Dreams of a Final Theory: The Scientist's Search for the Ultimate Laws of Nature*.[1] However, nature includes humans, and therefore the final theory must come to grips with the mystery of consciousness. As Weinberg says, "Of all the areas of experience that we try to link to the principles of physics by arrows of explanation, it is consciousness that presents us with the greatest difficulty."[2] He then goes on to discuss the objective correlates of consciousness. For example, when I experience pleasure or pain, there are neural correlates of my experience. Weinberg hopes that a sufficiently deep understanding of these correlates to consciousness will eventually lead to an understanding of consciousness itself in terms of the underlying laws of physics.

There is a fundamental flaw in this kind of analysis. As I have stressed in earlier chapters, and as Weinberg too stresses,[3] science has an objective orientation. This objective approach to consciousness is doomed, because consciousness can never be turned into an object like a quark or a flower. In other words, consciousness, by its very nature, cannot be objectified and thus cannot be fully encompassed by a strictly objective science.

Since this is such a fundamental point, so often obscured in the current literature, it is worth more careful consideration. As I write this, red roses are blooming next to my house. When I smell the rose, the consciousness that knows the smell is not directly given in the experience. Just as my visual perception of the rose does not reveal the physical eye that sees the rose, knowledge of an object does not reveal the true knower. The delightful smell and all the memories and associations that flow from it do not directly reveal that principle which knows the experience.

Now it is true that there are neural correlates of my experience of the rose. Such a simple act as smelling a rose is accompanied by an exceedingly complex set of occurrences in the brain. Of course, in the actual experience, I am not conscious of these brain processes as they would be studied by science, for example, exchanges of neurotransmitters in the olfactory region of my brain. Even if I later became fully informed of all the exquisitely complex processes that occurred in my body, that knowledge is not the smell of the rose as experienced. Every conscious experience, no matter how simple or complex, always has a subjective component that can never be captured in any objective analysis. For a simple image, let us return to the rose. If my eyes are free of cataracts and other defects, when I look out at the world, I see the red roses swaying in the breeze. What I *don't* see is my eye. The structure of my eye deeply conditions both what is seen and how it is seen; nevertheless, I don't see my eye. Analogously, my experience of seeing or smelling the rose does not explicitly contain that which delivers the experience—consciousness.

Therefore, point one is that *consciousness is never an object of knowledge, never known in an objective manner like other items of our experience.* For this reason, we can only experience the deeper consciousness at the core of our being through some meditation discipline that shuts down the thoughts that reflect consciousness. We must know consciousness itself by becoming it—knowledge through identity—not through objectification as in science and normal experience.

Notice that right in the midst of the experience of the rose, I am aware of having the experience. There is no need for a second experience telling me I saw a rose. The very nature of consciousness is such that, despite it never being an object of knowledge, it always makes us aware of its functioning right in the experience. In other words, conscious experience always entails the knowledge that it is occurring, right at the time of the experience. Therefore, the second critical point about consciousness is that *in the very act of knowing, we are aware that we are knowing.* In summary, *consciousness is never an object of knowledge, yet it is intrinsically self-knowing or self-illuminating.* This statement is just as true for a sublime meditation experience as it is for stubbing a toe on a piece of furniture.

Therefore, we must make a clear distinction between consciousness and the neural correlates of consciousness. Science can study the neural correlates and associated brain processes, certainly, but not consciousness per se. Philosopher David Chalmers also makes this distinction, although he arrives at it differently. According to Chalmers, this distinction gives rise to what he calls the easy and hard problems.[4] The easy problems include all the neural correlates of consciousness and the various kinds of associated brain processing, such as retrieving a memory or acting based on knowledge. These easy problems, which are actually extremely difficult, are only "easy" in relationship to the hard problem. The hard problem is understanding consciousness per se, which, Chalmers argues, today's science cannot do. He proposes to include conscious experience as a new and fundamental input to the ontology of science. I don't agree with everything Chalmers says. However, I do appreciate that a philosopher of his stature in consciousness studies clearly expresses how present-day science cannot directly deal with consciousness. He also explicitly says that consciousness cannot be a trivial add-on to science. Including it as a fundamental input will be a revolutionary change.

Along with its objective mode, as I stressed in chapter 9, modern science is thoroughly materialistic. It assumes that insentient matter is acted on by forces external to it, thereby generating the rich phenomena of our universe. Given this view, subjectively grounded and self-knowing consciousness would surely be a radical addition to the ontology of science. At this stage, nobody can predict how such an augmented science might look.

We can, however, ask how likely it is that such a radical augmentation might occur. With all due respect to Chalmers, in the history of physics there has never been a major change brought about by the urging of some philosopher or group of philosophers. As Weinberg says, "I know of *no one* who has participated actively in the advance of physics in the postwar period whose research has been significantly helped by the work of philosophers" [Weinberg's italics].[5] Given this and the disinterest, even disdain, physicists generally show for philosophy, it is very unlikely that such a radical change would result from the suggestions of philosophers. Physics always requires an internal earthquake to change. For example, a deep inconsistency between Maxwell's equations for electromagnetism and Newton's laws of mechanics, the two pillars of classical physics, drove Einstein to the discovery of special relativity. Quantum mechanics was born from numerous observations of atomic spectra that made no sense in terms of classical physics. Are there comparable pressures within today's physics?

Today the pressures are neither as great nor as obvious as in the two great revolutions just mentioned. Nevertheless, I will briefly discuss three major problems or pressures that might converge to require such a drastic step as adding consciousness to the foundational principles of physics. First, there is the drive for a theory of everything or grand unification scheme, mentioned briefly above. There can be no satisfactory theory of everything that omits consciousness. If you believe the argument that present-day physics cannot deal with consciousness, then the drive for a unifying theory must eventually lead to incorporating consciousness into physics at the deepest possible level. This pressure for such inclusion comes from within physics, through its inherent drive to comprehend greater and greater aspects of the universe, but there is added pressure from the new, multidisciplinary field of consciousness studies. That burgeoning field of physicists, philosophers, neurobiologists, cognitive scientists, and computer scientists draws inspiration from physics, but they are not waiting for a grand unification or theory of everything. They are pressing ahead to find a fundamental explanation for consciousness and thereby adding to the pressure from within physics. For the other two pressures that might be driving physics to include consciousness at a foundational level, I turn to two highly dissimilar topics: first, a thorny problem in physics known as the collapse of the wave function; and second, parapsychology.

THE COLLAPSE OF THE WAVE FUNCTION

Any group of physicists concerned with the foundations of physics would put the collapse of the wave function near the top of their list of outstanding problems. I will first state the problem generally and then give a simple example of it.

Every quantum system has a wave function, a mathematical entity that specifies the probabilities for any future measurements. The wave function is not a physical wave like a sound wave, electromagnetic wave, or the waves in your coffee cup. It is a set of "probability amplitudes" that propagate like those physical waves, but in abstract spaces of any number of dimensions, not just the three-dimensional space of our normal experience. According to quantum theory, while the system is undisturbed by external interactions and unmeasured, the wave function evolves completely deterministically, just like any wave in Newtonian physics. In other words, given the initial state of the wave function and the potentials (or forces) governing its evolution, quantum theory says that the wave function evolves in a completely predictable (causal or deterministic) way. However, upon measurement, which involves some disturbance of the system, one of the possible outcomes is actualized as the measured event. The statistical aspect of quantum theory arises right at this point of measurement. There is no way of predicting, in principle, which of the possibilities is actualized, nor exactly how it gets actualized. The wave function only gives probabilities for the results of measurement; no aspect of quantum theory explains *why* a particular outcome occurs or *how* it comes into spacetime. Most physicists consider this a serious missing piece, and many have labored hard to Resolve the problem. Despite all the effort, there is no generally agreed-upon solution. To illustrate the problem more concretely, consider the following example.

Rather than give an example from the microscopic domain where quantum theory reigns, let me modify a thought experiment first given by the great physicist Erwin Schrödinger[6] in 1935. (Thought experiments are not actually carried out but are imaginary experiments devised to illustrate a certain point.) This is the famous "Schrödinger's cat" example, which has been the source of endless discussion both at a technical and a popular level. It has been used in ways Schrödinger never intended! I'll use it to discuss the collapse of the wave function.

In Schrödinger's thought experiment, a cat is placed in a box containing a radioactive sample of material. Once prepared and closed, the box and anything that goes on inside it are entirely isolated from the outside world. When the radioactive sample decays, an apparatus inside the box senses the change and kills the cat. The question is this: what is the state of the cat before we look into the box to see whether the cat is alive? Since the introduction of a living system brings in unnecessary complications, I will simplify the apparatus.

In my version of the experiment, we have a box containing a radioactive sample and an apparatus that turns on a light when the sample decays. When closed, this box and its contents are entirely isolated from the rest of the world, so we cannot know if the light is on unless we open the box. The radioactive material has the property that it has a probability of one-half of decaying in one hour. This means that if you had a million identical boxes with identical radioactive samples and opened them all after one hour, half of them would have the light on, indicating the decay had occurred.

QUESTION 1: WHAT IS THE STATE OF THE LIGHT BEFORE MEASUREMENT? Since the box and its contents are completely isolated from the rest of the universe, we have no way of getting information about the state of the light other than opening the box and taking a measurement. Quantum theory clearly says that before the box is opened, the light is in an indefinite state—a "superposition" of both on and off. But what is meant by superposition here?

In classical physics, waves of all kinds, from sound to electromagnetic to water waves, superpose. That is, their amplitudes (heights) add according to their phase relationships (relative positions of troughs). For example, consider two surface water waves of the same amplitude that are out of phase by 180 degrees (that is, the peak of one occurs at exactly the same time and place as the trough of the other). When these two waves flow together, then the displacement of the water will be zero. While if two waves of the same amplitude arrive at the same place, at the same time, but are in phase, then the displacement of the water is twice that of one wave alone. Other phase relationships between the superposing waves give intermediate results between these two extremes. We can readily observe these superposition phenomena at the beach or in the kitchen sink. They are well understood in classical physics.

In quantum mechanics, the superposition takes the same mathematical form as in classical physics, but there is a major difference. In quantum mechanics, the waves superposing represent probability amplitudes, not physical waves. So although quantum mechanics is often called wave mechanics, as I stated earlier the waves are not physical processes in space and time, as in classical physics, but are probability amplitudes. These amplitudes represent potentials for events, not the events themselves. They are thus not entities in space and time. Returning to our thought experiment, before we open the box, the light is in a superposition of the possibilities of on and off. This superposition of possibilities refers to the likelihood of the light being on or off when measured, but not to a definite state of the light. Quantum superpositions do not correspond to well-defined states of the system and are never directly observed. However, we can easily measure the effects of superposition in a wide variety of experiments. Unfortunately, quantum superposition, despite being an indispensable feature of quantum mechanics, has no classical or macroscopic analogue. It is a prime example of the many situations in quantum mechanics where we understand and can use the mathematics but we have little understanding of its conceptual significance.

Although the probability of the light in the box being on increases with time, as the decay becomes more likely, prior to a conclusive measurement the light is in an indefinite superposition of on and off. (Note that this does not mean the light is on, but dim.) Most people would assume that before opening the box there is a definite state of the light. Only our ignorance forces probability statements on us. For example, imagine that I leave my office and cannot remember whether I turned off the light. I judge that it is equally likely that the light is off as on. In other words, there is a probability of one-half that the light is on. Here probability is an expression of my ignorance, but the state of the light in my office is well defined: it is either on or off. However, for quantum systems this is emphatically not the case. Before measurement, the box is in an indefinite state in which the possibilities of light on and light off superpose and change over time, evolving deterministically according to the Schrödinger equation. In summary, *systems isolated from measurements can be in a superposition of several possible outcomes that evolves deterministically until measurement occurs.*

This is strange, since we never see anything like a quantum superposition. Lights are either on or off. Cats are either alive or dead. The closest I can come to an example of a superposition is in psychology. Imagine that you have two possibilities and are completely deadlocked on a course of action. Both options or possibilities are alive in you. In some sense they interact and evolve and eventually, either through some outer or inner development, you make a choice. The shortcoming with this example is that the course of action you actually take can gradually develop, whereas in physics a measurement forces an instantaneous change from many possibilities to one actuality.

You might also ask what is actually meant by measurement. The answer is that a measurement involves an irreversible change in our knowledge of the system. Irreversible in this context means that the chance of reverting to the previous state is effectively zero. As an example of an irreversible process, consider pouring milk into coffee. The mixture quickly becomes homogeneous at one temperature. It is energetically possible for the milk to separate itself into one small region of the cup with pure coffee in the remaining part, but such an event is exceedingly unlikely. We thus say that pouring milk into coffee is an irreversible process, just like a quantum measurement.

As strange as superpositions are, our real task lies ahead.

QUESTION 2: WHAT OCCURS IN THE MEASUREMENT PROCESS? Just before the box is opened, the wave function, with its probabilities for light on and light off, evolves deterministically according to the Schrödinger's equation. Upon the box being opened, the wave function instantly collapses to one possibility—the actual measured event. Quantum theory has nothing to say about why one possibility is realized rather than another and this is where the statistical nature of quantum mechanics enters the picture. Even worse, quantum theory tells us absolutely nothing about what actually brings about the transformation from many possibilities to one actuality. In other words, there are no principles within quantum theory that help us understand how the instantaneous collapse, the transition from many possibilities to one actuality, takes place. We have well-defined procedures for predicting outcomes of possible measurements, but this vexing lacuna in quantum theory has been with us for seven decades.

DOES CONSCIOUSNESS COLLAPSE THE WAVE FUNCTION?

There have been many attempts at understanding the collapse more fully, but no single approach is generally agreed upon. Despite this uncertainty, it is worth discussing a suggestion that consciousness collapses the wave function, an idea that has persisted for more than sixty years in the work of several prominent physicists.[7] A small, respected minority of physicists hold this view. For many others, introducing consciousness into physics is as offensive as uniting church and state in the United States. To appreciate the motivation for including consciousness in the measurement process, we need to go a little more deeply into the heart of quantum measurement.

When we open a box and take a photograph of it, quantum theory tells us that as soon as the photographic film is exposed, but not yet developed, the new wave function for the system is an even larger superposition. Now in addition to the two possible states of the light, there must be new terms for the possibility that each grain of silver halide in the film is exposed. Simply exposing the film does not lead to a collapse, but to a more complex superposition of possibilities. Now extend the system to include the sensory functions and brain of the physicist looking at the picture. Then we get an even more complex superposition. Now there are terms for the quantum states for the light being on and off, the grains exposed or not, and the innumerable quantum states of the senses and brain. Nowhere has a collapse occurred.

Quantum theory works something like this. Imagine Jane, the CEO of Quantum Mechanics Inc., is in a state of uncertainty about a company policy, represented by a superposition of two different possible policies. Jane's superposition state includes these two possible policies and all the different states of her brain and body that go along with each of the policies. One vice president, Bill, tries to find out from Jane what the company policy is. He finds that his contact with Jane puts him into a complex superposition that includes both his own possible states and Jane's. Then along comes another vice president,

Henry, who wants to find out what the company policy is, only to find that he is put into an even more complex superposition that includes the possible states of Jane, Bill, and his own. In short, superposition is highly infectious and becomes progressively more complex upon each interaction with another system.

There are various ways, none of them entirely satisfactory, to break this infinite regress. The way under consideration here is to say that the consciousness of the physicist enters and triggers a collapse to a definite state. In other words, the intervention of consciousness brings about the transition from many superposed possibilities to the measured event.

There are several weaknesses in this suggestion, perhaps none of them catastrophic, but worth mentioning here. First, it is completely ad hoc. Consciousness is invoked as a means of breaking the infinite regress of ever-larger superpositions. There is no explanation nor reasoning for why it should enter here, except something unusual is needed. Second, no explanation is given for exactly how the collapse is brought about by the introduction of consciousness. In fact, consciousness plays a very peculiar role in this suggestion, unlike anything in physics. It acts on the quantum system to bring about the collapse but is not in turn acted upon by the quantum system. Third, with consciousness acting like a magic wand breaking the infinite regress of increasingly large superpositions, no explanation of consciousness comes out of this theory. In other words, consciousness is invoked to bring about the collapse, but a theory or explanation for consciousness does not come out of the model.

To my knowledge, something that has never been pointed out before is that the type of consciousness required by this theory is very special. Imagine that the consciousness responsible for the collapse has some sort of structure that can be objectified, that is turned into an item for scientific investigation. For example, your mind is happy, sad, agitated, confused, prejudiced, full of physics knowledge, and so on. These structures can be represented as a quantum state and thus must be part of the infinite regress predicted by quantum theory. This is a critical point, worth repeating. Any structure of consciousness that can be objectified is part of the wave function. This statement implies that the consciousness that ultimately collapses the wave function would have to be completely undifferentiated and unobjectifiable. This consciousness would also need to be self-knowing: there is no room to bring in another collapse process to find out whether you are aware of knowing that the light is on or off. In short, the very structure of the suggestion that consciousness collapses the wave function implies that consciousness would have to be unobjectifiable and self-illuminating.

To make this point about the nature of the consciousness required, let me introduce a little thought experiment. Imagine that you want to introspect directly into the nature of consciousness. This, of course, is not a scientific experiment, since personal introspection does not generate the public data required by science. Following the advice of any number of well-established traditions, you sit down and meditate on consciousness. Your first reaction will most likely be one of physical discomfort. Are those aches and pains consciousness? Clearly, they are known within consciousness, but are not consciousness per se. (They could be part of the wave function describing your state.) The same is true of the thoughts and feelings that spontaneously come into your mind. Those contents are illuminated or known by consciousness, but are not consciousness itself. (In other words, those contents are part of the superposition that characterizes your present state and not the consciousness that collapses the superposition.)

If you persist at this difficult meditation, you will find that you cannot look for consciousness as you would look for a black cat in a dark closet. Consciousness is not findable in this objective mode. It can never be an object of knowledge, which would require another consciousness as the knower, ad infinitum. This conclusion also implies that consciousness is self-knowing. You don't need another principle to become aware that you know. In this way, we learn that consciousness is ultimately undifferentiated, unobjectifiable, and self-knowing—just as it would have to be to collapse the wave function. Unfortunately, like many thought experiments, it is easier to do it intellectually than as a living experience of the nature of consciousness. However, if your meditation achieved knowledge of the unobjectifiable and self-knowing consciousness, it would be knowledge by identity—you becoming consciousness. Such experience is entirely outside the realm of objective scientific knowledge.

For the reasons discussed above, I don't believe that the idea that consciousness collapses the wave function is correct. It may be a step in the right direction, but the form sketched above seems unlikely to be the final one. There are too many fundamental difficulties with the theory and it is too much of an emergency "add-on," rather than fully integrated into physics.

The drive for a genuine theory of everything, along with the need to understand the collapse of the wave function, might actually force physics to include consciousness at a primordial level. Given the nature of consciousness, such a physical theory would have to encompass purely subjective phenomena, such as our most interior mental states. This step would certainly be a radical departure from the present state of science, but it will be necessary for achieving an encompassing theory of truly everything. Next, I turn to a field on the edge of physics that also encourages science to include consciousness: parapsychology.

MECHANICAL MICE AND ANOMALOUS PHENOMENA IN THE IVY LEAGUE

"Come here, you little critter! Damn it! Come here!" I am trying very hard and very unsuccessfully to get this little mechanical mouse moving around randomly in the middle of a table to come in my direction. After my effort, my wife, Elaine, tries to get the mouse to come to her. She has a very different strategy. "Come, little mouse. I'll give you some cheese. You little sweetie, come to me." That silly mouse is actually moving in her direction.

This mechanical mouse moves in equal-sized steps in a random direction on the surface of the table. Because each new direction is independent of the previous direction, there is no preferred direction of motion. We only know statistically that the average distance traveled from the starting point, irrespective of direction, equals the step length times the square root of the number of steps. This same "random walk," as it's called, describes the diffusion of photons from the center of the stars to their atmosphere and many similar processes. If it can be shown that human intention, whether threats or enticements, can statistically affect the direction of the mouse's movement, that result would be a documented case of mind over matter—telekinesis. Most of us have tried mentally to influence material events, whether a spinning roulette wheel or a sporting match, but the credibility of such phenomena would be greatly enhanced if they could be demonstrated under controlled laboratory conditions.

This mouse is a very small part of a large study at the Princeton Engineering Anomalies Research Laboratory (PEAR Lab). Rather than rely on spontaneous cases of parapsychological phenomena, they are employing all the methods of modern science to see whether such phenomena can be reproduced in rigorously controlled laboratory settings. Specifically, they are testing to see whether conscious intention can influence the generation of random numbers. For two decades, they have been carefully measuring the ability of untrained subjects willfully to bias the behavior of a variety of mechanical and electronic devices to conform to prestated intentions. In calibration tests these machines all produce strictly random outputs of zeroes and ones so that on average there are equal numbers of both. In a typical run, the operator sits in a comfortable setting in front of a random number generator and tries to make the machine generate more ones than zeros. This might be followed by a run with no intended bias, followed by another to generate more zeroes than ones, and so on.

No instructions are given as to how to affect the random number generator. Each operator brings their own style to the experiment, ranging from white-knuckled effort to a relaxed attitude of trying to get into "resonance" with the machine. A computer records the subject's intention and the numbers generated. Thousands of such experiments, involving many millions of trials, have been performed by more than a hundred operators, who usually have several sessions.

The observed biasing effects are small, a few parts in ten thousand, but they are statistically significant and operator-specific in their details. As one of the most recent reports from PEAR says, "Over the total database, the composite anomaly is unlikely by chance to less than one part in a trillion (10^{12})."[8] The effects of given operators on widely different machines tend to be similar in character and scale. In fact, examination of the details of the cumulative database shows that each operator has a particular "signature" or style in his or her ability to affect the random number generator. The operators can be located thousands of miles from the laboratory without any significant change in the details of the effect. Even more mysterious, the operators can exert their efforts as much as 73 hours before or 336 hours after the actual operation of the devices and still demonstrate the effect in detail.[9] For example, the researchers generate a large set of random numbers and carefully hide them from any observation. Then up to 336 hours after generating the numbers, the subject states her intentions. Comparing her intentions to the random numbers shows the same level of correlation as found in the more conventional version of the experiment. I find this result mind-boggling, but having read much of their research, spent a good deal of time with the PEAR staff, and visited their lab, I am confident it is real. This insensitivity to time sequence rules out any causal view of the relationship between the intention and the effect. Especially because these results are so anomalous by current scientific understanding, these experiments and the handling of the data are subject to careful scrutiny by skeptical outside observers. These extraordinary results are matched by equally astonishing data from *ganzfeld* experiments done at Cornell University.

The term *ganzfeld*, or "total field," describes the conditions under which standardized experiments test the ability of subjects to receive images from a distant sender—telepathy. The receiver wears headphones playing white noise. Halves of Ping-Pong balls are taped on the receiver's eyes and illuminated by red light. The resulting uniform auditory and visual experience gives a total undifferentiated perceptual field, or ganzfeld, believed to lower resistance to alien imagery. The working hypothesis is that anomalous perceptions, such as telepathy, are "weak signals" that easily go unnoticed in normal consciousness. The hope is that minimizing normal perceptions allows for easier access to telepathic knowledge. After the receiver undergoes a series of relaxation exercises, the isolated sender views a randomly chosen video clip from a randomly chosen group of four clips.

The isolated receiver's verbal reports are recorded and then the best match between these reports and the actual video clip shown is determined after the showing. In modern versions of the experiment, the receivers judge which of the four video clips matched their internal imagery, while in earlier efforts the experimenter decided which clip best fit the verbal reports of the receiver. The success rate according to blind chance is one-fourth. A variety of labs consistently find a rate of one-third for unselected subjects, and for gifted subjects the success rate can be over one-half.

Before the review article by Daryl Bem and Charles Honorton[10] in 1994 of the ganzfeld experiments, no mainstream academic psychology journal had ever published a major article about parapsychology. This is a significant phenomena itself and shows what an unwelcome guest parapsychology is and what a significant achievement it is that Bem and Honorton published their review article in the prestigious *Psychological Bulletin*.

In the last two decades, such experiments have benefited from skeptics' critiques of experimental protocols, data handling, and analysis. The result has been even more rigorous experiments. For example, in modern experiments, a computer does the random selecting and they are known as *autoganzfeld* tests. Tightening of the experimental protocols does not diminish the effect. These modern experiments, such as those done at Cornell University, where Daryl Bem is a faculty member, are done with great care. Bem and Honorton report:

The receiver's and sender's rooms were sound-isolated, electrically shielded chambers with single-door access that could be continuously monitored by the experimenter. There was two-way intercom communications between the experimenter and the receiver but only one-way communication into the sender's room; thus neither the experimenter nor the receiver could monitor events inside the sender's room. The archival record for each session includes an audiotape containing the receiver's mentation during the *ganzfeld* period and all verbal exchanges between the experimenter and the receiver throughout the experiment.

The automated *ganzfeld* protocol has been examined by several dozen parapsychologists and behavioral researchers from other fields, including well-known critics of parapsychology. Many have participated as subjects or observers. All have expressed satisfaction with the handling of security issues and controls.[11]

Although much more could be said about these autoganzfeld experiments, the essential points are the careful data collection and the statistically significant evidence for anomalous perception. The ability mentally to affect random number generators as studied at Princeton and the existence of anomalous perception as studied at Cornell are confirmed by many international laboratories performing these same experiments. For a good review of these two types of experiments, along with several others, see Dean Radin's 1997 book, *The Conscious Universe*.[12]

But how are we to evaluate the total statistical significance of data taken at different labs under different conditions? Let me clarify this question by considering a different example. For the last couple of decades, different studies suggest that smoking causes lung cancer and other diseases. Some studies found strong correlations between smoking and disease, while others found weaker or even no correlation. How seriously should we take this data?

Modern statistics comes to the rescue with a technique called meta-analysis. By using this technique, one can evaluate the overall statistical significance of different experiments, of differing quality, by different laboratories. Therefore, when we are told that smoking strongly correlates with disease, this conclusion is not the result of one experiment, or one set of lab results, but a meta-analysis of a variety of efforts.

Applying meta-analysis to ganzfeld data collected up to early 1997, which included 2,549 sessions from European and American labs, shows an average success rate of 33.2 percent. The odds against this occurring

by chance are smaller than one part in a million billion (10^{15}).[13] A 1987
meta-analysis of 832 studies conducted by 68 different investigators
suggesting the possibility of mentally biasing random number generators produced results with odds against chance of better than a trillion
to one.[14] The data collected since then strongly confirm the reality of
the effect.

Given all this impressive statistical data, why do conventional
scientists look so skeptically, even scornfully, on parapsychological
phenomena? This is a complex question, but some of their resistance is
simply built into science. There is always a good bit of healthy skepti-
cism in science toward anything controversial, especially something as
far-reaching in its implications as the phenomena just reviewed. However, that on its own hardly explains the conventional resistance. Surely
a large part of it must come from the realization, if only partly conscious, that the reality of these parapsychological phenomena seriously
challenges many of the fundamental presuppositions underlying modern science, such as those discussed in chapter 9. No scientist wants his
or her worldview turned upside down, especially if it's done by using
the tools of science. Allowing for all that, the resistance still seems
scandalous to me and many others. About the last third of *The Conscious Universe* examines this resistance to parapsychology, but no
satisfactory explanation emerges.

I had a painful firsthand experience of this resistance when I proposed a new course that included a section examining the two
parapsychological phenomena just reviewed. My generally capable and
well-meaning colleagues thought I had really gone astray. After a fair
amount of struggle back and forth, I finally got the new course ap-
proved. In the midst of the negotiations, they recommended that I
read Sagan's book *The Demon Haunted World*, a 450-page attempt to
destroy all the irrational and unscientific poisons in the minds of the
public, including some professors. Initially, I was offended that they
wanted me to read the book and return to the path of righteousness.
Only after my struggle for the course approval was over did I find the
following paragraph in Sagan's book:

> At the time of writing there are three claims in the ESP field
> which, in my opinion, deserve serious study: (1) that by
> thought alone humans can (barely) affect random number
> generators in computers; (2) that people under mild sensory
> deprivation can receive thoughts or images "projected" at them;
> and (3) that young children sometimes report the details of a

previous life, which upon checking turn out to be accurate and which they could not have known about in any other way than reincarnation.[15]

I have not shown this paragraph to those who wanted me to read the book. It seems better to let well enough alone and let the scientific studies of parapsychological phenomena guide us.

THE FUTURE OF SCIENCE AND CONSCIOUSNESS

Nobody can judge when or even whether science in general, or physics in particular, will embrace consciousness as a new element of its ontology. Certainly the pressures coming from the drive for a theory of everything, work in consciousness studies, a desire to solve the quantum measurement problem, and the quest to understand parapsychological phenomena are encouraging such a development. The history of science teaches us to avoid making too many predictions about the future form of science. Nevertheless, it is useful to ask some general question about what a science that included consciousness would look like.

What would the object of knowledge be for a physics with consciousness fully integrated into a unified structure of explanatory principles for all phenomena? Then a theory of everything would truly have as its study all phenomena on every level, both subjective and objective, including the knowing consciousness. Such a physics would include all subjective phenomena within it, and thus it could reveal what our personal contribution is to the form of knowledge. In the language from radio astronomy that I used in chapter 2 to discuss objectivity, this augmented science would allow for the possibility of knowing what I called our metaresponse function, our inevitable subjective contribution to knowledge. If we could actually know that in full, then we could discover genuine knowledge that is unconstituted by the knower—the ideal for the knowing approach to the absolute, according to Bhattacharyya (as discussed in chapter 10). However, such an approach to the absolute does not absorb or make irrelevant the willing and feeling approaches, which are still just as valid and valuable. Therefore, heroes and lovers need not fear the invasions of knowers.

At our present level of knowledge, there are rewards in just understanding more deeply both the objective phenomena studied by science and the subjective phenomena associated with consciousness. For example, if we appreciate the differences between scientific knowledge and transformative self-knowledge, then the opportunity for progress and growth in each arena improves. For example, we might more readily avoid scientism, which is the application of scientific values and methods where they don't belong. We might also avoid some of the dehumanizing sins of a strictly materialistic worldview, whether in modern medicine or foreign policy. From the other direction, seekers interested in cultivating an inner life can learn many valuable lessons in clear thinking from science. Those seekers have a special interest in the nature of consciousness. Appreciating the differences between the objective nature of science and the pivotal role of subjectivity in transformative self-knowledge sheds light on the mystery of consciousness. We may then get a better understanding of that principle which unifies the freaky kid brushing his hair with the complaining old man.

Chapter Twelve

HARMONIZING THE OPPOSITES

About five years ago, I had the following memorable dream:

> A great holy woman is coming to an Indian town where I
> am staying. There is much commotion and preparation for her
> arrival. Several of her devotees and attendants are bustling about
> with great excitement and anticipation. It is a very Indian scene.
> I am swept up in the excitement and am eager to see this great
> woman. I have never met her before, but I have a vague mental
> image of her as an older woman.
>
> A few of the close devotees or nuns with this great woman
> give me a frieze of elephants. It is approximately 18 inches on a
> side, made of heavy copper or bronze with a beautiful patina. I
> am very moved by their generous gift.
>
> I have a burning question to ask her. My wife says that I
> don't know the right protocol or how to address this great woman.
> I say, "I don't care about any of that. I will just throw myself at
> her feet and sincerely ask how I can harmonize the head and the
> heart."

The dream ended with a clear question, but, unfortunately, no
answer or experience of the holy woman. Here I'll amplify the
symbols in the dream.

It is not appropriate to be literal about the dream and assume that
it is about a real Indian holy woman. Nevertheless, just after the dream,
in an attempt to experience more fully the symbol of the holy woman,
I started thinking about those few Indian holy women of whom I had
heard. A friend gave me a catalog from which I sent off for some photographs of Anandamayi Ma, surely one of the greatest of India's modern
women saints. When I got the photograph shown in figure 46, I knew
it was a close approximation to my dream image of the holy woman.

Fig. 46. Anandamayi Ma (courtesy of Swami Bhaskarananda)

Anandamayi Ma was famous for her devotional approach to spiritual life within the Vedanta tradition and her spontaneous absorptions into the divine. However, in keeping with my desire to avoid being too literal, I am not interested in tying the dream closely to her or her doctrine. Rather, Anandamayi Ma embodies both the spiritual and physical qualities of the holy woman in my dream.

I associate the bronze frieze of elephants with my lovely experiences of temple elephants in India and their prominent appearances in both my dreams and waking experiences. My wife and I were the only Westerners around when Sankaracharya died in January 1994. We, along with so many others who loved him, were crushed by his death. Reflections on the great nondual truth that he taught brought us brief periods of comfort. However, all comfort was shattered when we returned to the mutt, where everybody from the man who cared for visitors' shoes while they were in the temples to Sankaracharya's closest attendants were covered in a steady stream of tears. Out of desperation, we visited the temple elephants. Once past the sobbing mahout, we found comfort among those enormous pachyderms. They too seemed sad, but an air of timeless beauty, dignity, and peace seemed to emanate from them.

One of the most popular gods in the Indian pantheon is Ganesh, the male elephant god. Because the frieze of elephants, surrounded by the feminine in the dream, is the only dream reference to the male principle (other than the dreamer), it takes on special emphasis. In Indian mythology, Ganesh was the son of the goddess Parvati, who made Ganesh out of the dirt from her own body. Parvati was preparing for the return of her husband, the great god Shiva, and asked Ganesh not to allow anyone into her bath. Ganesh, not knowing Shiva, tried to prevent him from entering, but Shiva flew into a rage and cut off the boy's head. When Parvati learned of the tragedy, she made Shiva restore the boy to life. He did so by replacing the severed head with the head of the next creature that came up the hill—an elephant. Ganesh was rewarded with the power to remove obstacles for any new undertaking. He is always propitiated at beginnings, whether of a worship of

Fig. 47. Ganesh with consort (photo by author)

other gods or the start of a day. He is also a god of wisdom, partly because he was the scribe for the Mahabharata, the poetical history of man. Ganesh is a special favorite of scholars and authors. Although I receive no answer to my question and no visit with the holy woman, I am given a gift associated with Ganesh, the god of wisdom who removes obstacles for new undertakings. In light of my question in the dream, I find Ganesh's unusual head problems particularly apt.

The photograph in figure 47 shows a statue I have of Ganesh. This one is different from the usual representations of Ganesh because his appearance with a consort and his pose have a decidedly Tantric flavor. The appearance of Ganesh with a female consort seems appropriate for the present dream discussion.

Another significant element of the dream is that I determined to throw myself at the holy woman's feet. The feet of gurus have a special significance for Indian devotees of all types, from the simplest *bhakti* or devotional person to the most sophisticated *jani* or philosophically oriented practitioner. For example, Adi Sankara wrote "Eight Stanzas in Praise of the Guru." Here are the first three stanzas, which illustrate the reverence toward the guru's feet:

> Though your body be comely and ever remain in perfect health,
> Though your name be unsullied, and mountain high your
>   hoarded gold,
> Yet if the mind be not absorbed in the guru's lotus feet,
> What will it all avail you? What, indeed will it all avail?

> Even if fortune bless you with riches and a virtuous wife,
> With children and their children, with friendship and the joys
>   of home,
> Yet if the mind be not absorbed in the guru's lotus feet,
> What will it all avail you? What, indeed will it all avail?

Though the lore of the Vedas take up its dwelling on your tongue,
Though you be learned in scripture, gifted in writing prose and
    verse,
Yet if the mind be not absorbed in the guru's lotus feet,
What will it all avail you? What, indeed will it all avail?[1]

In my spiritual journeys to visit with Sankaracharya, I was struck by how he would take offerings, anything from fruit and flowers to silk, and always touch them to the forward top of his head. I learned from his attendants that he believed that his forehead was always symbolically in contact with his guru's feet. Thus, touching offerings to the top of his head was symbolically offering them to the feet of his guru, to his incarnation of deity. Sankaracharya's devotees also did full prostrations at his feet. In summary, prostrating at the feet of the guru is a gesture of deepest reverence, an acknowledgment of our dependence on and need for the guru, and an expression of humility. All this may seem like Indian spiritual excess, until we think of Mary Magdalene washing and anointing the feet of Christ.

I now turn to the question posed in the dream of how to harmonize the head and the heart. The "head" for me means intellectual pursuits, such as science and philosophy—the masculine realm of the Sun. It is the active, willful, and analytical approach to knowledge, whether of the external world or the world of ideas. It usually apprehends the object by separating from it, by considering it in a detached way. It is thus functionally close to what Bhattacharyya defines as knowing, as discussed in chapter 10. Despite its detachment, there can be real satisfaction and joy in using the head, and it clearly yields results. As for the "heart," it is primarily associated with spiritual, psychological, moral, and aesthetic experiences, along with what I call transformative self-knowledge. Rather than active, willful, analytical, and detached, heart knowledge is receptive, intuitive, and gained through identification with the object—the feminine realm of the Moon. Although the head and the heart may have some overlap, they are two distinct principles, and one cannot be reduced to the other.

Let me give a concrete example of head and heart within one particular discipline. Over the last couple of decades, I have made a significant effort to understand the Mahayana Buddhist principle of emptiness, that all phenomena of both the inner and outer world are totally lacking in independent or inherent existence. To follow the philosophical arguments put forward for this view and the implications of the principle of emptiness is demanding head work, some of which appears in my first book. However, the other equally great principle within Mahayana Buddhism is the doctrine of universal compassion, that my entire feeling nature and value system must be reorganized so that the welfare of all sentient beings takes priority over my native selfishness. There are a few intellectual arguments for the doctrine of universal compassion. It is primarily a matter of the heart, of developing a sufficiently deep empathy for all suffering humanity and acting on that realization. Of course, developing universal compassion is a long and arduous process. With these amplifications, let me turn to a few analytical reflections on the dream.

As an unconscious compensation, this dream impresses upon me the critical importance of harmonizing the head and the heart. The head—the masculine, solar realm of action, reason, and will, is not in harmony with the heart—the feminine, lunar realm of receptivity, intuition, and empathy. This is not a happy realization, but the dream offers some hope that I can get help from this Sophia or wise feminine within, symbolized by the holy woman in the dream. In addition, representatives of this deep feminine present me with a masculine principle (Ganesh) that has special reference to head problems and may help with a fresh beginning in thought and writing—the head realm. Finally, the dream suggests that the way to the sought-for knowledge comes not from heroic action, but from humble prostration.

May Ganesh remove obstacles in my attempt to articulate in this chapter and the next some concluding thoughts about the relationship of science to the sacred, a critical example of relating the head to the heart. Part of that gift from Ganesh may be the realization that the dream only announces the importance of the problem, but I have not been given the answer. Nevertheless, I set out on the exploration.

PSYCHOLOGICAL WAYS OF RELATING THE HEAD AND THE HEART

I suggest that there are three fundamental modes of interaction between the head and the heart: domination, separation, and harmony through creative alternation. (As I'll show in the next section, these same modes also appear in different approaches to relating science and the sacred.)

In the mode of domination, either the head or the heart tries to do everything, including the work of the other principle. On the one hand, consider an extremely unbalanced intellectual. He may be a brilliant and daring thinker and have a great facility with ideas and their manipulations, but his heart is shriveled. His feelings and his ability to relate sensitively to others, empathize, and intuit deeper meanings are all atrophied. In a pinch, he substitutes the head for the heart. For example, he may be called upon to express sympathy for a victim of some tragedy. Then he will call upon his intellect to help frame the expected feeling response. Rather than speaking directly from the heart, he will gather ideas and try to plait them together into something that resembles a heartfelt response. He might even be able to get away with such a response. More likely, his response will be a wooden attempt at passing off a cold, mechanical heart for a one that truly throbs with compassion.

On the other hand, a person with an overdeveloped heart has great sensitivity of feeling, skill with human relationships, empathy, and intuition but has difficulty thinking clearly when life demands it. This person tries to make feelings substitute for clear thinking. For example, an important business investment requires a careful analysis of its responsibilities, risks, and advantages. Our person with the big heart and little head tries to *feel* his way to a decision or employ intuition or simply be receptive to what circumstances bring. On occasion, this may work, but always being receptive, intuitive, and empathetic when will, initiative, and detached analysis are required often leads to financial disaster.

In the separation mode, rather than trying to have one function do the work of the other, life is compartmentalized into head things and heart things, with little or no connection between them. This level of separation can generate the worst difficulties and tensions. For a historical example, consider the betrayal of Christ by Judas as interpreted by Father Panikkar.[2] Judas loved Christ, had a real heart connection with him. However, he was intellectually committed to the old tradition, to the old laws. He could not sustain the compartmentalization and the resulting tension. He allowed his head to betray his heart and delivered Christ to his enemies. The offended heart then retaliated with guilt so powerful that it led him to destruction through suicide. On a societal level, it is possible to view our ecological crisis as a destructive battle between the head and the heart, between the power of our technology and our moral paralysis at being unable to use it for the benefit of all.

Finally, there is the possibility of harmony through creative alternation and even synergy between the head and the heart. The realization that the head and heart are two different functions need not lead to domination or separation; rather, this realization can initiate a creative alternation and even cross-fertilization. In the latter case we have the ideal person who can initiate action, think deeply when the situation requires, and yet relate empathetically to others, access their feelings, and intuitively respond when life demands. I'll consider the present Dalai Lama as a specific example of such a person.

Although the public may not be aware of it, in Buddhist circles he is widely appreciated for his deep philosophical grasp of Buddhism and interest in how Buddhist thought relates to modern science. His interest in dialogue between Buddhism and science resulted in several intimate meetings with scientists over the years, two of which I attended. I, along with many others, was deeply impressed with his amazing ability to grasp subtle scientific ideas and go quickly to the essence of the matter. This achievement is all the more impressive because of his lack of formal scientific training, the obvious linguistic and cultural barriers, and the enormous time and energy he spends heading the Tibetan government in exile. I also have seen him show the tenderest compassion when relating to suffering Tibetan refugees. On a more personal and less tragic level, I, along with several fellow students, happened to be in the Dalai Lama's presence when our teacher Anthony died. We received his caring consolation and support. He did not present logical arguments on impermanence or some other philosophical panacea. Instead, he responded from the heart and related directly to our loss. I have also profited from his technical discussions of the philosophical doctrine of impermanence and its moral, psychological, and spiritual implications. Thus, in the person of the Dalai Lama we see that a harmonious and creative alternation and synergy between the head and the heart is not merely a fantasy, but a realizable ideal.

PHILOSOPHICAL WAYS OF RELATING THE HEAD AND THE HEART

Now I narrow the general discussion of the head and the heart to the relationship between science and religion. Here I use the term religion rather than spirituality, since by far the greater part of the writing on this subject deals not with spirituality, as I defined the term in the Introduction, but with conventional religions. In fact, most of the writing comes from those interested in how science relates to Christianity, a natural development given that modern science grew out of a Christian culture. I again group the modes of relationship under domination, separation, and harmony through creative alternation.

When science dominates religion, we have the scientific materialist who looks at religion and its concerns as either wishful thinking or simple error. Since matter and energy are the only reality and science is the only road to truth, errors and falsehoods must be scientifically eliminated. Then the universal themes of meaning, suffering, death, and salvation (the traditional concerns of religion) are addressed within scientific materialism. Issues such as meaning and salvation are either dismissed outright or shown to be incoherent ideas unworthy of discussion. I have already mentioned the great physicist Steven Weinberg as an example of a thoroughgoing scientific materialist. He exemplifies this attitude in his famous statement, "The more the universe seems comprehensible, the more it also seems pointless"[3] and in the equally revealing statement, "The [materialist] reductionist worldview *is* chilling and impersonal. It has to be accepted as it is, not because we like it, but because that is the way the world works."[4] Other good examples can easily be found, including such distinguished scientists as Carl Sagan, Francis Crick, Edward O. Wilson, and scores of others.

Those who would have religion dominate science are also easy to find. One of the most celebrated recent instances is the vote by the Kansas Board of Education to delete any mention of evolution in the state's science curriculum. As the *New York Times* reported on Thursday, August 12, 1999:

> The Kansas Board of Education voted on Wednesday to delete virtually any mention of evolution from the state's science curriculum, in one of the most far-reaching efforts by creationists in recent years to challenge the teaching of evolution in schools.
>
> While the move does not prevent the teaching of evolution, it will not be included in the state assessment tests that evaluate students' performance in various grades, which may discourage school districts from spending time on the subject.
>
> And the decision is likely to embolden local school boards seeking either to remove evolution from their curriculums, to force teachers to raise questions about its validity or to introduce creationist ideas. Some local boards have already said they will consider adopting creationist textbooks, while others have said they will continue teaching evolution.

The *Times* then goes on to report that even references to the big bang are eliminated from the state curriculum. Where does their attempt to dominate science stop? Would the Kansas Board of Education want an astronomy teacher to avoid telling students about the evolution of stars? Or that the oldest stars in our galaxy are more than ten billion years old, an instant contradiction of the much briefer exist-

ence claimed for the universe by many creationists? Whatever the answer to these questions, it is clear that the Christian fundamentalists
on the board are attempting to dictate what the pivotal ideas should be
in biology, geology, and astronomy.

In this book, I have been trying to distinguish clearly between
the kind of knowledge that comes through science and that which
comes in spiritual experiences, what I have called transformative self-
knowledge. Appreciating the differences between science and spirituality
(the core of religion) involves honoring each, without imposing the
values and practices of one on the other. The academic study of religion and science contains a well-known tradition that presents many
arguments, different from those presented here, that seek to fully separate science and religion.[5] As I said in the Introduction, it is necessary
to differentiate (clearly distinguish, but not fully separate) science and
the sacred before attempting to bring about some harmony between
them. I do not believe we can move from harmony to the stronger
notion of integration, which encompasses them in some larger whole.
As I have tried to show, there are too many points of divergence between science and spirituality, at least in their current forms, to permit
integration. However, full separation of science and religion, two of
the most powerful forces in modern culture, is even more problematic
then a full separation of the head and the heart. In the rest of this
chapter and the next, I attempt to show how we can move from separation of science and the sacred to a relationship of creative alternation,
dialogue, and even occasional synergy.

AN EXAMPLE OF SYNERGY BETWEEN THE
HEAD AND THE HEART

For a familiar example of a creative alternation and synergy between
religion and science, we can turn to Einstein. It is well known that he
sought a harmonious relationship between religion and science or, more
exactly, between spirituality and science.[6] For example, consider his
statement in the quotation discussed at the end of chapter 3: "The
contemplation of this [natural] world beckoned like a liberation,
and I soon noticed that many a man whom I had learned to esteem
and to admire had found inner freedom and security in devoted occu-
pation with it." For Einstein the study of physics was a spiritual
discipline.

However, for a less well-known, but even more compelling, example of a creative alternation and synergy between spirituality (not

formal religion) and science, consider the life and work of the internationally famous primatologist Dr. Jane Goodall. Her work revolutionized
thinking about chimpanzees and research modes in primatology. She
paved the way for primatology to become a science dominated by
women. Her work with chimpanzees gave us a new appreciation of our
biological relatives, with whom we share ninety-nine percent of our
DNA. It also has significant implications about what it means to be
human. In her recent autobiography, *Reason for Hope: A Spiritual
Journey*,[7] Goodall reveals something of the spiritual dimensions of her
life and their relationship to her field work on the behavior of chimpanzees.

She tells us of her early and abiding interest in the natural world,
along with her avid pursuit of careful observation and analysis. These
well-known traits were the foundation for her significant work as a
scientist. These traits show that she works from both the knowing and
the feeling consciousness, to use the language of Bhattacharyya discussed in chapter 10. The knowing approach, so characteristic of science,
seeks to reveal the object as unconstituted by the knowing subject, to
apprehend the object without interference from the empirical knower.
Broadly speaking, this is knowledge through the head. In contrast, according to Bhattacharyya, the feeling approach that characterizes
mysticism seeks a fusion with the object, a knowing by identity in a
higher unity. This is close to knowledge through the heart. Goodall
combines her strong tendency to be a scientific knower with the natural mystic's ability to find knowledge through identity with the object
through feeling. For example, writing about her late teens she says:

> Clearly, at that time I was starting to feel myself a part of a
> great unifying power of some kind. Certain things caused feel-
> ings of such profound happiness that tears would come to my
> eyes—"and in my heart the pain of joy that such could be." I
> never knew when such emotions would be triggered: an espe-
> cially beautiful sunset; standing under the trees when the sun
> suddenly burst from behind a cloud and a bird sang; sitting in
> the absolute hush of some ancient cathedral. At moments such
> as those, I felt strongly that I was within some great spiritual
> power—God. And as I moved through life I would gradually learn
> how to seek strength from this Power, this source of all energy,
> to bolster my flagging spirits or my exhausted body in times of
> need.[8]

Although Goodall was brought up as a Christian, when she was
nineteen she developed an interest in Theosophy and took courses in

it. She was especially drawn to the ideas of karma and reincarnation and learned something about elementary meditation from the Theosophists.[9] Meditation does not seem to have played a central role in her life; as she says, "There was a time when I practiced often; then, in the press of life, I had lost the art."[10] However, it is clear from several references in her book that she always appreciated the importance of a quiet mind in helping us attain what she calls "true awareness."

Early in her career as a scientist, she began combining scrupulous scientific knowing with the mystic's feeling quest for unity. For example, right in the midst of her early years of solitary field work, which involved groundbreaking observations of chimpanzees in their native environment, she experienced profound states of unity with nature. Describing those early years she says:

> I became totally absorbed into this forest existence. It was an unparalleled period when aloneness was a way of life. . . . All the time I was getting closer to animals and nature, and as a result, closer to myself and more and more in tune with the spiritual power that I felt all around. For those who have experienced the joy of being alone with nature there is really little need for me to say much more; for those who have not, no words of mine can ever describe the powerful, almost mystical knowledge of beauty and eternity that come, suddenly, and all unexpected. The beauty was always there, but moments of true awareness were rare. They would come, unannounced.[11]

Combining objective scientific fieldwork (knowledge by separation from the object) with mystical experiences of unity (knowledge by fusion) may seem like trying to mix oil and water. Either you get colorful reflections off the oil floating on the obscured water or you get a slippery mayonnaise. Despite the difficulty and dangers of combining such different approaches, Goodall and the science of primatology realized some unexpected benefits from combining the head and the heart. Her natural tendencies toward mysticism led her unselfconsciously to break, or at least bend, the rules for doing objective science. For example, she writes:

> As I got to know them [the chimpanzees] as individuals I named them. I had no idea that this, according to the ethological discipline of the early 1960s, was inappropriate—I should have given them more objective numbers. I also described their vivid personalities—another sin: only humans had personalities. It was an even worse crime to attribute humanlike emotions to the chimpanzees. And in those days it was held (at least by many

scientists, philosophers, and theologians) that only humans had minds, only humans were capable of rational thought. Fortunately, I had not been to university, and I did not know these things. And when I did find out, I just thought it was silly and paid no attention. I had always named the animals in my life. Moreover, Rusty [her childhood dog] and a series of cats, and assorted guinea pigs and golden hamsters, had taught me well. They had made it abundantly clear that animals had personalities, could reason and solve problems, had minds, had emotions—I thus felt no hesitation in ascribing these qualities to the chimpanzees. How right Louis [Leaky] had been to send someone to the field with a mind uncluttered by the theory of reductionist, oversimplistic, mechanistic science.[12]

Goodall clearly was not interested in being a completely detached observer. Her mode of studying the chimpanzees was something in between objective, detached observation on one hand and mystical union on the other. She studied the chimpanzees *in relationship* to humans, not behind glass or in a cage, but as entities with names, feelings, thoughts, and intentions—in other words, with an inner life that interacted with hers. Her relational approach opened primatology to new insights and appreciations both about chimpanzees and about what it means to be human.

An experience that had the most profound effect upon her, both as a scientist and as spiritual seeker, occurred after a long period of grief at the death of her much loved second husband. She describes this healing experience at length, but here is the core of the experience: "Lost in awe at the beauty around me, I must have slipped into a state of heightened awareness. . . . It seemed to me, as I struggled afterward to recall the experience, that *self* was utterly absent: I and the chimpanzees, the earth and trees and air, seemed to merge, to become one with the spirit power of life itself."[13] The lapsing of a finite, body-based center of consciousness, what she calls "self," was a precondition to her experience of merging and knowing the object by becoming one with it in a higher unity.

Let me close my discussion of Goodall by discussing her view of the relationship between science and spirituality. As the preceding quotations show, she certainly could combine them in her work. Philosophically, she takes a pluralistic view of their relationship. As I will discuss in more detail in the next chapter, my understanding of pluralism holds that reality is diffracted into many hues ranging from different religious and spiritual views on one hand to science on the other. Moreover, these unique hues cannot be reduced to each other: science can no more encompass spirituality than red can encompass blue, or vice versa. Reflecting on her experience, Goodall describes her pluralism when she writes:

> Yes, I thought, there are many windows through which we humans, searching for meaning, can look out into the world around us. There are those carved out by Western science, their panes polished by a succession of brilliant minds. Through them we can see ever farther, ever more clearly, into areas which until recently were beyond human knowledge. Through such a scientific window, I had been taught to observe the chimpanzees. For more than twenty-five years I had sought, through careful recording and critical analysis, to piece together their complex social behavior, to understand the workings of their minds. And this had not only helped us to better understand their place in nature but also helped us to understand a little better some aspects of our own human behavior, our own place in the natural world.
>
> Yet there are other windows through which we humans can look out into the world around us, windows through which the mystics and the holy men of the East, and the founders of the great world religions, have gazed as they searched for the meaning and purpose of our life on earth, not only in the wondrous beauty of the world, but also in its darkness and ugliness. And those Masters contemplated the truths that they saw, not with their minds only but with their hearts and souls too. From those revelations came the spiritual essence of the great scriptures, the holy books, and the most beautiful mystic poems and writings. That afternoon, it had been as though an unseen hand had drawn back a curtain and, for the briefest moment, I had seen through such a window. In a flash of "outsight" I had known timelessness and quiet ecstasy, sensed a truth of which mainstream science is merely a small fraction. And I knew that the revelation would be with me for the rest of my life, imperfectly remembered yet always within. A source of strength on which I could draw when life seemed harsh or cruel or desperate.
>
> How sad that so many people seem to think that science and religion are mutually exclusive. Science has used modern technology and modern techniques to uncover so much about the formation and the development of life-forms on Planet Earth and about the solar system of which our little world is but a minute part. . . . Alas, all of these amazing discoveries have led to a belief that every wonder of the natural world and the uni-

verse—indeed, of infinity and time—can, in the end, be understood through the logic and the reasoning of a finite mind. And
so, for many, science has take the place of religion.[14]

One of the most significant aspects of Goodall's life is that her
creative synthesis of the head and the heart, of her primatology and
mysticism, issued in an immense commitment to ecological action.
She now spends all but a few weeks a year on the road, lecturing, advis-
ing, and encouraging her listeners, especially the young, on the need
for grassroots ecological action—the focus of the Goodall Institute and
especially its "Roots and Shoots" program. Nature provided her with
an extraordinary laboratory for doing science, along with a great source
of spiritual experience. Now she seeks to protect that source. I would
find it satisfying, both theoretically and aesthetically, if harmonizing
the head and the heart always resulted in a deep commitment to action based on the dictates of these two masters. Although it might be
going too far to claim this as a general principle, I find that achieving a
genuine harmony between the head and the heart frequently leads to
inspired action. Perhaps that is the greatest benefit we can realize from
persisting in this often-difficult task.

PILGRIM AND PRODIGAL

I t is June 2000, and I am on my way to visit Raimon Panikkar. He is an eminent scholar of comparative religion and philosophy who lives in retirement in a small village in the mountains of Catalonia in Spain. I made a strong inner connection with him several months earlier when I organized his program on religion and human rights at Cornell University and Wisdom's Goldenrod. Just before seeing Panikkar, I am taking a short retreat at Montserrat, Spain, the site of a famous statue of a black virgin and one of the holiest pilgrimage sites in Spain. Months ago, when Panikkar recommended this place for a spiritual retreat, he could never have known that I would be wrestling with my own version of the dark feminine.

Fig. 48. Black Madonna of Montserrat (photo by author)

In the basilica at Montserrat, pilgrims are climbing the stairs behind the main altar to see and touch the black virgin. They move slowly and quietly, many of them saying their rosary. The statue is encased in Plexiglas with a hole in it, through which the pilgrims touch the globe held by the Virgin (fig. 48). Apparently, the dark virgin needs Plexiglas to protect her from our darkness.

As a young Catholic, I had a special attraction to the Virgin Mary. We were taught that she was the approachable intercessor to God. Like many Catholics, from popes to peasants, I thus directed much of my devotion and prayer to her. However, she is always portrayed as perfect, immaculate, and free of sin. As a child, I wondered how such a pure and ethereal nature, disconnected from the earthly realm, could be the intercessor or bridge between the divine and struggling humans.

In contrast, in the East, we often find a more complete integration of the light and dark sides of the divine feminine. In the West, some writers are paying more attention to the dark feminine in Christianity. The black virgins in Poland, Switzerland, Spain, and other places, although hardly prominent, are receiving long overdue recognition through the work of these writers, who seek a more embodied and fuller expression of the feminine spirit in matter, including those aspects of the feminine that are not all light and goodness.

However, in Montserrat, my attempt to make contact with the archetypal feminine in the form of the black virgin is not going well, despite my good intentions. Perhaps the four-decade absence of the Virgin from my mind is making it too difficult to light the old flame. Yes, the piety and devotion of the other pilgrims as well as the general sanctity of the site impress me, but I remain detached, even aloof. I work my way through the line and touch the Earth held by the Virgin. However, I am disappointed with my spiritual deadness and disturbed by compulsive ruminations about a nightmare from the previous week, one that featured the dark feminine.

That disturbing dream had its roots in the fierce thunderstorms early in May 2000, which forced the cancellation of my flight to London. After much frustration and three trips to the airport, I left two days late and missed two lectures I was scheduled to give in London. When I finally arrived, my plane hit the tarmac at 6:20 A.M. and my first lecture was scheduled to begin at 10:30 A.M. that same morning. I barely had time to get to my bed-and-breakfast inn for a shower and change of clothes. I had only been able to sleep about an hour and a half during the overnight flight. I feared that I would not be able to concentrate and have the energy necessary for a good lecture.

However, the first lecture went well. The audience seemed receptive and connected to my ideas. After lunch, my fatigue crashed in on me like a pile of boulders, but I had another lecture to give in the afternoon. In desperation, I decided to energize myself and reconnect to my body by going for a run along the streets of northwest London. The weather was uncharacteristically clear and warm. The flowering trees and tulips flowed by in a river of lavish colors as I ran through the streets. Tired as I was, my focus held until the second lecture and discussion ended around 4:00 P.M. In fact, the afternoon lecture went even better than the morning one. I was exhausted but delighted. That night I had the following dream:

> An English woman in her late twenties is standing in the hall of my bed-and-breakfast inn outside the bathroom. She looks so badly hung over that I ask if she needs help. She does not answer and stumbles into the bathroom. I stick my head in the door to ask her again if she needs help. She ignores me and urinates on the floor of the bathroom. "Are you OK? Do you need help?" She ignores me and defecates on the floor. I ask, "Why don't you use the toilet?" She growls fiercely, "It's hot in here!"

I awoke with a terrible feeling. It was clear that my inner feminine nature, my anima as Jung called her, was sick, making a mess, and ill-tempered. I thought I was doing well, but this imagery exposed the state of my sick feminine nature. My happiness about being able to give a long program under such adverse conditions completely vanished, plunging me into a subdued gloom.

I moped around all that morning trying to be a tourist and enjoy the beauties of a warm, sunny, and flower-filled day in London, but I had no enthusiasm for any of it. I tried not to immediately wrap the dream in an elegant intellectual construction, to disinfect it with theoretical knowledge. I knew the images had work to do, and I didn't want to inhibit them by using my head to save my heart the pain. Instead, I just tried to contemplate the images directly, embrace them, and let them work on me, despite the unpleasantness of the process. In the afternoon, I took a long run in Regent's Park. Sweat and endorphins helped lift my gloom, but I was still subdued for the next several days. Giving autonomy to the feminine often requires a painful replacement of heroism with receptivity to that which is rejected. As Sir Gawain and King Arthur learned, this is the route to transforming ugly hags into beautiful princesses.

THE DARK FEMININE

The key to my reflections on the London dream is Jung's point about self-regulation, quoted earlier:

As a rule, the unconscious content contrasts strikingly with the conscious material, particularly when the conscious attitude tends too exclusively in a direction that would threaten the vital needs of the individual. The more one-sided his conscious attitude is, and the further it deviates from the optimum, the greater becomes the possibility that vivid dreams with a strongly contrasting but purposive content will appear as an expression of the self-regulation of the psyche.[1]

My dream is about an English woman at my bed-and-breakfast inn. It thus seems connected to my activities in London. She has been involved in excess, in trying to get too much pleasure, and ends up sick with a massive hangover. She clearly has overindulged and made herself sick through her own actions.

It became clear to me that I had replaced anxiety about being able to give the lectures with excessive self-satisfaction and self-indulgence. More bluntly, I was in a drunken exultation about my heroic efforts in giving those successful lectures under difficult conditions. My identification with the willful hero also blinded me to any contribution from the mysterious feminine in me, the source of the few creative and inspired moments that did occur. The anima needs autonomy, attention, appreciation, and affirmation, otherwise our connection to that which is best and most creative in us is lost. When neglected, rather than being our personal intercessor to soul or our creative darkness within, she turns into a fearsomely ugly hag who causes all sorts of problems. However, in me, the anima also has a tendency toward vanity and excess. I plied her with the intoxication of my success, with excessive self-appreciation. Then we got sick. As Jung says, "The more one-sided his conscious attitude is, and the further it deviates from the optimum, the greater becomes the possibility that vivid dreams with a strongly contrasting but purposive content will appear as an expression of the self-regulation of the psyche." The unconscious responded to my excessive self-satisfaction with a pointed comeuppance. Immediately, before I had any understanding of the dream, it threw me roughly to the ground.

The vehicle for this painful realization was not the Virgin Mary, the approachable intercessor, the immaculate mother of Christ. Instead, it was the dark feminine, the one connected to the Earth, body, sickness, and fruitful darkness—the feminine spirit fully incarnated in matter—who served as the messenger. A powerful example of this dark feminine is Mother Kali, the great Hindu goddess, who combines the harvest bounty of an Earth mother with the death-dealing forces of nature, bringing infants into the world and then taking them away with pestilence or other natural disasters. Her statues often show her with a sheaf of grain in one hand and a brace of bloody skulls in the other. When devotees of Mother Kali experience some calamity, they recognize it as coming from her and often chant, "Victory to Kali, Victory to Kali."

Several writers have begun to explore how this aspect of feminine consciousness can become more fully integrated into Western culture.[2] They seek an expression of the divine feminine more fully conjoined with the body, the sorrows of the downtrodden, and that dark mysterious matrix out of which all life is born. They are recognizing and appreciating the darkness inherent in yin, both its positive aspect as creative matrix from which all springs and its negative aspect as the destructive forces of nature. In a sense, these writers seek autonomy for the archetypal feminine in all her complexity.

Although I could not connect emotionally to the Black Madonna of Montserrat, the dark feminine came to me nevertheless in a compelling form that related directly to my experience. That dream and its aftermath were painful and depressing, but upon reflection, I was thankful for the guidance, grateful that something higher than my ego and its insatiable need was operating in me.

The question naturally arises: What is it within me that knows when my "conscious attitude tends too exclusively in a direction that would threaten the vital needs of the individual"? What knows when I need correction? What sort of "vision" does this intelligence hold for me? Jung called this informing and directing intelligence the *self*; Plotinus calls it the *divisible aspect of soul*. Some call this intelligence, this directing force, the highest power in ourselves. For example, Marcus Aurelius, the great Roman general, emperor, and philosopher wrote:

> In the universe, respect the highest power, namely the creative force that directs and makes use of all things. In the same way, you must respect the highest power in yourself, for it is of the same creative kind.
> For this is what makes use of the rest of you and directs your life.[3]

This highest power in ourselves, the self, or divisible aspect of soul enters our lives in many ways. In the case of my dream in London, it entered through the dark feminine, not necessarily the one at Montserrat, but my symbolization of the feminine spirit in matter.

However, the darkness of the feminine depicted in the various black virgins is not just the darkness due to association with matter, body, and the instinctual life so evident in my dream. The darkness of the Virgin is also the womb of soul, the root of our being, and thus impenetrable by the light of intellect. Our entire personality is born out of this fruitful darkness, this primal yin element. She nurtures us and we die back into her, just as the devotees of Mother Kali understand. Although some expressions of this darkness are painful, its negative characterization results largely from the intellect's limited point of view and neglect. Recall that the fiercely ugly Ragnelle could be transformed only when rejection became embrace, when she was given love and autonomy. However, embracing our rejected traits takes many forms, as my experience with a Rembrandt drawing taught me.

The Return of the Prodigal Son

The Rijksmuseum in Amsterdam has an extraordinary art collection with a special strength in Rembrandt. A few days before going to Montserrat, I spent two afternoons there admiring the artwork. After several hours at the museum, I was saturated and ready to leave. On my way out, like a greedy child wanting one more piece of dessert, I wandered off into a side gallery containing smaller works of art. Suddenly, I was utterly captivated by Rembrandt's drawing *The Return of the Prodigal Son*, a theme I had not considered since my youth. It engaged me so powerfully that I felt inside the drawing, as if I were witnessing the original return of the prodigal son. Its expressiveness, power, and psychological depth stunned me. As preparation for commenting upon the experience, I quote the passage that inspires the drawing (Luke 15.11–32):

> Jesus said to them: "A man had two sons. The younger of them said to his father, 'Father, give me the share of the estate that is coming to me.' So the father divided up the property. Some days later this younger son collected all his belongings and went off to a distant land, where he squandered his money on dissolute living. After he had spent everything, a great famine broke out in that country and he was in dire need. So he attached himself to one of the propertied class of the place, who sent him to his farm to take care of the pigs. He longed to fill his belly with the husks that were fodder for the pigs, but no one made a move to give him anything. Coming to his senses at last, he said: 'How many hired hands at my father's place have more than enough to eat, while here I am starving! I will break away

and return to my father, and say to him, Father, I have sinned against God and against you; I no longer deserve to be called your son. Treat me like one of your hired hands.' With that, he set off for his father's house. While he was still a long way off, his father caught sight of him and was deeply moved. He ran out to meet him, threw his arms around his neck, and kissed him. The son said to him, 'Father, I have sinned against God and against you; I no longer deserve to be called your son.' The father said to his servants: 'Quick! Bring out the finest robe and put it on him; put a ring on his finger and shoes on his feet. Take the fatted calf and kill it. Let us eat and celebrate, because this son of mine was dead and has come back to life. He was lost and is found.' Then the celebration began.

"Meanwhile the elder son was out on the land. As he neared the house on his way home, he heard the sound of music and dancing. He called one of the servants and asked him the reason for the dancing and the music. The servant answered, 'Your brother is home, and your father has killed the fatted calf because he has him back in good health.' The son grew angry at this and would not go in; but his father came out and began to plead with him.

"He said to his father in reply: 'For years now I have slaved for you. I never disobeyed one of your orders, yet you never gave me so much as a kid goat to celebrate with my friends. Then, when this son of yours returns after having gone through your property with loose women, you kill the fatted calf for him.'

"'My son,' replied the father, 'you are with me always, and everything I have is yours. But we had to celebrate and rejoice! This brother of yours was dead, and has come back to life. He was lost, and is found.'"[4]

The prodigal son repudiated all his father's values. Despite the father's grief and pain, his love for his son persisted. Without hesitation, he warmly welcomes the returning prodigal son. "He ran out to meet him, threw his arms around his neck, and kissed him." Even with this warm reception, the son felt compelled to make his confession and seek forgiveness. The father forgives him immediately, showers gifts upon him, and calls for a celebration. Some jealousy arises as the older son returns. Rather than reason with the older son and explain his actions, as I would have done, the father responds with an extraordinary expression of unconditional love: "My son, you are with me always, and everything I have is yours. But we had to celebrate and rejoice! This brother of yours was dead, and has come back to life. He was lost, and is found."

Fig. 49. The Return of the Prodigal Son by Rembrandt (with permission of
the Teylers Museum, The Netherlands)

In Rembrandt's drawing (fig. 49), the father's grief seems to radiate outward from his body like intense heat. He is massive, powerful,
and grave. With his wide stance and bent knee, the father steadies himself against his son's weight while tenderly embracing him. His bodily
stance expresses both great power and receptive love. Usually, a relationship concerned with power drives out love and vice versa. However,
in this extraordinary father, unqualified loving generates his power.

The son clasps the father's right hand and buries his head in it,
while the father's left hand tenderly strokes his son's head. The son is
peaceful, bathed in forgiveness, and happy in the arms of his father. He
is home, safe, protected, loved, and sheltered by his great oak of a father. The father's luxurious robes contrast with the son's rags and bare
feet. Behind the father, the dark, womb-like entrance to the house beckons us inward. At the instant captured by Rembrandt, the son's primitive
walking stick, dropped when he embraced his father, has not quite
fallen to the ground. A young boy, maybe a servant, looks on intently
and tearfully with great tenderness. Perhaps the boy is just the father's
memory image of the returning son in his innocent youth.

When I first saw this drawing, I was surprised that people just
walked casually by it. "Can't they see this is the best piece in the museum?" The powerful attraction took me completely by surprise and
gave me the most moving experience of art I have ever had. Of course,

it does not affect everyone that profoundly. Why did this particular piece move me so? Certainly, we all want forgiveness for our transgressions, rebellions, and excesses by the loving father, whether the biological version or some other authority. We all want to come home to safety and to give and receive love. My own limited prodigality has always troubled me. Although my sons have not been prodigal, I can still relate to the theme from the side of the father.

Surely one reason this theme is especially compelling for me is that I have not had any significant contact with my father since before I could walk. Although there have been several important older men in my life, I have never felt love, protection, and support from my biological father. Without underestimating or denying this, I believe the drawing moved me profoundly for two additional reasons, one psychological, the other philosophical.

In thinking about any great parable, myth, vision, or dream, one useful psychological approach is to view each aspect of it as symbolizing parts of our own psyche, just as I did in my discussion of "The Wedding of Sir Gawain and Dame Ragnelle." My challenge is then to appreciate that both the prodigal son and the loving father live in me. Unconditionally loving the weak, lost, profligate, and despised aspects of myself is the most compelling theme in this drawing. Although I often make critical, even harsh, judgments of others, I usually keep them to myself, and generally, after the first flash of anger, disappointment, or condemnation, I don't have great difficulty forgiving others. Instead, I reserve the harshest criticisms and most unforgiving judgments for myself.

For example, chapter 8 describes the beautiful spiritual state that arose from my traffic accident in Phoenix, Arizona. I was in an unprecedented state of spiritual peace, devotion, and gratitude . . . until I castigated myself for giving an ineffectual lecture in Santa Fe, New Mexico, one week after the accident. Of course, I did not judge it significant that I gave the lecture with my arm in a sling and intense pain in several parts of my body. My anima not only gets drunk on success, but also (and just as easily) tears me apart with negative judgments. Then I even criticize myself for being too critical and unforgiving! What a healing balm it would have been if I could have embraced that pathetic fellow desperately seeking to impress his audience, bathed his wounds in their praise, and persuaded him to forgive, at least for a moment, that his own stupidity had nearly killed him. Forgiving myself, unconditionally loving the harsh critic, accepting my many weaknesses rather than despising them—all these are exceedingly difficult for me. Of course, this is a common problem. Jung says it beautifully when he writes about self-acceptance:

> Perhaps this sounds very simple, but simple things are always the most difficult. In actual life it requires the greatest art to be simple, and so acceptance of oneself is the essence of the moral problem and the acid test of one's whole outlook on life. That I feed the beggar, that I forgive an insult, that I love my enemy in the name of Christ—all these are undoubtedly great virtues. What I do unto the least of my brethren, that I do unto Christ. But what if I should discover that the least amongst them all, the poorest of all beggars, the most impudent of all offenders, yea the very fiend himself—that these are within me, and that I myself stand in need of the alms of my own kindness, that I myself am the enemy who must be loved—what then? Then, as a rule, the whole truth of Christianity is reversed: there is then no more talk of love and long-suffering; we say to the brother within us "Raca," and condemn and rage against ourselves. We hide him from the world, we deny ever having met this least among the lowly in ourselves, and had it been God himself who drew near to us in this despicable form, we should have denied him a thousand times before a single cock had crowed.[5]

A few lines later he says that this kind of self-acceptance is "the hardest of tasks, and one which it is almost impossible to fulfill. The very thought can make us sweat with fear." Is it any surprise that unconditional love of the prodigal son, the one so lost, so hungry, so desolate, can move me, the most bitter of self-critics, so deeply? I am challenged to become that unconditionally loving father, to embrace my inner prodigal son in all his wretchedness and excess, and yet not fall into limp acceptance of all weakness and evil, whether my own or others'. (My friend and colleague, Shimon Malin, rightly points out that the last phrase of the previous sentence shows that I am not yet unconditionally loving.)

This process of accepting, even welcoming, all the rejected aspects of our selves and our experience is captured beautifully in Rumi's poem "This Being Human,"[6] in which he refers to the divisible aspect of soul as the "Friend."

> This being human is a guest house.
> Every morning a new arrival.
>
> A joy, a depression, a meanness,

some momentary awareness comes
as an unexpected visitor.

Welcome and attend them all!
Even if they're a crowd of sorrows,
who violently sweep your house
empty of its furniture, still,
treat each guest honorably.
He may be clearing you out
for some new delight.
The dark thought, the shame, the malice,
meet them at the door laughing,
and invite them in.

Be grateful for whoever comes,
because each has been sent
as a guide from beyond.

Welcome difficulty.
Learn the alchemy True Human Beings know:
the moment you accept what troubles
you've been given, the door opens.

Welcome difficulty as a familiar
comrade. Joke with torment
brought by the Friend.

Sorrows are the rags of old clothes
and jackets that serve to cover,
and then are taken off.

That undressing, and the beautiful
naked body
       underneath,
              is the sweetness
                    that comes
                         after grief.

It is a challenge for me to appreciate that we should "Welcome difficulty as a familiar comrade. Joke with torment brought by the Friend."
Nevertheless, I have learned that acceptance of my faults and painful
experiences is the way beyond them, or "the moment you accept what
troubles you've been given, the door opens."

Beyond these psychological and spiritual reasons for my powerful attraction to *The Return of the Prodigal Son* lies a philosophical reason
I explored in Catalonia, Spain. There I returned home to a form of
catholicism—not to the narrow Roman Catholicism I fled four decades

ago, but to home in a deep sense, a truly universal, expansive, and liberal catholicism that can accommodate both science and the sacred. As with the prodigal son, this homecoming happened through the help of a fatherly figure.

CATALONIAN PILGRIMAGE

One of my earliest and most intense theological rebellions was over the old Roman Catholic idea that there is no salvation outside the Church. Even as a grammar-school child, I found this idea illogical, indefensible, and repugnant. As a child, I asked myself, "What about all those good people who died before Christ even appeared on Earth? Are these people eternally damned? Is this the action of a loving God?" At the time, I knew only vaguely of other religious traditions, because the nuns warned us about the sin of even wandering into their churches or temples.

Unfortunately, this "one true church" attitude is not exclusively a Western or Christian tendency. In fact, it is not just a competition between religious traditions; it is easily found even within a single tradition. For example, within Tibetan Buddhism (which, of course, is only one of many variants of Buddhism), four different schools or tenet systems exist. Jeffery Hopkins, a respected Tibetan Buddhist scholar and practitioner, writes:

> Can you attain Buddhahood through practicing the Bodhisattva path as it is explained in one of the lower tenet systems—the Great Exposition School, the Sutra School, the Mind Only School, or the Middle Way Autonomy School? According to the final system, the Middle Way Consequence School, it is not possible. It is not as if Buddhahood were situated at a crossroads with each of the four tenet systems leading directly to it. Only one path leads to it—that of the Consequence School—but the others feed into it.[7]

Of course, the other tenet systems or sects within Tibetan Buddhism do not agree that they are "lower"; nor do they agree with Hopkins and his "party line" from the Gelukpa sect (the Middle Way Consequence School). Here is a clear example of the "one true church" syndrome, expressed as "only one path leads to Buddhahood and it is my path." Much as I love the Gelukpa sect and its head the Dalai Lama, I cannot deny that this sectarianism is a nasty echo of the abuses that occur when a religion attains political power, as I discussed in chapter 7. In Catalonia, I found an alternative to religious chauvinism.

Fig. 50. From my balcony in Catalonia (photo by author)

Yesterday I left Montserrat in the rain, and today some clouds still linger. The rain made yesterday's trip to this little mountaintop village challenging, but the resulting profusion of wildflowers turns inconvenience into celebration. My bed-and-breakfast inn, built in 1776, is one of the newest houses in this town of a few hundred people. The view from my balcony (fig. 50), almost gives me vertigo. Best of all, I will be seeing Father Raimon Panikkar for lunch tomorrow. He was so warm and welcoming on the telephone this afternoon, even though he is already hosting some American students while I am in town. I look forward to asking him some philosophical questions about religious pluralism.

We meet at my bed-and-breakfast inn and walk to his house for lunch. Our conversation is relaxed and friendly and immediately moves to substantial issues. I talk to him about a recent psychological struggle, partly embodied in the dream of the English woman with the hangover. We soon move to philosophical topics. He tells me about the final revisions he is making to his Gifford lectures, a book he has been working on for eleven years. We use that as a jumping-off place to talk about religious pluralism, the idea that the nondual absolute expresses itself through a

Fig. 51. Raimon Panikkar (photo by author)

rainbow of diverse and sometimes doctrinally incompatible religious traditions. In a rainbow, red cannot be reduced to blue, nor is one color inherently superior to the others. Similarly, one religion cannot be reduced to another, nor is one inherently superior to another. Our conversation has much give and take. We wrestle with subtle ideas, tell stories, and laugh. He asks about my writing and is enthusiastic about my approach to the present book. He glows with warmth and, inappropriate as it is, treats me as an equal. After several hours, I return to my room. We meet again the next day for equally productive discussions and, just before leaving, I take a photograph of him (fig. 51). Our visit ends with a big hug and Father Panikkar blesses me, not in a formal Catholic way, but by tenderly putting his right palm on my forehead.

On the way back to the United States, the poignant realization slowly dawns on me that I have never experienced such fatherly interest, encouragement, and affection, even from my teacher Anthony, though he was the most benign of influences, never to be replaced nor duplicated. I am not interested in a guru-disciple relationship with Panikkar, and I told him so. He is not interested in having more students. However, because of his decades as an academic, prolific author, scientist, and Catholic priest, he has a deep appreciation of my world and my concerns. Because of this, his encouragement of my writing and suggestions for new directions have given me a profound sense of support.

The core of our discussions focused on religious pluralism, given in Panikkar's paper "The Metaphysical Challenge of Religious Pluralism"[8] and in his book *The Intrareligious Dialogue*.[9] I will briefly summarize his views by presenting a series of images. Although Panikkar does not use these images, he agrees that they represent his views. In the extreme view of "one true church," there is only one diamond and all the other religions are counterfeit jewels. This view makes dialogue between differing viewpoints impossible. In a more accommodating view, popular with many people with spiritual interests, there is one jewel of reality, one diamond, whose different facets represent all the various religious traditions. In this view, comparative religious studies relate the various facets and understand how they all express the same diamond or underlying reality. This view, which many find comfortable and resembles the view held by my own teacher, Anthony Damiani, is not Panikkar's position. Instead, the following image more accurately represents his view of pluralism.

Consider a ruby, sapphire, garnet, and innumerable other precious stones. Imagine that the ruby represents Christianity as a whole, while the sapphire represents Buddhism in all its various forms, the garnet Hinduism, and so forth. Now the various facets of the ruby signify the various traditions within Christianity, while the facets of the sapphire represent the various schools of Buddhism, and so on. Each jewel has reflections of the other jewels within it, just as many deep connections and reflections exist between religions. However, a ruby is not a sapphire, nor a garnet. One cannot be reduced to the other. In this metaphor, no one jewel is more precious or inherently superior to any other. Each of them expresses "jewelness" or reality in a unique and valuable way, without there being any inherent hierarchy among them. Finally, truth, reality, the nondual absolute, or the One (symbolized by "jewelness" in the analogy) by its very nature expresses itself pluralistically through the various competing religions. To assert that the diverse religions are different aspects of a unitary reality (one diamond with many facets) is neither warranted nor provable in the face of the variety of religious forms and the clear disparities among them.

If we hold firmly to this view of pluralism, the stage is set for a genuine interreligious dialogue. Nobody can be on top and dictate that the outcome must favor his or her view of reality. Another person's religious view may be offensive to me, but that view cannot simply be labeled as false and dismissed nor can that person become a target for reform or annihilation. Instead, Panikkar views all traditions, even those we judge aberrant, or even abhorrent, as different expressions of the nondual reality.

Such a view has many virtues, especially in providing a foundation for genuine dialogue, but it also presents serious challenges. For example, how do we keep from falling from the extreme of saying there is only one true church into the equally extreme view that anything goes? Panikkar explains (using the words truth and reality interchangeably):

> Before we explain a little more this inherent polarity [pluralism] of reality, we must meet a formidable difficulty: the problem of falsehood. Can there be a false religion? Does pluralism allow us to handle such cases? Have we no tools to condemn a racist religion, for instance, or a religiosity of hatred? We shall say that it is a wrong and a bad religion, but religion it is, and we shall have to reckon with it. Those people are not just cranky people. Evil is not a mere mistake, an error of vision or perspective. It is a hatred, an aberration, an incomprehensibility. Evil is by definition impervious to human comprehension. This does

not mean that everything unintelligible is evil, as the Gnostics are inclined to think. But it implies that there may be people grasped by the dark side of reality who put evil forward. It is the very pluralism of the real that gives to evil all its tragic seriousness.

Pluralism has a better answer than the already known and defeated answers of monism and dualism. These two latter systems are able to give excellent theoretical justifications, but they fail to discover a way to maintain dissent and still somehow embrace the dissenting party. No alternative is left besides the elimination of the wrong party. It has to be defeated because ultimately error is sin, evil. Pluralism, on the other hand, is neither individualistic subjectivism nor impersonal objectivism. With the former, we could condemn nothing. With the latter, we could condemn anything we disagree with. The nondualistic approach accepts the relativity of truth but not sheer relativism. This is to say, truth is constituted by the total relationship of things, because things are insofar as they are in relation to one another. But this relation is not a private relation between a subject and an object. It is a universal relationship so that it is not for any private individual or group to exhaust any relationship. Truth is relational, thus relational to me, but never private. There is no such thing as private truth. On the other hand, truth is not an immutable or absolute quality totally objectifiable in concepts or propositions independently of time, space, culture, and people. Each person, we said, is a source of self-understanding and of understanding, a knowing subject and not only a known object.

Here it is important to emphasize Panikkar's definition of truth or reality. He has clearly been influenced by his deep study of the Buddhist principle of emptiness, which asserts that no object or subject independently exists, or stated positively, that the fundamental nature of all objective and subjective phenomena is relational. In other words, all things, from microbe to galaxy, from human consciousness to the principle of emptiness itself, are empty of or lack independent existence. They cannot exist alone, independent, and self-defined. The ultimate nature of any phenomenon is interdependence and connection with other phenomena. Panikkar puts it this way: "truth is constituted by the total relationship of things, because things are insofar as they are in relation to one another." In other words, isolated existence is impossible. As the Tibetan Buddhists would say, independent existence is like a sweater made of turtle hair. You can say the words, but they make no sense. The ultimate reality or truth of any thing, from a dust particle to the entire Buddhist canon, is its relationships to the rest of the world, including the knower of the dust or canon. However, this truth or reality of a thing, despite its being in relationship to the knower, is not private, for that would exclude all the essential dependency relationships that extend out from the thing to the world in an infinite net of connections. Or as Panikkar says, "It is a universal relationship so that it is not for any private individual or group to exhaust any relationship." With this definition, Panikkar continues:

> How, then, shall we discriminate between true and false religion? When this constitutive relativity of truth is hampered by isolating it from this total relationship we fall into error. When a particular religion isolates itself from the rest of the world and does not accept relation, dialogue, or intercourse; when it becomes a sect refusing communication and communion with the wider world, then this kind of totalitarianism condemns itself by the very fact of implicitly condemning others.[10]

Because everything lacks independent existence, an isolated religious view or one independent of other views or the cultural, historical, political, geographical, economic, and literary tradition of a culture is impossible. Viewing reality or truth as relational, as inherently dependent for both its form and substance on the largest possible contextual relationships, implies that isolation is impossible. We are thus profoundly in error if we attempt to maintain isolation and refuse to engage in a discussion in which we consider the opposing person's view a legitimate expression of reality. Consequently, an isolationist religion is false. Panikkar restates this idea a few lines after the above quotation when he says, ". . . error entails isolation and breaking of relations. As long as there is dialogue, struggle, discussion, and disagreement, we have conflicting opinions, different and even contradictory views; but all this appertains to the very polarity of reality. In this view we also relativize error. From my vantage point, my opponent is wrong, but not absolutely wrong unless the group or person in question breaks loose from (*ab-solutus*) the rest of us."

As I discussed in chapter 6, science can be understood as a form of religion. Therefore, we must view science in a pluralistic context, as one of many expressions of reality, as one jewel among many. Pluralism is difficult for many scientists to accept for two reasons. First, we have been reared in a tradition in which there is always one and only one right answer to a question, one true view. Yes, theories change, such as when quantum mechanics replaced classical mechanics. However, the older theory is still applicable in its own realm. For instance, we know that understanding elementary particles requires quantum mechanics, while calculating planetary orbits requires classical mechanics. There is still one correct answer to a problem. Second, the astonishing success of science to shape our physical world and our understanding of it and ourselves leads many scientists to believe that *all* questions have one correct answer, one true understanding. Under these circumstances, it is difficult for many to accept that there may be several incompatible, yet legitimate, truths or views of reality.

However, pluralism claims that reality's very nature generates or expresses itself in different truths, just as the notion of "jewelness" expresses itself in rubies, sapphires, and garnets. Yet, no one truth or reality, whether articulated by a religion or a science, subsumes the others or is inherently superior. This is a truly catholic view, not in the Roman Catholic sense, but in the original sense of catholic as universal, broad, liberal, and all-encompassing. It is about as far from the "one true church" view as you can get. As Panikkar says:

> No religion, ideology, culture, or tradition can reasonably claim to exhaust the universal range of human experience or even the total manifestation of the Sacred. Thus *pluralism*, as distinct from the mere coexistence of a *plurality* of worldviews, becomes today the paramount human and religious imperative. It thus precludes the attempt at domination by any master perspective or absolutely privileged standpoint. Pluralism does not call for a superideology or a supersystem. It implies an almost mythical confidence that other perspectives are also plausible, or, more correctly, a mystical respect for the other that authenticates one's own religious experience.[11]

For Panikkar, divergences between traditions offer an opportunity for interreligious dialogue, wherein we sympathetically understand the other tradition and in so doing deepen and clarify our understanding of our own tradition. In this way, we cultivate tolerance for the other tradition and authenticate our own religious experience. Religious pluralism is not a call for compartmentalism, wherein everyone freely cultivates his or her own view of reality and avoids interfering with each other. Rather, the very relational nature of truth implies that my tradition is defined both by its own internal structure and by how it relates to other visions of reality. This is true whether my tradition is Zoroastrianism or science. Rather than compartmentalism, religious pluralism is a call for deep dialogue.

For example, let's imagine I am a Christian fundamentalist and troubled by the principles of Darwinian evolution as presented in modern science. Assuming that I am willing to experiment with this pluralistic view, I approach the issue in the following way. Rather than assume my view of reality is the only truth and therefore take the scientific view as an error that must be destroyed, I try to understand scientific evolution sympathetically. I try to understand how the various scientific arrows of explanation converge toward the evolutionary view and comprehend the fundamental presuppositions involved. I identify the strengths and weakness that characterize this view. Then I ask, "What are *my* arrows of explanation and fundamental presuppositions? How do these relate to the scientific view? What strengths and weakness characterize my view?" In this process, I come to understand scientific evolutionary theory while deepening and clarifying my own religious view and thereby become a better Christian. In this way, I allow for dissent and still embrace the dissenting party.

It follows that a genuine dialogue between religion and science cannot be built upon a hierarchical view, which claims the superiority of one view over the other, any more than a whole person can evolve from the belief that the head is more important than the heart or the other way around. Although there is no hierarchy, beautiful reflections and connections between the jewels of science and those of religion do exist. A scientific idea may illuminate or even challenge a religious view and vice versa. However, such challenges are not obstacles but opportunities for authenticating our religious commitments and experience.

Granted, such dialogue is extremely difficult. But two facts demand such deep dialogue if our planet is to survive. First, modern science and technology interconnect our world so thoroughly that separate islands of culture can no longer exist. This fact inevitably gives rise to widespread clashes between modernity and traditional cultures. Second, another "gift" of modern science and technology is the ready availability of weapons of mass destruction, whether nuclear, chemical, or biological. Today, a few people with appropriate scientific training and modest funding can threaten the entire globe. Now divergent views of reality easily blossom into major catastrophes. Thus, one religion—science, and the modernity so closely allied with it—creates the conditions that force the dialogue upon us.

Panikkar's religious pluralism, which provides the framework for genuine dialogue, is so universal, so comprehensive, that it has little to do with the usual Roman Catholicism, despite its articulation by a

Catholic priest. Nevertheless, in my personal psychological and spiritual journey, I see religious pluralism as a way to return home to catholicism in the true sense, a home transformed by my pilgrimage through "foreign lands" that ranged from psychedelic drugs to depth psychology, meditation, astrology, Buddhism, Hinduism, and Neoplatonism. Fortunately, my debauchery was limited, but I did wander far from Roman Catholicism and can no more return to it than the father and his prodigal son can return to their old relationship. In the eyes of the Roman Catholic Church, I have sinned deeply and repeatedly. However, unlike the prodigal son, I don't accept that evaluation, nor have I spent much time feeling lost like the prodigal. Nevertheless, corrosive self-doubt about my writing, my role as an unconventional academic, and about generally being "out there where the buses don't run" repeatedly besets me. With Raimon Panikkar I felt not only the deep kindness and support of the father, but also a sense of coming home to an accommodating philosophical worldview. Like the Biblical sons, I learned about support, encouragement, love, and blessing by example. I now feel a responsibility to embody those traits more fully in my daily life.

It is January 1993, and our return flight from India is delayed. The airline has arranged for my wife and me to stay in a five-star hotel in Bombay. It will be quite a luxury after the places where we have been staying. On the way to the hotel, we drive past an endless sea of hovels, shacks, and piles of cardboard and scrap lumber that serve as homes for the poor. Some of these areas are foul, smoldering heaps, where ghostly figures emerge from the smoke to poke through the ruins. We are struck by how many hovels were recently burned. Is it an urban renewal project?

When we arrive at the hotel, we are confronted with a round, windowless, fortresslike building. We discover that all the windows are on the inside, opening onto central gardens and a swimming pool area. I go up to the rooftop running track but decide the air is much too nasty for strenuous exercise. Instead I take some photographs. Standing on the roof, I point my camera down into the pool area (fig. 52). Despite the smoke that finds its way even into the central garden, all is calm and leisure as the members of the hotel staff serve the poolside patrons and silently glide about in a continuous dance of cleaning.

Fig. 52. Bombay's rich (photo by author)

From my rooftop perch, I rotate 180 degrees and shoot a photo of the squalid slums immediately outside the hotel (fig. 53). Sewers flow in the street; naked children run beside them. Now I understand why the hotel feels like a fortress. You need a lot of concrete and steel to sepa-

Fig. 53. Bombay's poor (photo by author)

rate the Garden of Eden from the reality of Bombay. A hotel whose windows open only into its interior luxury seems to symbolize the self-centeredness of the rich—including the guy taking these photographs with a camera and accessories worth about five times the per capita income of India.

I ask one of the hotel staff who ministers to the patrons using the rooftop track about the smoke. He explains that the Hindu fundamentalists are burning Muslim neighborhoods throughout the city. A few weeks earlier, Hindu fundamentalists had destroyed the ancient mosque in Ayodhya, about a thousand kilometers away in north-central India, reigniting the centuries-long animosity between Hindus and Muslims. That is why I can look in any direction, all the way to the horizon, and see clouds of thick, acrid smoke. I learn later that Hindu police stood idly by and sometimes joined the fundamentalist mobs in burning and pillaging Muslim homes.

Bombay has seen the fiercest riots, with nearly a thousand people killed (mostly Muslims), but similar riots are occurring in many cities in India, Pakistan, Nepal, and Bangladesh. The same culture that produced the greatest collection of religious and philosophical systems in the world, as well as towering adepts such as Sankaracharya, also produced this outrage. Just a few hours earlier, in Kanchi Puram in southern India, I had meditated with Sankaracharya in the shadow of a large Muslim mosque, whose inspiring calls to prayer several times a day mingle with Hindu chants. Now Hindu fundamentalist hatred, fanned by unscrupulous politicians, seeks (in the words of Deuteronomy) to "smite the unbeliever."

Today, in recalling that rooftop between the squalid slums and the luxurious pool, I can actually smell that smoke so reminiscent of a burning landfill. That hatred of Muslims, which played itself out in riots throughout the subcontinent, motivated India to build a nuclear bomb and threaten Muslim Pakistan, which quickly demonstrated its own nuclear bomb. Even before becoming nuclear powers, Pakistan and India fought three wars over their disputed border. At present, in early 2002, there is fear for a fourth war, since continuing tension between these two nuclear powers has resulted in a massive military buildup along their border. Now, enmity and intolerance could become unimaginable catastrophe. All this, when seventy percent of Indians have no access to a toilet or indoor plumbing, and Pakistan is even poorer.

However, fundamentalism and intolerance are hardly limited to the Indian subcontinent. I think of those in my own country who seek to change the science curriculum to fit their narrow interpretation of scripture, those who wed politics to fundamentalist Christianity, and those who breed killers of doctors of obstetrics and gynecology. The self-centered architecture of the luxury hotel in Bombay also reminds me of the growing gap between the rich and poor, both within my country and between countries. According to the World Bank, of the thirty richest nations in the world, the United States gives the lowest fraction of its gross national product to foreign aid.[12] Lack of compassion, fundamentalism, hatred, and intolerance are universal.

These observations, and the catastrophe of the terrorist attacks of September 11, 2001, convince me that religious pluralism is not just an academic plaything, something to amuse professors entombed in the bell jars of their intellects. Religious fundamentalists of all types need to consider pluralism as much as professors do. A pluralistic view of all the competing "-isms," from Hindu fundamentalism to scientific materialism, can provide the intellectual framework for tolerance and understanding. Yet this knowledge by itself is not adequate. Understanding that each religion is a nonhierarchical expression of the nondual absolute, that each religion and its relationship to the others offers an opportunity to understand the opposing tradition and our own more fully, is not enough. "Head knowledge" cannot by itself issue in action. It will not help the naked child playing alongside the open sewer.

However, pluralism in conjunction with the "heart knowledge" of the sacredness of each individual *can* help a poor child, whether in the slums of Bombay, at the construction site at the Madras airport, or among the underprivileged in my part of Appalachia. A naïve pluralist might retort that the sacredness of the individual is a notion peculiar to just a few of the traditions and really comes out of the Western Renaissance. Then, in the spirit of pluralism, the sacredness of each individual should not be held as an absolute and applied to all.

I suggest, however, that equivalent principles to the sacredness of each individual do exist in nearly every religion. For example, a Hindu claims that the light of Brahman glows in the heart of each person, from the poor man who kept our shoes at the entrance to the mutt in Kanchi Puram to the "diamond people" who swept in with their servants, jewels, and fine clothing. Ultimately, everyone from shoe man to head of state is capable of the highest realization and is therefore in principle of equal value. The Christian uses different language to make the same point and complements it with the second of the two greatest commandments: to love thy neighbor as thyself. A nontheistic Buddhist claims that the seed of Buddhahood resides in each person.

Buddhism complements this view with the principle of universal compassion, that the highest good is the reduction of suffering for all sentient beings. Equivalent or analogous statements could be made for enough of the other religions to ensure that affirming the sacredness of the individual is not merely a parochial view that I am wrongly applying to the whole. Despite the egregious violations of this principle that have occurred in most religions, it is universal.

The sacredness of the individual is not an exaltation of the ego, but a call for less selfishness, a call to grant each individual on our planet the right to realize his or her unique expression of divinity. This sacredness is not to be confused with mere material wealth; rather, it is a plea for the opportunity for each person to cultivate a meaningful life, in his or her unique way. Although under special conditions this can be done even in extreme poverty, the sacredness of each individual demands that each person on the planet have adequate food, housing, health care, and human rights. Anything less is not justice, but "just us," as Panikkar frequently says.

Therefore, the head knowledge of religious pluralism must be made dynamic and fertile by complementing it with the heart knowledge of the sacredness of the individual. Intellectual understanding must be vitalized with the milk of human kindness.

In this, we can again be guided by the medieval tale with which I began, "The Wedding of Sir Gawain and Dame Ragnelle." Up to this point, I have interpreted this tale psychologically, as calling for each man and woman to pay attention to feminine consciousness and allow it an opportunity to flower. Of course, intrinsic to the feminine, built into its very nature, is caring for others. As I said earlier, this very aspect of the feminine can also make it fragile and in need of our support. No doubt, some of my respected feminist friends would say that caring for others, unlike childbirth, is not intrinsic to the feminine. They would say that, like most characteristics ascribed to the feminine, it is actually a construct of our culture. I agree that many so-called feminine qualities are culturally conditioned, but I also recall something that my wife and I learned with the birth of our first child.

Our first son was born when we lived in an idyllic cottage on Cayuga Lake in Ithaca, New York, while I was a graduate student at Cornell. Like many new parents, the miracle of birth and the joy of being parents wrapped us in a cocoon of light while it simultaneously devoured us. My wife, Elaine, noticed that when our child cried, milk flowed from her breasts even before she picked him up. Sometimes, when she was away from home without the baby, simply a loving thought of him could trigger this spontaneous flow, which is called the letdown reflex. Nature evolved women so that their childrens' cries automatically, through mysterious pathways from the mind to the hormones and to the breasts, release the true milk of human kindness. I loved our baby too, but his cry did not evoke such powerful biological responses in me. This experience and many others convince me that caring for others really is built into the feminine at the deepest levels. This conviction also contributed to my shock and confusion when the mother in the Madras airport attempted to give me her little girl.

In light of these biological realities, allowing the feminine autonomy entails having a genuine concern for the naked child playing alongside the open sewer and then extending such concern to every person on the planet. In other words, granting autonomy to the feminine can generate in us a psychological letdown reflex, a compassion that responds to the cries of the planet and all its citizens. When this heart knowledge is combined with the head knowledge of religious pluralism, the despair of the hungry and sick will surely be answered. Alternatively, withholding autonomy from the feminine creates monsters, whether the despised Dame Ragnelle or the Islamic fundamentalist regime of the Taliban.

However, autonomy for the feminine and religious pluralism are only meaningful from the point of view of the divisible, changing, or finite aspect of soul. From the perspective of the indivisible, unchanging, or infinite aspect of soul, all pairs of opposites are aspects of soul's unity. From this lofty position, there is no question of conflict between the head and the heart, masculine and feminine, the outer and inner worlds, or science and the sacred. All knowledge and experience are merely different aspects of the indivisible or unified soul. From this view, the divine is as much in my innermost thoughts as in the farthest galaxies, an idea echoed by mystics around the world, an idea that makes the entire world truly sacred. Equally then, the pain of another is my pain; another's joy is my joy. In this interplay of the infinite soul and the finite soul we can find the meaning of the great commandment, "Love thy neighbor as thyself." Limited and finite though I am, in the majestic unity of soul I have the responsibility of relieving the pain of those around me.

I had the idea that the world's so full of pain
it must sometimes make a kind of singing.

And that the sequence helps, as much as order helps—
First an ego, and then pain, and then the singing.

—Robert Hass[13]

NOTES

Introduction

1. Ravi Ravindra, *Science and Spirit* (New York: Paragon House, 1991), 146.

2. Victor Mansfield, *Synchronicity, Science, and Soul-Making* (Chicago: Open Court Publishing, 1995).

3. Ralph Waldo Emerson, *Selected Essays* (New York: Penguin Books, 1982), 97.

4. Albert Einstein, "Autobiographical Notes," in *Albert Einstein, Philosopher-Scientist*, vol. 1, ed. P. A. Schlipp (New York: Harper & Row, 1959), 3–5.

Chapter 1

1. I summarize the tale as it is presented in Thomas Hahn, ed., *Sir Gawain: Eleven Romances and Tales (Middle English Texts)* (Kalamazoo, Mich.: Western Michigan University Press, 1995).

2. See, for example, John Matthews, *Gawain: Knight of the Goddess* (London: Aquarian Press, 1990).

3. C. G. Jung, "Psychology of the Transference," in *Collected Works*, vol. 16 (Princeton, N.J.: Princeton University Press, 1966).

4. I follow Edward Whitmont, *Symbolic Quest* (Princeton, N.J.: Princeton University Press, 1978) in turning to the yin-yang doctrine for insight into the feminine. However, I do not use his definitions of yin and yang, preferring to go back to original sources.

5. Wing-Tsit Chan, trans. and comp., *A Source Book in Chinese Philosophy* (Princeton, N.J.: Princeton University Press, 1973), 244.

6. Rudolf Ritsema and Stephen Karcher, *I Ching* (Shaftesbury, Dorset, England: Element Books Ltd., 1994), 68–69.

Chapter 2

1. Meister Eckhart, *Meister Eckhart: A Modern Translation*, trans. Raymond B. Blakney (New York: Harper & Row, 1941), 96.

2. Paul Reps, ed., *Zen Flesh, Zen Bones* (Rutland, Vt.: Charles Tuttle Co., 1958), 19.

3. Victor Mansfield, *Synchronicity, Science, and Soul-Making* (Chicago: Open Court Publishing, 1995).

4. Ruth Bieler, *Feminist Approaches to Science* (New York: Pergamon Press, 1986), 3.

5. Ravi Ravindra, *Science and Spirit* (New York: Paragon House, 1991), 129.

6. Sheldon Glashow, "We Believe That the World Is Knowable," *New York Times*, 22 October 1989, p. 24.

7. Daniel Dennett, *Consciousness Explained* (Boston: Little, Brown & Co., 1991).

Chapter 3

1. Sogyal Rinpoche, *Tibetan Book of Living and Dying* (San Francisco: HarperSanFrancisco, 1992), 41.

2. Anthony J. Damiani, *Astronoesis: Philosophy's Empirical Context, Astrology's Transcendental Ground* (Burdett, N.Y.: Larson Publications, 2000).

3. Paul Brunton, *Perspectives: The Notebooks of Paul Brunton* (Burdett, N.Y.: Larson Publications, 1984), 18.

4. Victor Mansfield, "The Guru-Disciple Relationship: Making Connections and Withdrawing Projections." Available at http://www.lightlink.com/vic.

5. Rachel Naomi Remen, *My Grandfather's Blessings* (New York: Riverhead Books, 2000), 345.

Chapter 4

1. These options have become more complex with the distinct possibility that there is a nonzero cosmological constant. In the interest of simplicity, I omit that discussion. It does not hinder my analogical use of cosmology.

2. C. G. Jung, "General Aspects of Dream Psychology," in *Collected Works*, vol. 8 (Princeton, N.J.: Princeton University Press, 1978), 253.

3. C. G. Jung, "On the Nature of Dreams," in *Collected Works*, vol. 8 (Princeton, N.J.: Princeton University Press, 1978), 289–90.

4. C. G. Jung, *Memories, Dreams, Reflections,* trans. Richard and Clara Winston (New York: Vantage Books, 1963), 3.

5. James Hillman, *Anima: An Anatomy of a Personified Notion* (Dallas, Tex.: Spring Publications, 1985).

6. C. G. Jung, "The Personification of the Opposites," in *Collected Works*, vol. 14 (Princeton, N.J.: Princeton University Press, 1974), 110.

7. *Ibid.*, 148.

8. Anthony Damiani, founder of Wisdom's Goldenrod Center for Philosophic Studies, Valois, New York, often used this analogy in creative ways.

9. All Plotinus quotations are from *Plotinus: The Enneads*, trans. Steven MacKenna (Burdett, N.Y.: Larson Publications, 1992).

10. Mundaka Upanishads, in *The Enlightened Heart,* trans. Stephen Mitchell (New York: Harper & Row, 1989), 4.

Chapter 5

1. In fact, the weak nuclear force is not time-reversible. However, we know that this time asymmetry does not play a role in generating the arrow of time or the asymmetry between the past and the future.

2. Jorge Luis Borges, "A New Refutation of Time," in *Labyrinths, Selected Stories and Other Writings*, ed. D. A. Yates and J. E. Irby (New York: New Directions Books, 1964), 234.

3. Victor Mansfield, "Time in Madhyamika Buddhism and Modern Physics," *The Pacific World Journal of the Institute of Buddhist Studies*, 11–12 (1995–1996): 10. Also available at http://www.lightlink.com/vic.

4. The time interval $\Delta t = \Delta t_0 / \sqrt{1 - (v/c)^2}$ where Δt_0 is the rest frame value (70 days in our example) and v/c is the relative velocity between the system and the observer divided by the speed of light, c.

5. Mansfield, "Time in Madhyamika Buddhism."

6. P. C. W. Davies, "Stirring up Trouble," in *Physical Origins of Time Asymmetry*, ed. J. J. Halliwell et al. (Cambridge, England: Cambridge University Press, 1994), 119–130.

7. Albert Einstein, "Autobiographical Notes" in *Albert Einstein, Philosopher-Scientist*, vol. 1, ed. P. A. Schlipp (New York: Harper & Row, 1959), 3–5.

Chapter 6

1. All biblical quotations are from the King James Version unless noted otherwise.

2. Roy B. Chamberlain and Herman Feldman, *The Dartmouth Bible* (Boston: Houghton Mifflin, 1950), 166.

3. Raimon Panikkar, "Religious Pluralism: The Metaphysical Challenge" in *Religious Pluralism*, Boston University Studies in Philosophy and Religion, vol. 5, ed. Leroy S. Rouner (South Bend, Ind: University of Notre Dame Press, 1984), 97–115.

4. National Aeronautics and Space Administration, National Science Foundation, Department of Energy, Defense Advanced Research Projects Agency, National Institutes of Health, National Institute of Mental Health.

5. Paul Feyerabend, *Against Method* (London: Verso, 1975), 295.

6. Reginald A. Ray, *Indestructible Truth: The Living Spirituality of Tibetan Buddhism* (Boston: Shambhala, 2000), 221.

7. Dean Radin, *The Conscious Universe* (New York: HarperCollins Publishers, 1997).

8. Paul Feyerabend, *Science in a Free Society* (London: NLB, 1978); *Against Method* (London: Verso, 1975); *Farewell to Reason* (London: Verso, 1996).

9. Bart J. Bok and Lawrence E. Jerome, "Objections to Astrology," *The Humanist* 35 (Sept./Oct. 1975).

10. Bart J. Bok and Lawrence E. Jerome, *Objections to Astrology* (Buffalo, N.Y.: Prometheus Books, 1975).

11. Feyerabend, *Science in a Free Society*, 91–96.

12. Carl Sagan, "Readers Forum," *The Humanist* 36 (Jan./Feb. 1976).

13. Feyerabend, *Science in a Free Society*, 92.

14. Sagan, "Readers Forum."

15. Feyerabend, *Science in a Free Society*, 93–94.

16. C. G. Jung, "Synchronicity: An Acausal Connecting Principle," in *Collected Works*, vol. 8 (Princeton, N.J.: Princeton University Press, 1978), 460.

17. Feyerabend, *Science in a Free Society*, 91, fn. 13.

18. Michel Gauquelin, *L'influence des Astres. Étude critique et expérimentale* (Paris: Le Dauphin, 1955).

19. Suitbert Ertel and Kenneth Irving, *The Tenacious Mars Effect* (London: Urania Trust, 1996), KI-7.

20. *Ibid.*

21. An extensive critique of astrology, by one of its most active critics, is I. W. Kelly, "Modern Astrology: A Critique," *Psychological Reports* 81 (1997): 1035–1066.

Chapter 7

1. C. G. Jung and Wolfgang Pauli, "Synchronicity: An Acausal Connecting Principle," in *The Interpretation of Nature and the Psyche* (New York: Pantheon Books, 1955).

2. Victor Mansfield, "An Astrophysicist's Sympathetic and Critical View of Astrology," *The Mountain Astrologer*, August 1997, 46.

3. Jane Goodall, *Reason for Hope: A Spiritual Journey* (New York: Warner Books, 1999), 2–3.

4. Joseph Campbell, *The Power of Myth with Bill Moyers* (New York: Doubleday, 1988), 151.

5. Rabindranath Tagore, *Gitanjali* (Song Offerings) (Boston: International Pocket Books, 1992), 27–28.

6. C. G. Jung, "Synchronicity: An Acausal Connecting Principle," in *Collected Works*, vol. 8 (Princeton, N.J.: Princeton University Press, 1978).

7. *Ibid.*, 434.

8. Marie-Louise von Franz, *Psyche and Matter* (Boston: Shambhala, 1992), 234.

9. *Ibid.*, 231.

10. Jung, "Synchronicity," 516.

11. *Ibid.*, 519.

12. *Ibid.*, 485.

13. *Ibid.*, 486.

14. *Ibid.*, 486, fn. 3.

15. *Ibid.*, 486.

16. *Ibid.*, 487.

17. *Ibid.*, 488.

18. Victor Mansfield and Marvin Spiegelman, "On the Physics and Psychology of the Transference as an Interactive Field," *Journal of Analytical Psychology* 41 (1996): 179–202.

19. C. G. Jung, "General Aspects of Dream Psychology," in *Collected Works*, vol. 8 (Princeton, N.J.: Princeton University Press, 1978), 241.

20. Victor Mansfield, *Synchronicity, Science, and Soul-Making* (Chicago: Open Court Publishing, 1995), 14–16.

21. Von Franz, *Psyche and Matter*, 258.

22. C. G. Jung, "On the Nature of Dreams," in *Collected Works*, vol. 8 (Princeton, N.J.: Princeton University Press, 1978), 289.

23. Jung, "Synchronicity," 493.

24. Jung, "General Aspects of Dream Psychology," 253.

25. Marie-Louise von Franz, *C.G. Jung: His Myth in Our Time*, trans. William H. Kennedy (London: Hodder & Stoughton, 1975), 247.

26. von Franz, *Psyche and Matter*, 272.

27. Jean Shinoda Bolen, *The Tao of Psychology: Synchronicity and the Self* (San Francisco: Harper & Row, 1979), 7.

28. Jelaluddin Rumi, *The Essential Rumi,* trans. Colmean Barks et al. (San Francisco: Harper San Francisco, 1995), 142.

Chapter 8

1. C. G. Jung, "VI. The Conjunction," in *Collected Works*, vol. 14 (Princeton, N.J.: Princeton University Press, 1974), 437–438.

2. C. G. Jung, "Synchronicity: An Acausal Connecting Principle," in *Collected Works*, vol. 8 (Princeton, N.J.: Princeton University Press, 1978), 518.

3. *Ibid.*, 516–517.

4. *Ibid.*, 512.

5. Marie-Louise von Franz, *Psyche and Matter* (Boson: Shambhala, 1992), 28–29, 234–235.

6. Jung, "Synchronicity," 456.

7. *Ibid.*, 515.

8. Marie-Louise von Franz, *Number and Time: Reflections Leading toward a Unification of Depth Psychology and Physics* (Evanston, Ill.: Northwestern University Press, 1974), ix.

9. von Franz, *Psyche and Matter*, 28.

10. Jung, "Synchronicity," 511.

11. von Franz, *Psyche and Matter*, 198.

12. *Ibid.*, 237.

13. Victor Mansfield, Sally Rhine-Feather, and James Hall, "The Rhine-Jung Letters: Distinguishing Synchronicity from Parapsychological Phenomena," *The Parapsychology Journal*, 62 (March 1998): 3–25. Victor Mansfield, "Distinguishing Synchronicity from Parapsychological Phenomena: An Essay in Honor of Marie-Louise von Franz," parts I and II, *Quadrant, The Journal of Contemporary Jungian Thought*, 28, no. 2 (1998): 16–37; 29, no. 1 (1999): 37–45; also available at http://www.lightlink.com/vic.

14. Jung, "Synchronicity," 478.

15. *Ibid.*, 477.

16. See Mansfield, "Distinguishing Synchronicity from Parapsychological Phenomena," for a review of recent parapsychological research.

Chapter 9

1. Ravi Ravindra, *Science and Spirit* (New York: Paragon House, 1991), especially chapters 7 and 8.

2. Richard Feynman, *The Feynman Lectures in Physics*, vol. 1 (New York: Addison-Wesley Publications, 1989), 1.

3. A. A. Penzias and R. W. Wilson, "Cosmic Black-Body Radiation," *Astrophysical Journal*, 142 (1965): 419.

4. R. H. Dicke, P. J. E. Peebles, P. G. Roll, and D. T. Wilkinson, "A Measurement of Excess Antenna Temperature at 4080 mc/s," *Astrophysical Journal*, 142 (1965): 414.

5. C. G. Jung, "On the Nature of the Psyche," in *Collected Works*, vol. 8 (Princeton, N.J.: Princeton University Press, 1978), 169.

6. Galileo Galilei, *The Assayer (1623)*, translated in Stillman Drake, *Galileo* (Oxford: Oxford University Press, 1969), 70.

7. Peter Medawar, *The Art of the Soluble* (London: Methuen, 1967), 114.

8. Steven Weinberg, *Dreams of a Final Theory: The Scientist's Search for the Ultimate Laws of Nature* (New York: Vantage Books, 1993), 50.

9. Robert Jahn and Brenda Dunne, *Margins of Reality: The Role of Consciousness in the Physical World* (New York: Harcourt Brace Jovanovich, 1987).

10. Plotinus, *The Enneads*, trans. Steven MacKenna (Burdett, N.Y.: Larson Publications, 1992), I.6.9.

11. James Hillman, *Re-Visioning Psychology* (New York: Harper & Row, 1976), 5.

12. Weinberg, *Dreams of a Final Theory*, 53.

13. Marie-Louise von Franz, *Psyche and Matter* (Boston: Shambhala, 1992), 257.

14. Victor Mansfield, *Synchronicity, Science, and Soul-Making* (Chicago: Open Court Publishing, 1995).

15. von Franz, *Psyche and Matter*, 237-238.

16. *Ibid.*, 238.

17. C. G. Jung, "Synchronicity: An Acausal Connecting Principle," in *Collected Works*, vol. 8 (Princeton, N.J.: Princeton University Press, 1978).

18. von Franz, *Psyche and Matter*.

19. Mansfield, *Synchronicity*.

20. Dean Radin, *The Conscious Universe* (New York: HarperCollins Publishers, 1997).

21. von Franz, *Psyche and Matter*, 198.

22. *Ibid.*, 262.

Chapter 10

1. My source for all references to the writings of Bhattacharyya is Krishnachandra Bhattacharyya, *Studies in Philosophy*, vols. 1 and 2 (New Delhi: Motilal Banarsidass, 1983).

2. *Ibid.*, 113.

3. *Ibid.*, 491.

4. Albert Einstein, "Autobiographical Notes," in *Albert Einstein: Philosopher-Scientist*, vol. 1, ed. P. A. Schlipp (New York: Harper & Row, 1959), 5.

5. Neils Bohr, *Atomic Theory and the Description of Nature* (Cambridge, England: Cambridge University Press, 1934), 115.

6. Victor Mansfield, *Synchronicity, Science, and Soul-Making* (Chicago: Open Court Publishing, 1995), chapters 5–9.

7. John Wheeler, "Law without Law," in *Quantum Theory and Measurement*, ed. J. Wheeler and W. Zurek (Princeton, N.J.: Princeton University Press, 1983), 194.

8. Bhattacharyya, *Studies in Philosophy*, 491.

9. Nelson Mandela, *Long Walk to Freedom* (Boston: Little, Brown & Co., 1994), 322.

10. Jelaluddin Rumi, *The Essential Rumi*, trans. Coleman Barks et al. (San Francisco: HarperSanFrancisco, 1995), 100–101.

11. Swami Nikhilananda, *Self-Knowledge*, translations of Ātmabodha (New York: Ramakrishna-Vivekananda Center, 1970), 182–183.

12. Bhattacharyya, *Studies in Philosophy*, 503–504.

13. Rabindranath Tagore, *Gitanjali* (Song Offerings) (Boston: International Pocket Library, 1992), 43.

14. *Ibid.*, 29–30.

15. *Ibid.*, 25.

Chapter 11

1. Steven Weinberg, *Dreams of a Final Theory: The Scientist's Search for the Ultimate Laws of Nature* (New York: Vintage Books, 1993).

2. *Ibid.*, 44.

3. *Ibid.*, 184–190.

4. David Chalmers, *The Conscious Mind* (New York: Oxford University Press, 1996).

5. Weinberg, *Dreams of a Final Theory*, 168–169.

6. Erwin Schrödinger, "Discussion of Probability Relations between Separated Systems," *Proceedings of the Cambridge Philosophic Society* 31 (1935): 1903–1905.

7. For two early and influential examples, see Fritz London and Edmond Bauer, "The Theory of Observation in Quantum Mechanics," in *Quantum Theory and Measurement*, ed. J. Wheeler and W. Zurek (Princeton, N.J.: Princeton University Press, 1983), and Eugene Wigner, "Interpretation of Quantum Mechanics," in the same volume.

8. Robert G. Jahn and Brenda J. Dunne, "Science of the Subjective," *Journal of Scientific Explorations* 11, no. 2 (1997): 209.

9. R. G. Jahn, B. J. Dunne, R. D. Nelson, Y. H. Dobyns, and G. J. Bradish, "Correlations of Random Binary Sequences with Pre-stated Operator Intention: A Review of a 12-Year Program," *Journal of Scientific Explorations* 11, no. 3 (1997): 358.

10. D. J. Bem and C. Honorton, "Does Psi Exist?" *Psychological Bulletin* 115, 1 (1994).

11. *Ibid.*

12. Dean Radin, *The Conscious Universe* (New York: HarperCollins Publishers, 1997).

13. *Ibid.*, 88.

14. *Ibid.*, 140.

15. Carl Sagan, *The Demon Haunted World* (New York: Random House, 1995), 302.

Chapter 12

1. Adi Sankara, "Eight Stanzas in Praise of the Guru," translated in Swami Nikhilananda, *Self-Knowledge* (New York: Ramakrishna-Vivekananda Center, 1970), 175.

2. Raimon Panikkar, private communication, October 1999.

3. Steven Weinberg, *The First Three Minutes* (New York: Basic Books, 1977), 131–132.

4. Steven Weinberg, *Dreams of a Final Theory: The Scientist's Search for the Ultimate Laws of Nature* (New York: Vantage Books, 1993), 53.

5. Ian Barbour, *Religion in an Age of Science* (San Francisco: Harper & Row, 1990), 10–16.

6. Max Jammer, *Einstein and Religion: Physics and Theology* (Princeton, N.J.: Princeton University Press, 1999).

7. Jane Goodall, *Reason for Hope: A Spiritual Journey* (New York: Warner Books, 1999).

8. *Ibid.*, 30.

9. *Ibid.*, 32–33.

10. *Ibid.*, 79.

11. *Ibid.*, 72.

12. *Ibid.*, 74.

13. *Ibid.*, 173.

14. *Ibid.*, 174–176.

Chapter 13

1. C. G. Jung, "General Aspects of Dream Psychology," in *Collected Works*, vol. 8 (Princeton, N.J.: Princeton University Press, 1978), 253.

2. China Galland, *Longing for Darkness: Tara and the Black Madonna* (New York: Penguin Books, 1990) and *The Bond Between Women: A Journey to Fierce Compassion* (New York: Riverhead Books, 1998); Marion Woodman, *The Pregnant Virgin: A Process of Psychological Transformation* (Toronto, Canada: Inner City Books, 1985).

3. Marcus Aurelius, *The Spiritual Teachings of Marcus Aurelius*, trans. Mark Forstater (New York: HarperCollins, 2000), 154–155.

4. Luke 15.11–32, *New American Bible* (New York: P.J. Kenedy & Sons, 1970).

5. C. G. Jung, "Psychotherapy or the Clergy," in *Collected Works,* vol. 11, (Princeton, N.J.: Princeton University Press, 1969), 339.

6. Jelaluddin Rumi, *The Illuminated Rumi*, trans. Coleman Barks (New York: Broadway Books, 1997), 77.

7. Jeffery Hopkins, *The Tantric Distinction: An Introduction to Tibetan Buddhism* (London: Wisdom Publications, 1984), 93.

8. Raimon Panikkar, "Religious Pluralism: The Metaphysical Challenge," in *Religious Pluralism,* Boston University Studies in Philosophy and Religion, vol. 5, ed. Leroy S. Rouner (South Bend, Ind.: University of Notre Dame Press, 1984).

9. Raimon Panikkar, *The Intrareligous Dialogue* (New York: Paulist Press, 1999).

10. Panikkar, "Religious Pluralism," 113–114.

11. Raimon Panikkar, *Intrareligous Dialogue*, 106.

12. Jeff Madrick, "Rich Nations Have Been Too Insensitive to Poverty," *New York Times*, 1 November 2001.

13. Robert Hass, "Faint Music," in *Sun Under Wood: New Poems* (Hopewell, N.J.: Ecco Press, 1996), 41.

BIBLIOGRAPHY

Aurelius, Marcus. *The Spiritual Teachings of Marcus Aurelius*. Trans. Mark Forstater. New York: HarperCollins, 2000.

Barbour, Ian. *Religion in an Age of Science*. San Francisco: Harper and Row, 1990.

Bem, D. J. and C. Honorton. "Does Psi Exist?" *Psychological Bulletin* 115, 1 (1994):4–18.

Bhattacharyya, Krishnachandra. *Studies in Philosophy*, vols. 1 and 2. New Delhi, India: Motilal Banarsidass, 1983.

Bieler, Ruth. *Feminist Approaches to Science*. New York: Pergamon Press, 1986.

Bohr, Neils. *Atomic Theory and the Description of Nature*. Cambridge, England: Cambridge University Press, 1934.

Bok, Bart J., and Lawrence E. Jerome. *Objections to Astrology*. Buffalo, NY: Prometheus Books, 1975.

Bolen, Jean Shinoda. *The Tao of Psychology: Synchronicity and the Self*. San Francisco: Harper and Row, 1979.

Borges, Jorge Luis. "A New Refutation of Time," in *Labyrinths, Selected Stories and Other Writings*, ed. D. A. Yates, and J. E. Irby. New York: New Directions Books, 1964.

Brunton, Paul. *Perspectives: The Notebooks of Paul Brunton*. Burdett, N.Y.: Larson Publications, 1984.

Chalmers, David. *The Conscious Mind*. New York: Oxford University Press, 1996.

Chamberlain, Roy B., and Herman Feldman. *The Dartmouth Bible*. Boston: Houghton Mifflin, 1950.

Chan, Wing-Tsit, trans. and comp. *A Source Book in Chinese Philosophy*. Princeton, N.J.: Princeton University Press, 1973.

Damiani, Anthony J. *Astronoesis: Philosophy's Empirical Context, Astrology's Transcendental Ground*. Burdett, N.Y.: Larson Publications, 2000.

Davies, P. C. W. "Stirring up Trouble," in *Physical Origins of Time Asymmetry*, ed. J. J. Halliwell, et al. Cambridge, England: Cambridge University Press, 1994.

Dennett, Daniel. *Consciousness Explained*. Boston: Little, Brown & Co., 1991.

Dicke, R. H., P. J. E. Peebles, P. G. Roll, and D. T. Wilkinson. "A Measurement of Excess Antenna Temperature at 4080 mc/s." *Astrophysical Journal* 142 (1965):414–419.

Eckhart, Meister *Meister Eckhart: A Modern Translation*, trans. Raymond B. Blakney. New York: Harper & Row, 1941.

Einstein, Albert. "Autobiographical Notes," in P.A. Schlipp (ed.). *Albert Einstein, Philosopher-Scientist*. Vol. I. New York: Harper and Row, 1959.

Emerson, Ralph Waldo. *Selected Essays*. New York: Penguin Books, 1982.

Ertel, Suitbert, and Kenneth Irving. *The Tenacious Mars Effect*. London: Urania Trust, 1996.

Feyerabend, Paul. *Against Method*. London: Verso, 1975.

_____. *Science in a Free Society*. London: NLB, 1978.

_____. *Farewell to Reason*. London: Verso, 1996.

Feynman, Richard. *The Feynman Lectures in Physics*. Vol. 1. New York: Addison-Wesley Publications, 1989.

Frost, Robert. *Complete Poems of Robert Frost*. New York: Henry Holt, 1964.

Galilei, Galileo. *The Assayer* (1623), translated in Stillman Drake, *Galileo*. Oxford: Oxford University Press, 1969.

Galland, China. *Longing for Darkness: Tara and the Black Madonna*. New York: Penguin Books, 1990.

_____. *The Bond Between Women: A Journey to Fierce Compassion*. New York: Riverhead Books, 1998.

Gauquelin, Michel. *L'influence des Astres. Étude critique et expérimentale*. Paris: Le Dauphin, 1955.

Glashow, Sheldon. "We Believe That the World Is Knowable." *New York Times*, 22 October 1989.

Goodall, Jane. *Reason for Hope: A Spiritual Journey*. New York: Warner Books, 1999.

Hahn, Thomas, ed. *Sir Gawain: Eleven Romances and Tales (Middle English Texts)*. Kalamazoo, Mich.: Western Michigan University Press, 1995.

Hass, Robert. *Sun Under Wood: New Poems*. Hopewell, N.J.: Ecco Press, 1996.

Hillman, James. *Anima: An Anatomy of a Personified Notion*. Dallas, TX: Spring Publications, 1985.

_____. *Re-Visioning Psychology*. New York: Harper & Row, 1976.

Hopkins, Jeffery. *The Tantric Distinction: An Introduction to Tibetan Buddhism.* London: Wisdom Publications, 1984.

Jahn, R. G., B. J. Dunne, R. D. Nelson, Y. H. Dobyns, and G. J. Bradish. "Correlations of Random Binary Sequences With Pre-stated Operator Intention: A Review of a 12-Year Program." *Journal of Scientific Explorations* 11, 3 (1997):345–367.

Jahn, Robert, and Brenda Dunne. *Margins of Reality: The Role of Consciousness in the Physical World.* New York: Harcourt Brace Jovanovich, 1987.

_____. "Science of the Subjective." *Journal of Scientific Explorations* 11, 2 (1997):201–224.

Jammer, Max. *Einstein and Religion: Physics and Theology.* Princeton, N.J.: Princeton University Press, 1999.

Jung, C. G. *Memories, Dreams, Reflections.* New York, N.Y.: Vintage Books, 1962.

_____. *Mysterium Coniunctionis, Collected Works.* Vol. 14. Princeton, N.J.: Princeton University Press, 1974.

_____. *Psychology and Religions: West and East, Collected Work.* Vol. 11. Princeton, N.J.: Princeton University Press, 1969.

_____. *The Practice of Psychotherapy, Collected Works.* Vol. 16 Princeton, N.J.: Princeton University Press, 1966.

_____. *The Structure and Dynamics of the Psyche, Collected Work.* Vol. 8. Princeton, N.J.: Princeton University Press, 1978.

Kelly, I. W. "Modern Astrology: A Critique." *Psychological Reports* 81 (1997):1035–1066.

London, Fritz, and Edmond Bauer. "The Theory of Observation in Quantum Mechanics," in *Quantum Theory and Measurement*, ed. J. Wheeler and W. Zurek. Princeton, N.J.: Princeton University Press, 1983.

MacKenna, Steven, trans. *Plotinus: The Enneads.* Burdett, N.Y.: Larson Publications, 1992.

Madrick, Jeff. "Rich Nations Have Been Too Insensitive to Poverty." *New York Times*, 1 November 2001.

Mandela, Nelson. *Long Walk to Freedom.* Boston: Little, Brown & Company, 1994.

Mansfield, Victor. "An Astrophysicist's Sympathetic and Critical View of Astrology." *The Mountain Astrologer* (1997):46–54.

Mansfield, Victor. "Distinguishing Synchronicity from Parapsychological Phenomena: An Essay in Honor of Marie-Louise von Franz," parts I and II.

Quadrant, The Journal of Contemporary Jungian Thought, 28, no. 2 (1998):16–37; 29, no. 1 (1999):37–45.

_____. "The Guru-Disciple Relationship: Making Connections and Withdrawing Projections." Available at http://www.lightlink.com/vic.

_____. "Time in Madhyamika Buddhism and Modern Physics." *The Pacific World Journal of the Institute of Buddhist Studies* 11–12 (1995–1996) 10–27.

_____. *Synchronicity, Science, and Soul-Making.* Chicago: Open Court Publishing, 1995.

Mansfield, Victor, and Marvin Spiegelman. "On the Physics and Psychology of the Transference as an Interactive Field." *Journal of Analytical Psychology* 41 (1996):179–202.

Mansfield, Victor, Sally Rhine-Feather, and James Hall. "The Rhine-Jung Letters: Distinguishing Synchronicity from Parapsychological Phenomena." *The Parapsychology Journal* 62:1 (March 1998):3–25.

Matthews, John. *Gawain: Knight of the Goddess.* London: Aquarian Press, 1990.

Medawar, Peter. *The Art of the Soluble.* London: Methuen, 1967.

Mitchell, Stephen, trans. "Mundaka Upanishads," in *The Enlightened Heart.* New York: Harper & Row, 1989.

New American Bible. New York: P.J. Kenedy & Sons, 1970.

Nikhilananda, Swami. *Self-Knowledge, Translations of Atmabodha.* New York: Ramakrishna-Vivekananda Center, 1970.

Panikkar, Raimon. "Religious Pluralism: The Metaphysical Challenge" in *Religious Pluralism*, Boston University Studies in Philosophy and Religion. Vol. 5. Edited by Leroy S. Rouner. South Bend, Ind: University of Notre Dame Press, 1984.

Panikkar, Raimon. *The Intrareligous Dialogue.* New York: Paulist Press, 1999.

Penzias, A. A., and R. W. Wilson. "Cosmic Black-Body Radiation." *Astrophysical Journal* 142 (1965):419–421.

Radin, Dean. *The Conscious Universe.* New York: HarperCollins Publishers, 1997.

Ravindra, Ravi. *Science and the Sacred.* Wheaton, Ill: Theosophical Publishing House 2000.

Ray, Reginald A. *Indestructible Truth: The Living Spirituality of Tibetan Buddhism.* Boston: Shambhala, 2000.

Remen, Rachel Naomi M.D. *My Grandfather's Blessings.* New York: Riverhead Books, 2000.

Reps, Paul, ed. *Zen Flesh, Zen Bones*. Rutland, Vt.: Charles Tuttle Co., 1958.

Rinpoche, Sogyal. *Tibetan Book of Living and Dying*. San Francisco: HarperSanFrancisco, 1992.

Ritsema, Rudolf, and Stephen Karcher. *I Ching*. Shaftesbury, Dorset, England: Element Books Ltd., 1994.

Rumi, Jelaluddin. *The Illuminated Rumi*. Trans. Coleman Barks. New York: Broadway Books, 1997.

_____. *The Essential Rumi*. Trans. Coleman Barks, et al. New York: Harper-Collins, 1995.

Sagan, Carl. "Readers Forum." *The Humanist* 36 (Jan./Feb. 1976):2.

_____. *The Demon Haunted World*. New York: Random House, 1995.

Sankara, Adi. "Eight Stanzas in Praise of the Guru," translated in Swami Nikhilananda, *Self-Knowledge*. New York: Ramakrishna-Vivekananda Center, 1970.

Schrödinger, Erwin. "Discussion of Probability Relations between Separated Systems," *Proceedings of the Cambridge Philosophic Society* 31 (1935):1903–1905.

Tagore, Rabindranath. *Gitanjali, Song Offerings*. Boston: International Pocket Library, 1992.

von Franz, Marie-Louise. *C.G. Jung: His Myth in Our Time*. Trans. William H. Kennedy. London: Hodder and Stoughton, 1975.

_____. *Number and Time: Reflections Leading toward a Unification of Depth Psychology and Physics*. Evanston, Ill.: Northwestern University Press, 1974.

_____. *Psyche and Matter*. Boston: Shambhala, 1992.

Weinberg, Steven. *Dreams of a Final Theory*. New York: Vantage Books, 1993.

_____. *The First Three Minutes*. New York: Basic Books, 1977.

Wheeler, John. "Law without Law," in *Quantum Theory and Measurement*, ed. J. Wheeler and W. Zurek. Princeton, N.J.: Princeton University Press, 1983.

Whitmont, Edward. *Symbolic Quest*. Princeton, N.J.: Princeton University Press, 1978.

Wigner, Eugene. "Interpretation of Quantum Mechanics," in *Quantum Theory and Measurement*, ed. J. Wheeler and W. Zurek. Princeton, N.J.: Princeton University Press, 1983.

Woodman, Marion. *The Pregnant Virgin: A Process of Psychological Transformation*. Toronto: Inner City Books, 1985.

INDEX

QUEST BOOKS
are published by
The Theosophical Society in America,
Wheaton, Illinois, 60189-0270,
a branch of a world fellowship,
a membership organization
dedicated to the promotion of the unity of
humanity and the encouragement of the study of
religion, philosophy, and science, to the end that
we may better understand ourselves and our place in
the universe. The Society stands for complete
freedom of individual search and belief.
For further information about its activities,
write, call 1-800-669-1571, e-mail olcott@theosmail.net
or consult its Web page: http://www.theosophical.org

The Theosophical Publishing House
is aided by the generous support of
THE KERN FOUNDATION,
a trust established by Herbert A. Kern
and dedicated to Theosophical education.

PRAISE for HEAD AND HEART

In clear and engaging language, Victor Mansfield explores the great mystery of human consciousness. . . . A warm and lively investigation of the most important questions anyone can ask of themselves and the world.
　　　　　—Nick Herbert, author of *Quantum Reality* and *Elemental Mind*

Mansfield's riveting stories illustrate how the insights of astrophysics, cosmology, and depth psychology are directly (and often humorously) relevant to the pressures, pleasures, and paradoxes of daily living and human relationships. If you are looking for an exhilarating journey from cosmology and individuation to yoga and scientific knowledge, you have come to the right place. Here is a foundation for the science of the new millennium.
　　　　　—Greg Bogart, Ph.D., Professor of Psychology, Graduate School for
　　　　　　　　　　　Holistic Studies, John F. Kennedy University

Victor Mansfield reminds us that while science involves a search for objective laws of nature, its origin always lies in a sense of wonder. . . . He reminds us that the deeper science goes the more it encounters mysteries, in particular the mystery of human consciousness and the nature of subjective experience. He shows us that true understanding must involve an integration of all dimensions of our being—the rational, intuitive, social, and mystical.
　　　　　—F. David Peat, Ph.D., author of
　　　　　Synchronicity: The Bridge between Matter and Mind

Vic Mansfield takes the reader along an inspiring journey across the realms of the scientific method and transformative self-knowledge. . . . He also courageously discusses synchronicity, parapsychology, and astrology—concepts still considered controversial within the scientific community. After clearly analyzing the major differences between objective, scientific knowledge and subjective knowledge obtained by identification, Mansfield outlines the way to harmony between the head and the heart.
　　　　　—Paul H. L. Groenenboom, Ph.D.,
　　　　　　　　　　　Physicist, Hague, the Netherlands

Vic Mansfield's inner journey and work toward resolution of Cartesian conflict is in perfect harmony with our global ethos. As Jung would say, the greatest work for the human race is the resolution of psychic conflict *mysterium coniunctio*—the union of that mystery called "soul and body," "mind and psyche," or, as Vic says, "head and heart."
　　　　　—Erin Sullivan, author of
　　　　　Retrograde Planets: Traversing the Inner Landscape

Inspired by Carl Jung's insights into the balancing of opposite tendencies in the human psyche, Mansfield does a brilliant job of comparing and contrasting science and spirituality as alternative paths to the understanding of reality, and explaining the adverse consequences of leaning too heavily on one at the expense of the other.
　　　　　—John Palmer, Ph.D., Director of Research, Rhine Research Center

Vic Mansfield's new book uniquely combines his personal spiritual quest with his vision as a physicist to bring science and the sacred together. Scientists will relate to the way in which he boldly integrates parts of his life that some people leave in separate compartments, while nonspecialist readers will appreciate the breadth and clarity of his vision.
　　　　　—David Lorimer, Director of the Scientific and Medical Network